Data Preparation and Analysis

An easy approach to master data science

Dr. Pooja Sharma

bpb

www.bpbonline.com

First Edition 2025

Copyright © BPB Publications, India

ISBN: 978-93-65896-190

LIMITS OF LIABILITY AND DISCLAIMER OF WARRANTY

To View Complete
BPB Publications Catalogue
Scan the QR Code:

www.bpbonline.com

Dedicated to

My students
and
my family

About the Author

Dr. Pooja Sharma, assistant professor, in computer science and engineering, has teaching and research experience of more than 18 years. She is a gold medalist in postgraduate, and her other academic achievements include a fellowship for regular PhD from UGC, New Delhi, after qualifying UGC NET and JRF, several merit certificates, gold and silver medals in matric, higher secondary, undergraduate, and postgraduate levels. She was awarded a PhD in 2013 on Content-Based Image Retrieval under the supervision of Dr. Chandan Singh from Punjabi University, Patiala. She has several research publications in peer-reviewed international journals of Springer and Elsevier with significant Thomson Reuters impact factors. She is the author of various research book chapters in Taylor and Francis, Scrivener, and CRC. She has published books, viz. *Programming in Python* and *Simplified Machine Learning*. She is the reviewer of various international journals of Elsevier, IET (IEEE Computer Society), Scientific Reports, The Journal of Supercomputing, and Scientific Research and Essays. She has participated in various conferences and workshops. Her areas of specialization include data analysis, machine learning, content-based image retrieval, face recognition, pattern recognition, and digital image processing. Through her YouTube channel, she offers free guidance on effective research, academic publishing, journal writing, and the use of AI tools. She worked and was selected at various eminent Universities and Colleges, including Central University. She had been the head of department at DAV University for 3 years. Currently, she holds the position of assistant professor in the department of computer science and engineering, IKG Punjab Technical University, Main Campus, Kapurthala.

About the Reviewer

Susmitha Nair is an accomplished software engineer with over 19 years of experience in the technology industry, specializing in the design and deployment of scalable software systems. With expertise in Java, Python, JavaScript, and emerging fields like artificial intelligence and deep learning, she has played a key role in delivering high-impact solutions across the retail and automotive sectors.

In addition to her professional work, Susmitha is an independent researcher with a strong interest in artificial intelligence and data analytics. Her deep-rooted curiosity drives her to explore innovative applications of machine learning and AI in solving real-world problems. Known for her ability to bridge technical depth with strategic vision, Susmitha consistently leads projects that improve efficiency, enhance user experience, and embrace the latest in intelligent automation. Her work reflects a commitment to lifelong learning, innovation, and excellence in software engineering.

Acknowledgement

I am always indebted and grateful to the Almighty for making me capable of writing this book. I extend my gratitude to my parents for their encouragement and support in every sphere of life. I would like to acknowledge my husband, Rajkumar, for his persistent encouragement and support throughout the writing this book, and my daughter, Angel.

I convey my heartiest thanks to the authorities of IKG Punjab Technical University, Kapurthala, and the head of department and my colleagues in the department of computer science and engineering for their support and cooperation.

I would like to acknowledge BPB Publications for their direction and expertise in bringing this book to completion. It was a long journey of writing and revising this book, with valuable assistance and guidance from reviewers, technical experts, and editors.

To all the readers, thank you for your interest in this book and for the unwavering support that helped bring it to life. Your engagement means the world to me.

Preface

In the era of digital transformation, data has become the most powerful asset in shaping decisions, driving innovations, and transforming industries. At the core of this revolution lies data science, a multidisciplinary field that blends statistics, programming, and domain expertise to extract meaningful insights from raw data. A vital branch of **artificial intelligence** (**AI**), data science enables machines and systems to learn from patterns and make intelligent decisions from recommendation engines, fraud detection, to medical diagnosis, and climate modeling.

Data analysis is one of the most critical stages in the data science workflow. It bridges the gap between raw data and actionable insights. However, before any sophisticated modelling or machine learning can take place, a solid foundation in data preparation and analysis is essential. This book has been designed to equip readers with that foundation, ensuring they understand not only the tools but also the techniques and best practices for handling data effectively and efficiently.

This book is structured into eight comprehensive chapters, each focusing on key aspects of data preparation and analysis:

Chapter 1: Introduction to Data Science – Introduces data science, its key objectives, and its evolution over time. It highlights the vital role data science plays in modern industries and outlines the main stages of a typical data science project. The chapter also addresses data security issues and clearly differentiates data science from data analysis, machine learning, and artificial intelligence. Career opportunities in this field are discussed, along with the essential skills required. Lastly, it offers a practical guide to installing Anaconda and Python, helping readers set up their environment for hands-on data science work.

Chapter 2: NumPy – Focuses on various concepts of NumPy, creating NumPy arrays, array attributes, array operations, broadcasting, indexing, slicing, fancy indexing, advanced indexing techniques, reshaping arrays, combining and splitting arrays, random numbers and simulations, performance and optimization in NumPy are elaborated with programming exercises.

Chapter 3: Pandas – Covers all the concepts of Pandas, including series and DataFrame creation with programming exercises.

Chapter 4: Data Collection and Data Preprocessing – This chapter elaborates on gathering data from various sources and preparing it for analysis through transformation and formatting. In this chapter, data collection, various types of datasets, different data formats, parsing of data, data transformations, and real-time issues with data are explained with programming illustrations.

Chapter 5: Data Cleaning – In this chapter, techniques for handling missing values, duplicate records, and inconsistencies to ensure data quality. Heterogeneous data, data consistency, missing data, data transformation, and segmentation are elaborated.

Chapter 6: Exploratory Data Analysis – This chapter elaborates descriptive statistics, comparative statistics, clustering, association, and hypothesis generation with programming details.

Chapter 7: Data Visualization - Explains creating effective, insightful, and interactive visual representations of data to aid interpretation and storytelling. Time series analysis, geolocated analysis, correlations, networks and hierarchies, and interactivity are explored with programming illustrations.

Chapter 8: Projects - Implements real-world problems for a deep understanding of data science and machine learning models. A comprehensive practical approach is followed to implement a recommender system, a chatbot, and a customer segmentation system, which are used in the real-world.

Code Bundle and Coloured Images

Please follow the link to download the
Code Bundle and the *Coloured Images* of the book:

https://rebrand.ly/da582c

The code bundle for the book is also hosted on GitHub at
https://github.com/bpbpublications/Data-Preparation-and-Analysis.
In case there's an update to the code, it will be updated on the existing GitHub repository.

We have code bundles from our rich catalogue of books and videos available at
https://github.com/bpbpublications. Check them out!

Errata

We take immense pride in our work at BPB Publications and follow best practices to ensure the accuracy of our content to provide with an indulging reading experience to our subscribers. Our readers are our mirrors, and we use their inputs to reflect and improve upon human errors, if any, that may have occurred during the publishing processes involved. To let us maintain the quality and help us reach out to any readers who might be having difficulties due to any unforeseen errors, please write to us at :

errata@bpbonline.com

Your support, suggestions and feedbacks are highly appreciated by the BPB Publications' Family.

Did you know that BPB offers eBook versions of every book published, with PDF and ePub files available? You can upgrade to the eBook version at www.bpbonline. com and as a print book customer, you are entitled to a discount on the eBook copy. Get in touch with us at :

business@bpbonline.com for more details.

At www.bpbonline.com, you can also read a collection of free technical articles, sign up for a range of free newsletters, and receive exclusive discounts and offers on BPB books and eBooks.

Piracy

If you come across any illegal copies of our works in any form on the internet, we would be grateful if you would provide us with the location address or website name. Please contact us at business@bpbonline.com with a link to the material.

If you are interested in becoming an author

If there is a topic that you have expertise in, and you are interested in either writing or contributing to a book, please visit www.bpbonline.com. We have worked with thousands of developers and tech professionals, just like you, to help them share their insights with the global tech community. You can make a general application, apply for a specific hot topic that we are recruiting an author for, or submit your own idea.

Reviews

Please leave a review. Once you have read and used this book, why not leave a review on the site that you purchased it from? Potential readers can then see and use your unbiased opinion to make purchase decisions. We at BPB can understand what you think about our products, and our authors can see your feedback on their book. Thank you!

For more information about BPB, please visit www.bpbonline.com.

Join our Discord space

Join our Discord workspace for latest updates, offers, tech happenings around the world, new releases, and sessions with the authors:

https://discord.bpbonline.com

Table of Contents

CHAPTER 1
Introduction to Data Science

Introduction

Data science is an interdisciplinary field that combines techniques from statistics, computer science, and domain expertise to extract meaningful insights from data. It involves collecting, processing, analyzing, and interpreting large volumes of structured and unstructured data to solve complex problems and support decision-making. For example, in the retail industry, data science is used to analyze customer purchasing behavior to personalize marketing campaigns and improve customer retention. In healthcare, it aids in predicting disease outbreaks by analyzing patient records and environmental data, enabling proactive measures and better resource allocation. Financial institutions leverage data science for fraud detection by identifying unusual transaction patterns and predicting credit risks. Additionally, social media companies use data science to analyze user interactions and preferences, optimizing content delivery and enhancing user engagement. Data scientists employ various tools and techniques, such as machine learning algorithms, statistical models, and data visualization, to uncover hidden patterns and trends within the data. They might use Python or R for coding, SQL for database queries, and tools like Tableau for visualizing data insights. The field's scope extends to predictive analytics, where future trends are forecasted based on historical data, and prescriptive analytics, which suggests actions to achieve desired outcomes. By transforming raw data into actionable insights, data science empowers organizations across different sectors to make data-driven decisions, innovate, and maintain a competitive edge in their respective industries.

Structure

The chapter covers the following topics:

- Data science objectives
- Evolution of data science
- Role of data science in various domains
- Stages of a data science project
- Data security issues
- Data science vs. data analysis vs. machine learning vs. artificial intelligence
- Career in data science
- Steps to install Anaconda and Python

Objectives

By the end of this chapter, you will be able to understand the core concept of data science, its needs, objectives, and real-world applications in diverse areas. The reader will comprehend the evolution of data science along with all the stages of developing a data science project. You will also come to know the requirements to make a career in data science. The differences among data science, data analysis, **machine learning (ML)**, and **artificial intelligence (AI)** will be known to you. You will learn the steps to install Anaconda (Python) for learning and implementing data science projects.

Data science objectives

The core objective of data science is to transform raw data into actionable knowledge that can be used to drive decisions and strategic initiatives across various industries. The data science process involves several key stages:

- **Data collection**: Gathering data from various sources, including databases, web scraping, and APIs, ensuring the data is relevant and sufficient for analysis.

- **Data cleaning**: Preparing the data by handling missing values, correcting inconsistencies, and transforming the data into a suitable format for analysis.

- **Exploratory data analysis (EDA)**: Utilizing statistical tools and visualization techniques to understand the underlying patterns, trends, and relationships within the data.

- **Data modeling**: Applying machine learning algorithms and statistical models to make predictions or classify data. This step often involves selecting the right model, training it on a subset of data, and validating its performance.

- **Interpretation and communication**: Translating the model's findings into understandable insights and visualizations. This is crucial for stakeholders to make informed decisions based on the data.

Data science leverages tools and programming languages like Python, R, and SQL, and platforms like Hadoop and Spark for big data processing. It encompasses various disciplines, including machine learning, artificial intelligence, and statistical analysis, making it a versatile and powerful field.

In essence, data science is pivotal in today's data-driven world, enabling organizations to harness the power of data for improved efficiency, innovation, and competitive advantage. By uncovering hidden patterns and predicting future trends, data science helps in making better-informed decisions that can significantly impact business strategies and outcomes.

Evolution of Data Science

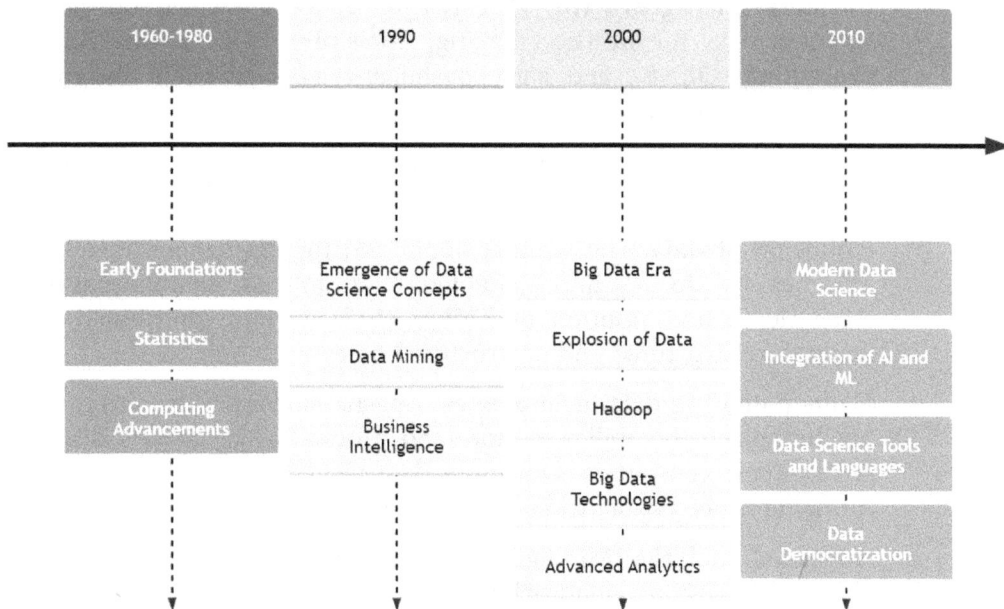

Figure 1.1: Evolution of data science

Evolution of data science

Data science has evolved from basic statistical analysis to a comprehensive field that integrates advanced ML, big data technologies, and domain-specific knowledge. This evolution continues as technology advances and the demand for data-driven insights grows across all sectors. The evolution of data science can be traced through several key phases, reflecting advancements in technology, data availability, and analytical techniques, is displayed in *Figure 1.1* and its detailed overview of its developments is given as follows:

- **Early foundations:** It includes statistics and data analysis (1960s-1980s) as follows:

  - **Statistics:** The roots of data science lie in statistics, which have been used for centuries to analyze and interpret data. Techniques like regression analysis, hypothesis testing, and probability theory were foundational.

  - **Computing advancements:** With the advent of computers in the mid-20th century, statistical analysis became more sophisticated and efficient. Early computers were used for basic data processing and analysis.

- **Emergence of data science concepts (1990s):** It includes data mining and business intelligence as follows:

  - **Data mining:** In the 1990s, the term **data mining** became popular. It refers to the process of discovering patterns and knowledge from large datasets using techniques from statistics, machine learning, and database systems.

  - **Business intelligence (BI):** The rise of BI tools enabled businesses to leverage data for decision-making. Tools like SQL, **online analytical processing (OLAP)**, and early dashboard tools provided insights into business performance.

- **Big data era (2000s):** It includes an explosion of data and big data technologies as follows:

  - **Explosion of data:** The internet boom and the digitization of numerous activities led to an unprecedented explosion of data. Social media, e-commerce, and **Internet of Things (IoT)** devices contributed to vast amounts of structured and unstructured data.

  - **Hadoop and big data technologies:** Apache Hadoop, introduced in 2006, revolutionized the ability to store and process large datasets distributed across many computers. Other big data technologies like Apache Spark further enhanced data processing capabilities.

  - **Advanced analytics:** ML algorithms became more sophisticated, and the ability to process and analyze big data enabled predictive analytics and real-time data processing.

- **Modern data science (2010s-present):** It includes AI and ML, data science tools and languages, data democratization, and cloud computing as follows:

  - **Integration of AI and ML:** AI and ML have become integral parts of data science. Deep learning, neural networks, and advanced algorithms have pushed the boundaries of what can be achieved.

  - **Data science tools and languages:** Python and R emerged as the dominant programming languages for data science due to their extensive libraries and community support. Tools like TensorFlow, PyTorch, and scikit-learn have become standard.

o **Data democratization**: Platforms like Tableau, Power BI, and Google Data Studio have made data visualization and analysis accessible to non-technical users. This democratization has empowered more people to make data-driven decisions.

o **Cloud computing**: The proliferation of cloud services (AWS, Azure, Google Cloud) has enabled scalable data storage and processing, making advanced analytics accessible to organizations of all sizes.

- **Future of data science**: It includes the following:

    o **Automated ML (AutoML)**: The development of AutoML tools is simplifying the creation and deployment of machine learning models, making data science more accessible.

    o **Ethics and privacy**: As data science becomes more pervasive, ethical considerations and data privacy are becoming critical issues. There is a growing focus on ensuring data is used responsibly and transparently.

    o **Interdisciplinary approach**: Data science is increasingly becoming interdisciplinary, integrating domain knowledge from fields like healthcare, finance, and social sciences to solve complex problems.

    o **Edge computing and real-time analytics**: With the growth of IoT, edge computing is enabling real-time data analysis at the source, reducing latency and enhancing decision-making.

Role of data science in various domains

Data science is a transformative field that touches almost every aspect of modern life. Leveraging data enables organizations to optimize operations, innovate new solutions, and make data-driven decisions that improve efficiency and effectiveness. As technology and methodologies continue to evolve, the role of data science is expected to become even more integral to organizational success and societal advancement. Data science plays a pivotal role across numerous domains by providing insights that drive decision-making, improve processes, and foster innovation. The detailed role of data science is categorized into various sectors as follows:

- **Business and finance**: It includes the following:

    o **Customer insights**: Data science helps businesses understand customer behavior through segmentation, customer lifetime value analysis, and sentiment analysis. This leads to personalized marketing strategies and improved customer experience.

    o **Risk management**: In finance, data science is used to assess and mitigate risks by analyzing transaction patterns, predicting default probabilities, and detecting fraudulent activities.

- o **Algorithmic trading**: Advanced algorithms analyze market data in real-time to make high-frequency trading decisions, optimizing returns while minimizing risks.

Note: In bank fraud detection, ML is used to analyze large volumes of transaction data to identify suspicious patterns. For example, an ML model can learn normal spending behavior of customers, such as usual transaction amounts, locations, and timings, and flag unusual activities like a sudden high-value transaction from a foreign country. Algorithms like logistic regression, decision trees, or neural networks help classify transactions as legitimate or fraudulent in real-time, allowing banks to prevent financial losses and protect customer accounts.

- **Healthcare**: It includes the following:

  - o **Predictive analytics**: Data science enables the prediction of disease outbreaks, patient readmissions, and treatment outcomes. Predictive models can identify at-risk patients and suggest preventive measures.

  - o **Medical imaging**: ML algorithms assist in the analysis of medical images, improving the accuracy of diagnoses in radiology, pathology, and other fields.

  - o **Personalized medicine**: By analyzing genetic data and patient history, data science facilitates the development of personalized treatment plans, leading to more effective healthcare solutions.

- **E-commerce and retail**: It includes the following:

  - o **Recommendation systems**: Data science powers recommendation engines that suggest products to users based on their browsing history and purchase patterns, enhancing user engagement and sales.

  - o **Inventory management**: Predictive analytics forecast demand, optimizing inventory levels, and reducing stockouts or overstock situations.

  - o **Customer churn prediction**: By analyzing customer behavior, data science identifies potential churners, enabling targeted retention strategies to keep customers engaged.

- **Transportation and logistics**: It includes the following:

  - o **Route optimization**: Data science algorithms optimize delivery routes and schedules, reducing costs and improving efficiency in logistics and supply chain management.

  - o **Predictive maintenance**: Analyzing data from sensors on vehicles and machinery helps predict failures before they occur, minimizing downtime and maintenance costs.

    o **Traffic management**: Data science models traffic patterns and helps in designing smart traffic systems that reduce congestion and improve urban mobility.

Note: Amazon uses ML for route optimization by analyzing vast amounts of data, such as traffic conditions, weather, delivery time windows, and customer locations, to determine the most efficient delivery routes. ML algorithms help predict delays, cluster deliveries based on proximity, and assign packages to drivers in real-time. This not only reduces delivery times and fuel costs but also improves customer satisfaction by ensuring faster and more reliable deliveries.

- **Manufacturing**: It includes the following:

    o **Quality control**: ML models detect defects in products by analyzing data from production lines, ensuring higher quality and consistency.

    o **Process optimization**: Data science analyzes production data to identify bottlenecks and optimize manufacturing processes, leading to increased efficiency and reduced waste.

    o **Supply chain optimization**: By forecasting demand and optimizing inventory levels, data science helps maintain a balance between supply and demand.

- **Energy and utilities**: It includes the following:

    o **Energy forecasting**: Predictive models forecast energy demand, aiding in efficient resource allocation and grid management.

    o **Smart grids**: Data science enables the development of smart grids that optimize the distribution of electricity, reduce outages, and integrate renewable energy sources.

    o **Equipment monitoring**: Data from sensors on equipment is analyzed to predict failures and schedule timely maintenance, improving the reliability of utilities.

- **Education**: It includes the following:

    o **Personalized learning**: Data science creates adaptive learning platforms that tailor educational content to individual student needs, enhancing learning outcomes.

    o **Student performance prediction**: Analyzing student data helps predict performance and identify those at risk of falling behind, allowing for timely interventions.

- o **Curriculum development**: Data-driven insights inform curriculum development, ensuring it meets the evolving needs of students and the job market.

- **Government and public policy**: It includes the following:

  - o **Public health monitoring**: Data science tracks and predicts disease outbreaks, guiding public health interventions and resource allocation.

  - o **Crime prediction and prevention**: Analyzing crime data helps predict and prevent criminal activities, enhancing public safety.

  - o **Economic planning**: Data science informs economic policies by analyzing trends in employment, inflation, and other economic indicators.

Stages of a data science project

A data science project involves a systematic approach, starting from problem definition and data collection, through exploration, modeling, deployment, interpretation, and iteration. Each stage is interconnected and iterative, requiring collaboration between data scientists, domain experts, and stakeholders to deliver valuable insights and solutions that address business objectives. A data science project typically follows a series of stages or phases, each essential for the successful completion of the project. A figure representing phases of a data science project is depicted in *Figure 1.2*. The detailed elaboration of these stages is given as follows:

1. **Problem definition**:

   a. **Identify objectives**: Clearly define the goals and objectives of the project in collaboration with stakeholders. Understand the problem domain and the business context.

   b. **Define metrics for success**: Establish **key performance indicators (KPIs)** or metrics that will be used to evaluate the success of the project.

   c. **Scope of the project**: Determine the scope of the project, including the data available, resources required, and constraints such as time and budget.

2. **Data collection and cleaning**:

   a. **Data acquisition**: Gather relevant data from various sources, including databases, APIs, files, and external datasets. Ensure data is collected ethically and legally.

   b. **Data cleaning**: Preprocess the data by handling missing values, removing duplicates, correcting errors, and standardizing formats. This stage is crucial for ensuring data quality and integrity.

3. **EDA**:

    a. **Data visualization**: Explore the dataset visually using charts, graphs, and plots to identify patterns, trends, and anomalies. Understand the distribution of variables and the relationships between them.

    b. **Statistical analysis**: Compute descriptive statistics, such as mean, median, variance, and correlations, to gain insights into the data distribution and characteristics.

4. **Feature engineering**:

    a. **Feature selection**: Identify relevant features or variables that are most predictive of the target variable. Use domain knowledge and statistical techniques to select informative features.

    b. **Feature transformation**: Transform variables through techniques like normalization, standardization, encoding categorical variables, and creating new features through transformations or interactions.

5. **Model development**:

    a. **Model selection**: Choose appropriate machine learning algorithms or statistical models based on the problem type (classification, regression, clustering) and data characteristics.

    b. **Model training**: Train the selected models using a portion of the dataset. Tune hyperparameters and optimize model performance using techniques like cross-validation.

    c. **Model evaluation**: Evaluate model performance using appropriate metrics (accuracy, precision, recall, F1-score, ROC-AUC) on a separate validation dataset or through cross-validation.

6. **Model deployment**:

    a. **Integration**: Integrate the trained model into the production environment or application where it will be used to make predictions or recommendations.

    b. **Testing**: Test the deployed model thoroughly to ensure it performs as expected and meets the defined success criteria.

    c. **Monitoring**: Continuously monitor the model's performance in production, tracking metrics, and detecting any drift or degradation in performance.

7. **Interpretation and communication**:

    a. **Interpret results**: Interpret the model predictions or insights generated from the analysis in the context of the problem domain. Understand the implications and actionable recommendations.

   b. **Communication**: Present findings, insights, and recommendations to stakeholders using visualizations, reports, and presentations. Tailor communication to the audience, highlighting key takeaways and actionable insights.

8. **Iteration and improvement**:

   a. **Feedback loop**: Collect feedback from stakeholders and users of the system to identify areas for improvement or refinement.

   b. **Iterative development**: Iterate on the data science process, incorporating feedback and new data to improve model performance and address emerging challenges.

   c. **Continuous learning**: Stay updated with the latest advancements in data science techniques, tools, and technologies to enhance skills and capabilities.

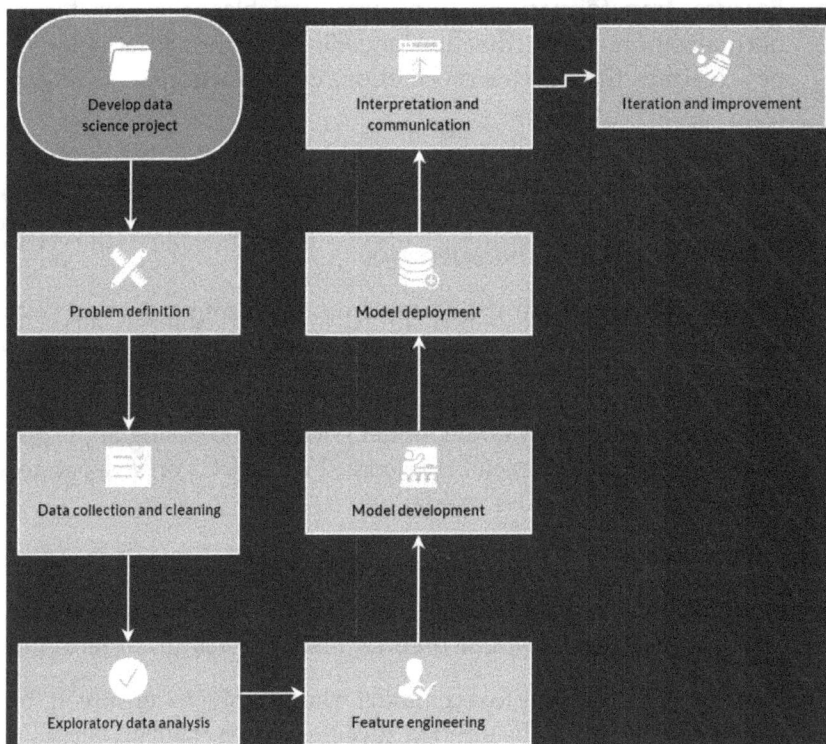

Figure 1.2: Phases of a data science project

Data security issues

Data security issues pose significant risks to organizations that handle sensitive data. Addressing potential data security issues requires a comprehensive approach involving robust cybersecurity measures, risk management strategies, employee training, and compliance with regulatory requirements. Organizations must continually assess and mitigate security risks to protect their data assets, safeguard customer trust, and maintain business continuity in today's digital landscape. Some potential data security issues that organizations may face are described as follows:

- **Unauthorized access**:
  - **Data breaches**: Unauthorized access to sensitive data by hackers or malicious actors can lead to data breaches, resulting in theft, loss, or exposure of sensitive information. For example, the Equifax data breach, one of the largest in history, occurred in 2017 and exposed sensitive personal information of over 147 million people, including social security numbers, birth dates, addresses, and credit card details. This breach happened due to a failure in data security: Equifax did not patch a known vulnerability in its Apache Struts web application software. Hackers exploited this flaw to gain unauthorized access to the system over several months. The breach highlights the critical importance of regular software updates, strong cybersecurity practices, and prompt vulnerability management to protect user data and maintain trust in digital systems.
  - **Insider threats**: Employees, contractors, or partners with access to sensitive data may misuse their privileges, intentionally or unintentionally, leading to data breaches or leaks.

- **Data loss or corruption**:
  - **Accidental deletion**: Data can be lost due to accidental deletion, hardware failure, or software errors, leading to data loss and disruption of business operations.
  - **Data corruption**: Errors in data storage, transmission, or processing can corrupt data, rendering it unusable or inaccurate, which can have serious implications for decision-making and business processes.

- **Data theft and espionage**:
  - **Intellectual property theft**: Theft of intellectual property, trade secrets, or proprietary information can occur through cyber espionage, insider threats, or unauthorized access, causing financial and reputational damage to organizations.
  - **Corporate espionage**: Competitors or adversaries may target organizations to steal sensitive data for competitive advantage or sabotage, posing significant risks to business continuity and competitiveness.

- **Regulatory compliance violations**:
  - **Data privacy regulations**: Failure to comply with data privacy regulations such as the **General Data Protection Regulation (GDPR)** or the **California**

Consumer Privacy Act (CCPA) can result in hefty fines, legal penalties, and reputational damage for organizations.

- o **Industry compliance**: Industries such as **Healthcare Insurance Portability and Accountability Act (HIPAA)**, finance **(Payment Card Industry Data Security Standards (PCI-DSS))**, and government **(Federal Information Security Management Act (FISMA))** have specific data security regulations and compliance requirements that organizations must adhere to; failure to do so can lead to regulatory action and legal consequences.

- **Data interception and tampering**:
  - o **Man-in-the-middle attacks**: Attackers intercept and eavesdrop on data transmissions between parties, gaining unauthorized access to sensitive information or injecting malicious content into data streams.
  - o **Data tampering**: Attackers modify or manipulate data in transit or storage to disrupt business operations, spread misinformation, or commit fraud, compromising data integrity and trust.

- **Insider threats**:
  - o **Malicious insider actions**: Employees or insiders with privileged access may intentionally sabotage systems, steal data, or leak confidential information for personal gain or malicious intent.
  - o **Negligent insider actions**: Accidental actions by employees, such as clicking on phishing links, mishandling sensitive data, or failing to follow security protocols, can inadvertently expose organizations to security risks and data breaches.

- **Inadequate security controls**:
  - o **Weak authentication**: Inadequate authentication mechanisms, such as weak passwords, a lack of **multi-factor authentication (MFA)**, or improper access controls, can make it easier for attackers to gain unauthorized access to systems and data.
  - o **Inadequate encryption**: Failure to encrypt sensitive data in transit and at rest leaves it vulnerable to interception and unauthorized access, increasing the risk of data breaches and privacy violations.

- **Supply chain risks**:
  - o **Third-party risks**: Organizations may face security risks from third-party vendors, suppliers, or service providers who have access to their data or systems. Failure to assess and manage third-party risks can lead to security breaches and data exposure.

Data science vs. data analytics vs. machine learning vs. artificial intelligence

Data science, data analytics, ML, and AI are related but distinct fields within the broader domain of data-driven decision-making and artificial intelligence. The differentiation between these terms is described as follows:

- **Data science**:
  - **Definition**: Data science is an interdisciplinary field that involves extracting insights and knowledge from structured and unstructured data using various techniques, including statistics, ML, data mining, and data visualization.
  - **Focus**: Data science focuses on the entire data lifecycle, from data collection and cleaning to analysis, modeling, and interpretation. It aims to uncover patterns, trends, and correlations in data to support decision-making and solve complex problems.
  - **Applications**: Data science is applied across various domains, including business, healthcare, finance, marketing, and social sciences, to derive actionable insights, optimize processes, and drive innovation.

- **Data analytics**:
  - **Definition**: Data analytics involves analyzing datasets to discover meaningful patterns, insights, and trends that can inform decision-making and drive business outcomes.
  - **Focus**: Data analytics focuses on descriptive and diagnostic analysis, answering questions like *What happened?* and *Why did it happen?* It involves summarizing and visualizing data to identify patterns and trends.
  - **Applications**: Data analytics is used to track performance metrics, monitor KPIs, and gain insights into customer behavior, market trends, and operational efficiency.

- **ML**:
  - **Definition**: ML is a subset of AI that involves developing algorithms and statistical models that enable computers to learn from and make predictions or decisions based on data, without being explicitly programmed.
  - **Focus**: ML focuses on building predictive models that learn from data and improve their performance over time through experience. It involves tasks such as classification, regression, clustering, and anomaly detection.
  - **Applications**: ML is applied in various fields, including predictive analytics, recommendation systems, natural language processing, computer vision, and autonomous systems.

- **AI**:
  - o **Definition**: AI refers to the simulation of human intelligence processes by machines, including learning, reasoning, problem-solving, perception, and decision-making.

  - o **Focus**: AI aims to create systems that can perform tasks that typically require human intelligence, such as understanding natural language, recognizing patterns in data, making decisions, and solving complex problems.

  - o **Applications**: AI is applied in diverse domains, including robotics, autonomous vehicles, virtual assistants, healthcare diagnostics, financial trading, gaming, and cybersecurity.

Career in data science

A career in data science requires a diverse set of skills and qualifications that span technical, analytical, and domain-specific knowledge. GitHub plays a vital role in data science projects by providing a collaborative platform for version control, code sharing, and project management. Data scientists use GitHub to store and track changes in their code, notebooks, and datasets, ensuring that their work is organized and reproducible. It enables team collaboration through features like pull requests, issue tracking, and code reviews. GitHub also supports integration with tools like Jupyter Notebooks, making it easier to share analyses and visualizations. Additionally, open-source data science projects hosted on GitHub foster learning, knowledge sharing, and innovation within the community. Some essential skills and qualifications for aspiring data scientists are described as follows:

- **Technical skills**: The details are given as under:
  - o **Programming languages**: The knowledge of at least one of the following programming languages is required:
    - ▪ **Python**: Widely used for data analysis, machine learning, and scripting.
    - ▪ **R**: Popular for statistical analysis and data visualization.
    - ▪ **SQL**: Essential for querying and manipulating databases.
  - o **Statistics and mathematics**: The knowledge of the following mathematical skills is mandatory:
    - ▪ **Probability theory**: Understanding distributions, Bayesian statistics, etc.
    - ▪ **Hypothesis testing**: Conducting t-tests, chi-square tests, ANOVA, etc.
    - ▪ **Linear algebra and calculus**: Fundamental for understanding ML algorithms.
  - o **Data manipulation and analysis**: If you opt for Python programming then following libraries are to be learnt with the knowledge of Excel.

- **Pandas**: For data manipulation and analysis in Python.
- **NumPy**: For numerical computations in Python.
- **Excel**: Basic tool for data analysis and visualization.

  o **Machine learning**: The following packages of ML will be helpful:

- **Scikit-learn**: Library for ML in Python.
- **TensorFlow/PyTorch**: Libraries for deep learning.
- **Algorithm knowledge**: Understanding of classification, regression, clustering, and dimensionality reduction techniques.

  o **Data visualization**: To get a better understanding of data, the following visualization libraries need to be focused on:

- **Matplotlib/Seaborn**: Libraries for plotting in Python.
- **Tableau/Power BI**: Tools for interactive and business-oriented visualizations.
- **D3.js**: JavaScript library for creating dynamic and interactive data visualizations.

- **Analytical skills**: The details are given as under:

  o **Data cleaning and preprocessing**: Handling missing values, outliers, and data normalization.

  o **EDA**: Identifying patterns, trends, and anomalies in data.

  o **Critical thinking**: Ability to interpret data and draw actionable insights.

  o **Problem-solving**: Formulating and testing hypotheses to solve business problems.

- **Domain knowledge**: One must have domain knowledge on the following subjects:

  o **Business acumen**: Understanding industry-specific challenges and opportunities.

  o **Subject matter expertise**: Knowledge in fields like finance, healthcare, marketing, etc., to contextualize data insights.

- **Soft skills**: One must have strong communication skills as described follows:

  o **Communication skills**: Ability to convey complex findings in a clear and concise manner to non-technical stakeholders.

  o **Collaboration**: Working effectively within multidisciplinary teams.

  o **Project management**: Planning, executing, and monitoring data science projects.

- **Educational background**: To get a place in a good company/industry, one needs to acquire a degree in per following streams:

  o **Degrees**:

    ▪ A bachelor's degree in a relevant field such as computer science, statistics, mathematics, engineering, or data science.

    ▪ Advanced degrees (master's or PhD) can be advantageous for specialized roles or research positions.

- **Practical experience**: Hands-on practice is required to get expertise in data science as follows:

  o **Projects and internships**: Hands-on experience through personal projects, internships, or co-op programs.

  o **Competitions**: Participation in data science competitions like Kaggle to hone skills and gain practical exposure.

  o **Certifications**: Professional certifications from recognized platforms (e.g., Coursera, edX, DataCamp) in data science, machine learning, or specific tools and technologies.

- **Continuous learning**: One must keep in mind the following points:

  o **Staying updated**: Keeping abreast of the latest trends, tools, and techniques in data science.

  o **Professional development**: Attending workshops, webinars, conferences, and joining data science communities.

By developing these skills and qualifications, individuals can build a strong foundation for a successful career in data science, enabling them to tackle complex data-driven problems and contribute valuable insights to their organizations.

Steps to install Anaconda and Python

Although data science implementation can be done in R programming and other software packages, in the course of this book, we implement all constructs and algorithms of data science in Python. Python provides all libraries and packages for statistics, visualizations, and machine learning. Therefore, one needs to learn only one programming language to obtain the optimum results. For this, you need to install Anaconda. It is a distribution that includes Python and a wide range of libraries and tools commonly used in data science and machine learning. Installing Anaconda and Python is a straightforward process. The following are the steps to install Anaconda and Python:

1. **Download Anaconda**: Visit the Anaconda website (**https://www.anaconda.com/products/distribution**) and download the **Anaconda Distribution** that matches your operating system (Windows, macOS, or Linux), as shown in *Figure 1.3*:

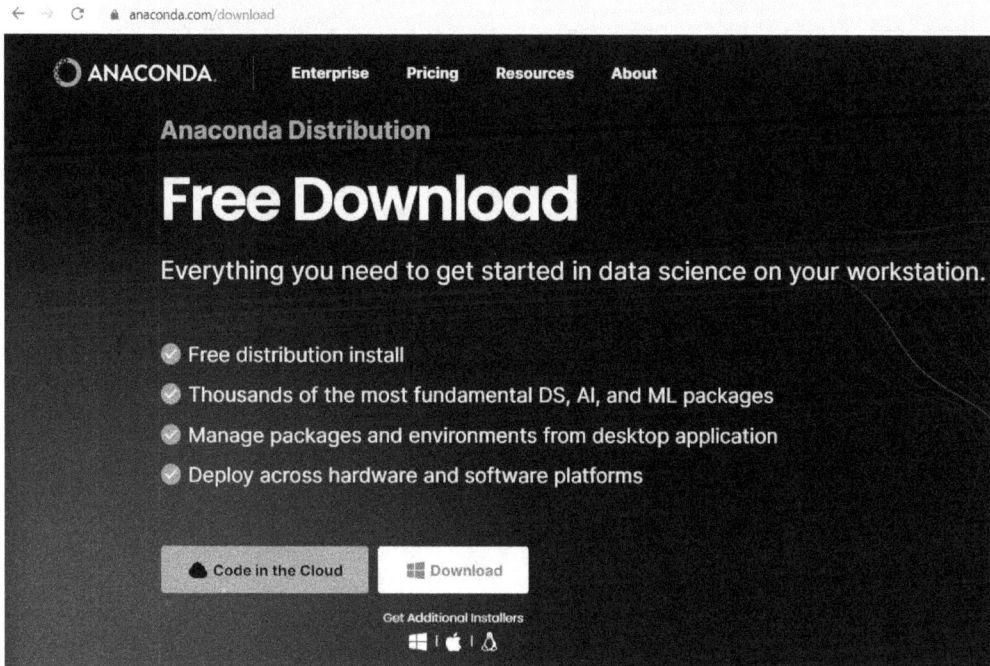

Figure 1.3: Open www.anaconda.com

2. **Run the installer**:

    a. **Windows**: Double-click the downloaded **.exe** file and follow the installation wizard's instructions.

    b. **macOS**: Open the downloaded **.pkg** file and follow the installation prompts.

    c. **Linux**: Open a terminal, navigate to the directory containing the downloaded script, and run the following command:

    ```bash
    bashCopy code
    bash Anaconda3-<version>-Linux-x86_64.sh
    Replace <version> with the version number in the downloaded file's
    name.
    ```

As we are working in Windows, the complete process of installing Anaconda is presented in the following steps:

1. As we can see in *Figure 1.4* and *Figure 1.5,* the installer asks for agreement with the license agreement:

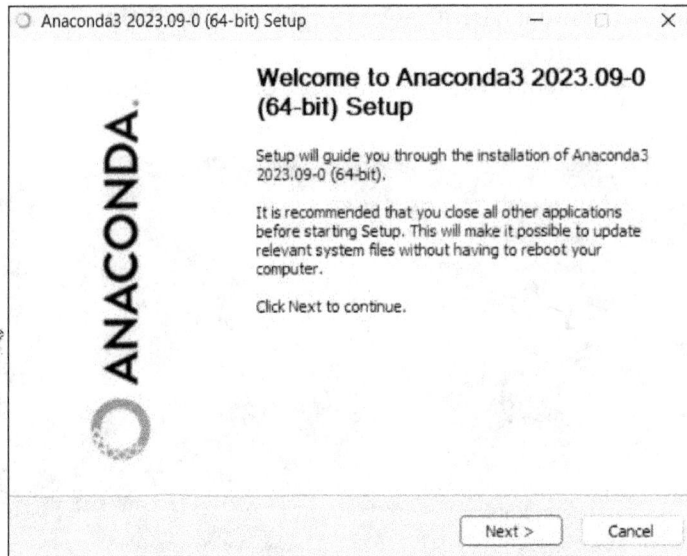

Figure 1.4: *anaconda.exe file ready to be installed*

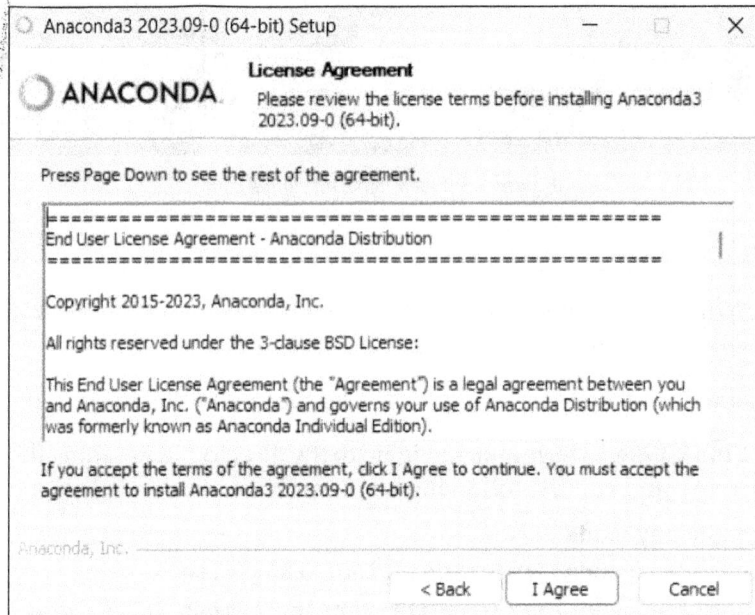

Figure 1.5: *License agreement*

2. Thereafter, the user has to select the installation type, either single-user or server-based, as shown in the following figure. Here we select just for me.

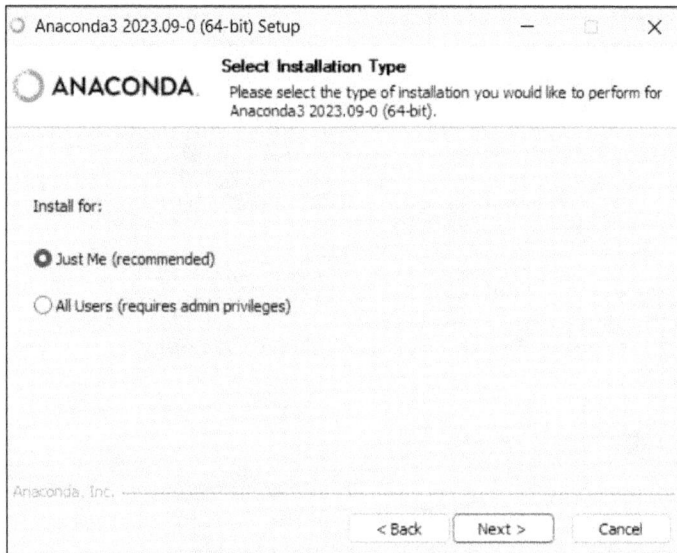

Figure 1.6: Choose installation type

3. After that, it asks for the location where you want to install Anaconda:

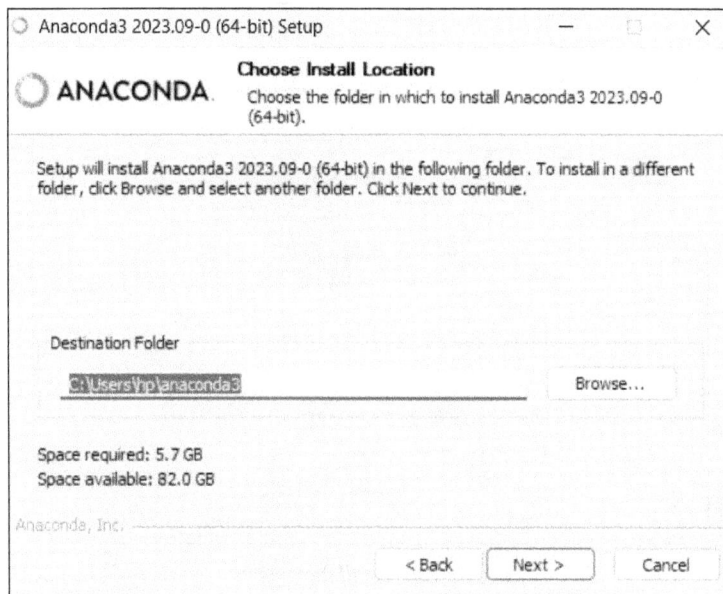

Figure 1.7: Choose the installation location on your system

4. Then, the usual recommended options are already set by the installer, like the shortcut menu, and setting Anaconda as the default for Python, as shown here:

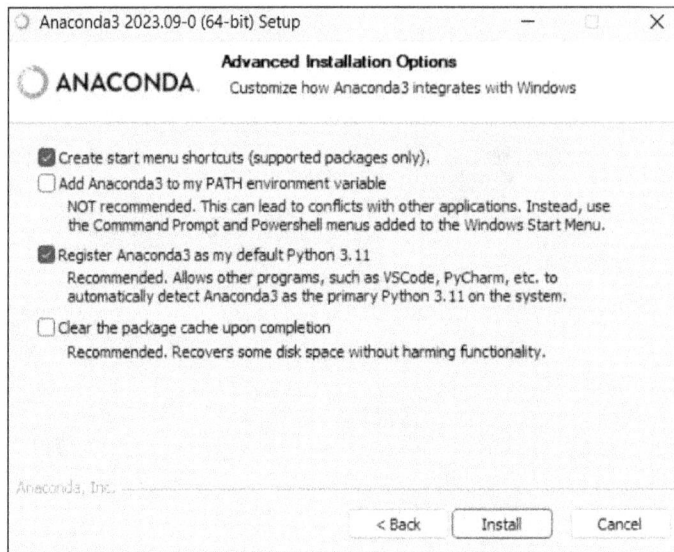

Figure 1.8: *Click on Install*

5. Finally, the installation begins, as shown in the following figure:

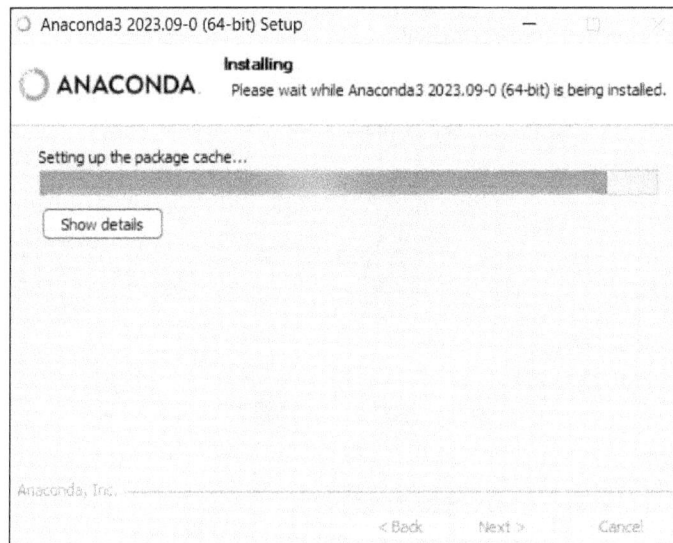

Figure 1.9: *Installation starts*

6. After the successful installation, the user can open the Jupyter Notebook by simply clicking on its icon on the desktop. It opens in the web browser as shown in *Figure 1.10*:

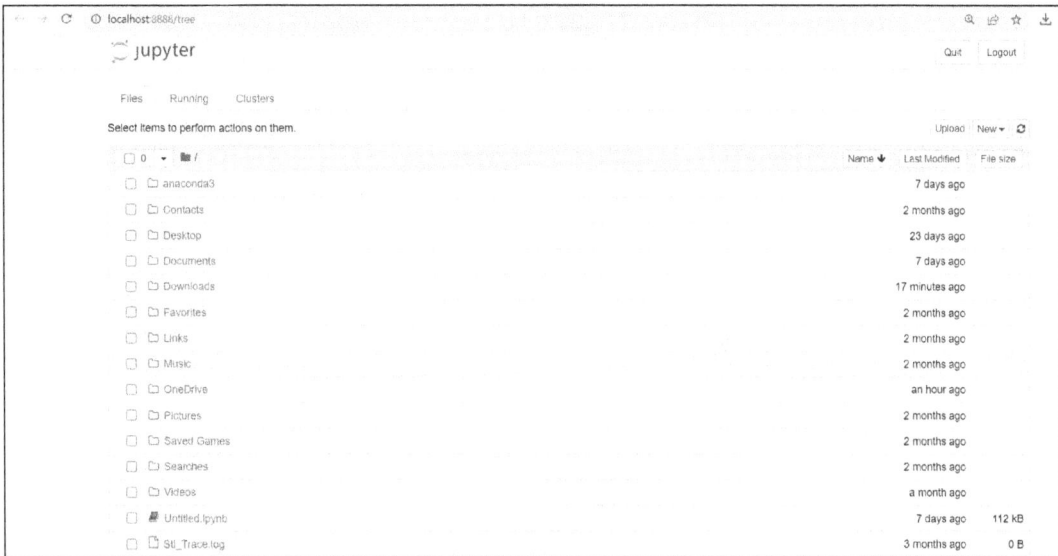

Figure 1.10: Jupyter Notebook opened in browser

7. You can click on the **New** button on the right side and write your first statement as displayed in *Figure 1.11*. In the rest of the chapters, the code is developed in Jupyter Notebook.

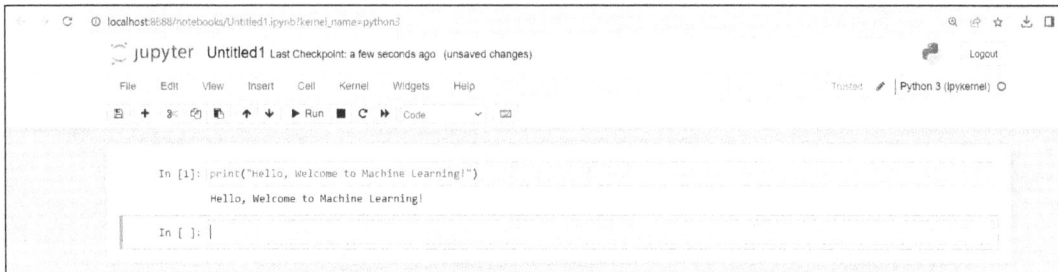

Figure 1.11: First program in Jupyter Notebook

Conclusion

In this chapter, we have discussed an introduction to data science and its significance by means of various applications in diverse domains. The evolution of data science, starting from early foundations to the future of data science, is discussed in detail. Thereafter, stages for developing a complete data science project are also described. Further, various data security issues are discussed. The difference between data science, data analytics, machine learning, and artificial intelligence is also elaborated to get a better understanding of the subject matter. Subsequently, the requirements to build a career as a data scientist are explained in depth. The steps to install Anaconda for Python are included at the end of the chapter.

In the next chapter, we will discuss **Numerical Python** (**NumPy**) and its usage in detail, which serves as the first step to learn data science and ML.

Multiple choice questions

1. **What is the primary objective of data science?**

    a. To create mobile apps

    b. To visualize charts only

    c. To extract knowledge and insights from data

    d. To build websites

2. **Which of the following best represents the evolution of data science?**

    a. Excel | PowerPoint | Python

    b. Statistics | Data mining | Data science

    c. Machine learning | Excel | Tableau

    d. Database | Java | Data analysis

3. **Which of the following is not a typical application of data science?**

    a. Fraud detection

    b. Recommender systems

    c. Facial recognition

    d. Writing poetry

4. **What is the first stage of a data science project?**

    a. Model building

    b. Data collection

    c. Data cleaning

    d. Deployment

5. **Which stage comes after data cleaning in a typical data science workflow?**

    a. Deployment

    b. Visualization

    c. EDA

    d. Requirement gathering

6. **What is a major concern regarding data security in data science?**

    a. File compression

    b. Cloud backups

    c.   Unauthorized access to sensitive data

    d.   File size limits

7. **Which of the following is true about data science and ML?**

    a.   They are completely unrelated

    b.   ML is a subset of data science

    c.   Data science is a branch of ML

    d.   They are synonyms

8. **Which of these fields focuses primarily on human-like decision making?**

    a.   Data science

    b.   Data analysis

    c.   AI

    d.   Business intelligence

9. **Which of the following is not a role a data scientist might perform?**

    a.   Data engineer

    b.   Business analyst

    c.   Software tester

    d.   ML engineer

10. **What is one of the most important skills for a data scientist?**

    a.   Video editing

    b.   Statistical analysis

    c.   CAD design

    d.   Typing speed

11. **What is usually the minimum education requirement for a data scientist role?**

    a.   High school diploma

    b.   Associate degree

    c.   Bachelor's or master's degree in a quantitative field

    d.   Certificate course

12. **Which tool is commonly used for managing data science environments?**

    a.   WordPress

    b.   Android Studio

    c.   Anaconda

    d.   Canva

13. **What is the first step in installing Anaconda?**

    a.   Install Python separately

    b.   Download it from the official Anaconda website

    c.   Open Jupyter Notebook

    d.   Set up a GitHub account

14. **After installing Anaconda, which IDE is available by default for Python?**

    a.   Visual Studio

    b.   Eclipse

    c.   Jupyter Notebook

    d.   Android Studio

15. **Which command is used in the terminal to launch Anaconda Navigator?**

    a.   anaconda

    b.   launch-anaconda

    c.   anaconda-navigator

    d.   start anaconda

16. **Which of the following best describes data analysis?**

    a.   Creating AI models

    b.   Understanding data through summary statistics and visuals

    c.   Creating games

    d.   Making mobile apps

17. **Which of the following is an AI application?**

    a.   Excel graphs

    b.   Voice assistants like Siri and Alexa

    c.   Google Docs

    d.   Notepad

18. **What is one major advantage of using Python in data science?**

    a.   High memory usage

    b.   Easy-to-read syntax and rich libraries

    c.   Requires complex setup

    d.   Limited community support

19. **Which of the following is a popular Python library for ML?**

    a. NumPy

    b. Matplotlib

    c. Scikit-learn

    d. WordPress

20. **What does the .ipynb file extension stand for?**

    a. iPad notebook

    b. IPython notebook

    c. Interactive presentation notebook

    d. Internet Python block

Answers

1. c
2. b
3. d
4. b
5. c
6. c
7. b
8. c
9. c
10. b
11. c
12. c
13. b
14. c
15. c
16. b
17. b
18. b
19. c
20. b

Questions

1. Define data science and explain its significance in today's digital world.

2. What are the key components of the data science process, and how do they contribute to extracting insights from data?

3. Trace the evolution of data science from its early foundations to its current state.

4. How have advancements in technology, such as big data and cloud computing, influenced the evolution of data science?

5. Discuss the role of data science in addressing modern challenges and driving innovation across various industries.

6. Describe the roles and responsibilities of a data scientist in an organization.

7. How does a data engineer differ from a data analyst or a machine learning engineer?

8. Discuss the importance of interdisciplinary collaboration in data science projects and the roles that domain experts play.

9. What are some essential skills and qualifications required for a career in data science?

10. Explain the significance of communication skills for data science professionals.

11. Outline the key stages involved in a typical data science project lifecycle.

12. How does the problem definition stage influence the overall success of a data science project?

13. Provide examples of real-world applications of data science in various industries, such as healthcare, finance, and retail.

14. How does data science contribute to improving customer experience and personalization in e-commerce platforms?

15. Identify and discuss potential data security threats that organizations may face in handling sensitive data.

16. How can organizations mitigate the risk of unauthorized access and data breaches in their data systems?

17. Explain the importance of regulatory compliance and data privacy regulations in addressing data security issues.

CHAPTER 2
NumPy

Introduction

NumPy is a fundamental library for numerical and scientific computing in Python. It provides support for large multi-dimensional arrays and matrices, along with a comprehensive collection of mathematical functions to operate on these arrays. NumPy enables efficient array operations, vectorization, and broadcasting, making it faster and more memory-efficient than Python's native lists. It also includes advanced linear algebra, random number generation, and integration capabilities with other scientific libraries like Pandas, SciPy, and Matplotlib. NumPy's efficiency and versatility make it indispensable for data science and machine learning tasks. A real-world example of NumPy in use is in financial market analysis. Analysts and data scientists use NumPy to handle large arrays of stock price data for tasks like calculating moving averages, daily returns, or portfolio risk. For instance, NumPy can quickly compute the mean and standard deviation of thousands of stock prices, helping identify trends and volatility. Its ability to perform fast vectorized operations makes it ideal for processing time-series financial data efficiently, which is essential for making real-time investment decisions.

Structure

The chapter covers the following topics:

- Introduction to NumPy

- Creating NumPy arrays
- NumPy array attributes
- NumPy array operations
- Broadcasting
- Indexing, slicing, and iterating NumPy arrays
- Fancy indexing in NumPy
- Advanced indexing techniques
- Reshaping arrays in NumPy
- Combining and splitting NumPy arrays
- Random numbers and simulations in NumPy
- Input and output in NumPy
- Performance and optimization in NumPy

Objectives

The objective of this chapter is to provide a comprehensive understanding of NumPy, the foundational library for numerical computing in Python. By studying this chapter, readers will grasp the core features of NumPy, such as its speed, efficiency, and capability to handle large multi-dimensional arrays and matrices. It covers various ways to create arrays, including manual methods, list conversion, and built-in functions like **zeros()**, **ones()**, and **arange()**. The chapter also looks into input and output operations, including reading from and writing to text and binary files. The learners will become proficient in performing arithmetic, statistical, and **universal functions (ufuncs)** for efficient computations. Additionally, concepts such as indexing, slicing, iterating, reshaping, and splitting arrays are explained to enhance data manipulation skills. The chapter further explores the use of the random module for generating random numbers, handling binary data, and understanding broadcasting rules. Overall, the objective is to equip readers with the practical knowledge and skills required to effectively use NumPy for data analysis, simulations, and scientific computing.

Introduction to NumPy

NumPy is a powerful library in Python used for numerical and scientific computing. It provides support for arrays, matrices, and a wide variety of mathematical functions to operate on these data structures efficiently. Here are some key aspects of NumPy:

- **N-dimensional arrays**: At the core of NumPy is the **ndarray** object, which is a multi-dimensional array that supports a variety of data types. These arrays are more efficient for numerical operations compared to Python's native lists.

- **Broadcasting**: NumPy allows operations on arrays of different shapes through a process known as broadcasting, which avoids the need for explicitly reshaping arrays to perform element-wise operations.

- **ufuncs**: These are functions that operate element-wise on arrays, such as trigonometric functions, arithmetic operations, and more. They are implemented in C for efficiency, making NumPy operations very fast.

- **Vectorization**: NumPy operations are vectorized, meaning they are optimized to operate on entire arrays without the need for explicit loops. This leads to concise and fast code.

- **Linear algebra**: NumPy provides extensive support for linear algebra operations, including matrix multiplication, determinants, eigenvalues, and singular value decomposition.

- **Random number generation**: The library includes a robust random number generation module (`np.random`) for creating arrays of random numbers from various distributions.

- **Integration with other libraries**: NumPy serves as the foundation for other scientific computing libraries in Python, such as SciPy, Pandas, and Matplotlib, making it integral to the scientific Python ecosystem.

Importance of NumPy in data science

NumPy is essential in data science for several reasons:

- **Efficiency**: Operations on NumPy arrays are faster and more memory-efficient than on Python lists.

- **Ease of use**: It simplifies complex mathematical and statistical computations with concise code.

- **Foundation for other libraries**: Many other data science libraries, like Pandas (for data manipulation), SciPy (for scientific computations), and Matplotlib (for plotting), are built on top of NumPy, making it a fundamental tool for any data scientist.

NumPy basics

Before working on NumPy, you need to install its package. To install NumPy, you can use the Python package manager, **pip**. Open your command line or terminal and run the following command:

```
pip install numpy
```

This will download and install the latest version of NumPy available from the **Python Package Index (PyPI)**. If you are using a Jupyter Notebook, you can install NumPy by running:

```
!pip install numpy
```

Creating NumPy arrays

NumPy provides a variety of methods to create arrays, ranging from simple conversions of Python sequences to generating arrays filled with specific patterns or random numbers. In this section, we discuss six methods to create NumPy arrays.

From Python lists and tuples

Creating NumPy arrays from lists and tuples is straightforward. You can use the **np.array()** function to convert these Python data structures into NumPy arrays. The following code demonstrates how to do this:

```
import numpy as np
```

This line imports the NumPy library and assigns it the alias **np**, which is a common convention. NumPy provides support for large, multi-dimensional arrays and matrices, along with a collection of mathematical functions to operate on these arrays. The following code demonstrates creating arrays from lists:

- **Creating a 1D array from a list:**

```
# Creating 1D array from list
list_1D = [1, 2, 3, 4, 5]
array_1D = np.array(list_1D)
print("1D Array from list:", array_1D)
```

  o   The details are as follows:

  - **list_1D = [1, 2, 3, 4, 5]:** This line creates a Python list containing five integers.

  - **array_1D = np.array(list_1D):** This line converts the Python list **list_1D** into a NumPy array using the **np.array()** function.

  - **print("1D Array from list:", array_1D):** This line prints the NumPy array created from the list.

- **Creating a 2D array from a list of lists:**

```
# Creating 2D array from list of lists
list_2D = [[1, 2, 3], [4, 5, 6]]
array_2D = np.array(list_2D)
print("2D Array from list of lists:\n", array_2D)
```

  o   The details are as follows:

  - **list_2D = [[1, 2, 3], [4, 5, 6]]:** This line creates a Python list of lists, which is a 2-dimensional structure (a list containing two lists, each with three integers).

- **array_2D = np.array(list_2D)**: This line converts the Python list of lists `list_2D` into a 2D NumPy array using the **np.array()** function.

- **print("2D Array from list of lists:\n", array_2D)**: This line prints the 2D NumPy array created from the list of lists.

- **Creating a 1D array from a tuple**:

```
# Creating 1D array from tuple
tuple_1D = (1, 2, 3, 4, 5)
array_1D_from_tuple = np.array(tuple_1D)
print("1D Array from tuple:", array_1D_from_tuple)
```

  - The details are as follows:

    - **tuple_1D = (1, 2, 3, 4, 5)**: This line creates a Python tuple containing five integers.

    - **array_1D_from_tuple = np.array(tuple_1D)**: This line converts the Python tuple **tuple_1D** into a NumPy array using the **np.array()** function.

    - **print("1D Array from tuple:", array_1D_from_tuple)**: This line prints the NumPy array created from the tuple.

- **Creating a 2D array from a tuple of tuples**:

```
# Creating 2D array from tuple of tuples
tuple_2D = ((1, 2, 3), (4, 5, 6))
array_2D_from_tuple = np.array(tuple_2D)
print("2D Array from tuple of tuples:\n", array_2D_from_tuple)
```

  - The details are as follows:

    - **tuple_2D = ((1, 2, 3), (4, 5, 6))**: This line creates a Python tuple of tuples, which is a 2-dimensional structure (a tuple containing two tuples, each with three integers).

    - **array_2D_from_tuple = np.array(tuple_2D)**: This line converts the Python tuple of tuples **tuple_2D** into a 2D NumPy array using the **np.array()** function.

    - **print("2D Array from tuple of tuples:\n", array_2D_from_tuple)**: This line prints the 2D NumPy array created from the tuple of tuples.

The combined code with output is given as follows:

```
# Creating 1D array from list
list_1D = [1, 2, 3, 4, 5]
```

```
array_1D = np.array(list_1D)
print("1D Array from list:", array_1D)

# Creating 2D array from list of lists
list_2D = [[1, 2, 3], [4, 5, 6]]
array_2D = np.array(list_2D)
print("2D Array from list of lists:\n", array_2D)

# Creating 1D array from tuple
tuple_1D = (1, 2, 3, 4, 5)
array_1D_from_tuple = np.array(tuple_1D)
print("1D Array from tuple:", array_1D_from_tuple)

# Creating 2D array from tuple of tuples
tuple_2D = ((1, 2, 3), (4, 5, 6))
array_2D_from_tuple = np.array(tuple_2D)
print("2D Array from tuple of tuples:\n", array_2D_from_tuple)
```

The output is as follows:

```
1D Array from list: [1 2 3 4 5]
2D Array from list of lists:
 [[1 2 3]
 [4 5 6]]
1D Array from tuple: [1 2 3 4 5]
2D Array from tuple of tuples:
 [[1 2 3]
 [4 5 6]]
```

A summarized table of comparison of creating different kinds of arrays is shown in *Table 2.1*:

Method	Input type	Example input	Resulting array	Dimensions (shape)
1D array from a list	List	`[1, 2, 3, 4, 5]`	`[1 2 3 4 5]`	1D (5,)
2D array from a list of lists	List of lists	`[[1, 2], [3, 4]]`	`[[1 2] [3 4]]`	2D (2, 2)
1D array from a tuple	Tuple	`(10, 20, 30, 40)`	`[10 20 30 40]`	1D (4,)
2D array from a tuple of tuples	Tuple of tuples	`((1, 0), (0, 1))`	`[[1 0] [0 1]]`	2D (2, 2)

Table 2.1: Comparison of creating different types of lists (arrays) in NumPy

Creating arrays with specific values

There are four types that fall into this category as follows:

- **Zeros array**: If you want to create an array filled with zeros, then the following code is used:

```
array_zeros = np.zeros((3, 4))
print("Zeros Array:\n", array_zeros)
```

Output:
```
Zeros Array:
 [[0. 0. 0. 0.]
 [0. 0. 0. 0.]
 [0. 0. 0. 0.]]
```

- **Ones array**: If you want to create an array filled with ones, then the following code is used:

```
array_ones = np.ones((2, 3))
print("Ones Array:\n", array_ones)
```

Output:
```
Ones Array:
 [[1. 1. 1.]
 [1. 1. 1.]]
```

- **Full array**: If you want to create an array filled with a specific value, then the following code is used:

```
array_full = np.full((2, 3), 7)
print("Full Array:\n", array_full)
```

Output:
```
Full Array:
 [[7 7 7]
 [7 7 7]]
```

- **Identity matrix**: If you want to create a 2D identity matrix, then the following code is used:

```
array_identity = np.eye(3)
print("Identity Matrix:\n", array_identity)
```

Output:
```
Identity Matrix:
 [[1. 0. 0.]
 [0. 1. 0.]
 [0. 0. 1.]]
```

Creating arrays with a range of values

There are two types that fall into this category, listed as follows:

- **np.arange()**: It creates an array with values in a specified range. The code is as follows:

```
array_arange = np.arange(10)
print("Arange Array:\n", array_arange)
```

- **np.linspace()**: It creates an array with a specified number of evenly spaced values between two bounds. The code is as follows:

```
array_linspace = np.linspace(0, 1, 5)
print("Linspace Array:\n", array_linspace)
```

Creating random arrays

There are two types that fall into this category:

- **np.random.rand()**: It creates an array of the given shape with random values between 0 and 1 as shown in the following code:

```
array_random = np.random.rand(3, 3)
print("Random Array:\n", array_random)
```

- **np.random.randint()**: It creates an array with random integers within a specified range, as shown in the following code:

```
array_random_int = np.random.randint(0, 10, (3, 3))
print("Random Integer Array:\n", array_random_int)
```

Creating empty and uninitialized arrays

Empty and uninitialized arrays are created as follows:

- **np.empty()**: It creates an array without initializing the values as in the following code:

```
array_empty = np.empty((2, 2))
print("Empty Array:\n", array_empty)
```

- **np.empty_like()**: It creates an uninitialized array with the same shape and type as another array, as shown in the following code:

```
array_base = np.array([[1, 2, 3], [4, 5, 6]])
array_empty_like = np.empty_like(array_base)
print("Empty Like Array:\n", array_empty_like)
```

Creating arrays with patterns

There are two types that fall in this category:

- **np.tile()**: It repeats an array a specified number of times along each axis, as in the following code:

```
array_tile = np.tile([1, 2], (3, 2))
print("Tiled Array:\n", array_tile)
```

- **np.repeat()**: It repeats elements of an array as in the code given below:

```
array_repeat = np.repeat([1, 2, 3], 2)
print("Repeated Array:\n", array_repeat)
```

The combined code with output is given as follows:

```
import numpy as np

# 1D array from list
list_1D = [1, 2, 3, 4, 5]
array_1D = np.array(list_1D)

# 2D array from tuple of tuples
tuple_2D = ((1, 2, 3), (4, 5, 6))
array_2D = np.array(tuple_2D)

# Zeros array
array_zeros = np.zeros((3, 4))

# Ones array
array_ones = np.ones((2, 3))

# Full array
array_full = np.full((2, 3), 7)

# Identity matrix
array_identity = np.eye(3)

# Arange array
array_arange = np.arange(10)

# Linspace array
array_linspace = np.linspace(0, 1, 5)

# Random array
array_random = np.random.rand(3, 3)

# Random integer array
array_random_int = np.random.randint(0, 10, (3, 3))
```

```
# Empty array
array_empty = np.empty((2, 2))

# Empty like array
array_base = np.array([[1, 2, 3], [4, 5, 6]])
array_empty_like = np.empty_like(array_base)

# Tiled array
array_tile = np.tile([1, 2], (3, 2))

# Repeated array
array_repeat = np.repeat([1, 2, 3], 2)

# Display results
print("1D Array from list:", array_1D)
print("2D Array from tuple of tuples:\n", array_2D)
print("Zeros Array:\n", array_zeros)
print("Ones Array:\n", array_ones)
print("Full Array:\n", array_full)
print("Identity Matrix:\n", array_identity)
print("Arange Array:\n", array_arange)
print("Linspace Array:\n", array_linspace)
print("Random Array:\n", array_random)
print("Random Integer Array:\n", array_random_int)
print("Empty Array:\n", array_empty)
print("Empty Like Array:\n", array_empty_like)
print("Tiled Array:\n", array_tile)
print("Repeated Array:\n", array_repeat)
```

The output is as follows:

```
1D Array from list: [1 2 3 4 5]
2D Array from tuple of tuples:
 [[1 2 3]
  [4 5 6]]
Zeros Array:
 [[0. 0. 0. 0.]
  [0. 0. 0. 0.]
  [0. 0. 0. 0.]]
Ones Array:
 [[1. 1. 1.]
  [1. 1. 1.]]
```

```
Full Array:
 [[7 7 7]
  [7 7 7]]
Identity Matrix:
 [[1. 0. 0.]
  [0. 1. 0.]
  [0. 0. 1.]]
Arange Array:
 [0 1 2 3 4 5 6 7 8 9]
Linspace Array:
 [0.   0.25 0.5  0.75 1.  ]
Random Array:
 [[0.76872367 0.96800122 0.16147715]
  [0.26456885 0.25314601 0.85930394]
  [0.78695712 0.41474333 0.90940164]]
Random Integer Array:
 [[8 7 4]
  [9 6 1]
  [3 1 8]]
Empty Array:
 [[2.14321575e-314 2.10077583e-312]
  [4.94065646e-324 0.00000000e+000]]
Empty Like Array:
 [[2.14321575e-314 2.10077583e-312 4.94065646e-324]
  [0.00000000e+000 0.00000000e+000 0.00000000e+000]]
Tiled Array:
 [[1 2 1 2]
  [1 2 1 2]
  [1 2 1 2]]
Repeated Array:
 [1 1 2 2 3 3]
```

The above output is explained as follows:

- **1D array from list**: [1 2 3 4 5]—A simple 1D array created from the list [1, 2, 3, 4, 5].

- **2D array from tuple of tuples**: [[1 2 3] [4 5 6]] —A 2D array created from a tuple of tuples.

- **Zeros array**: A 3x4 array filled with zeros.

- **Ones array**: A 2x3 array filled with ones.

- **Full array**: A 2x3 array filled with the value 7.

- **Identity matrix**: A 3x3 identity matrix.

- **Arange array**: An array with values ranging from 0 to 9.

- **Linspace array**: An array with 5 evenly spaced values between 0 and 1.

- **Random array**: A 3x3 array filled with random values between 0 and 1.

- **Random integer array**: A 3x3 array filled with random integers between 0 and 10.

- **Empty array**: A 2x2 array with uninitialized values.

- **Empty like array**: An uninitialized array with the same shape and type as **array_base**.

- **Tiled array**: An array created by repeating the array **[1, 2]** three times along the first axis and two times along the second axis.

- **Repeated array**: An array where each element of **[1, 2, 3]** is repeated twice.

NumPy array attributes

NumPy arrays have several attributes that provide information about their size, shape, data type, and memory layout. These attributes are useful for understanding and manipulating arrays effectively. The most commonly used array attributes in NumPy are as follows:

- **shape**: It returns a tuple indicating the size of each dimension of the array. For example, a 2D array with shape (3, 4) has 3 rows and 4 columns.

- **ndim**: It returns the number of dimensions (axes) of the array.

- **size**: It returns the total number of elements in the array.

- **dtype**: It returns the data type of the elements in the array, such as int, float, etc.

- **itemsize**: It returns the size in bytes of each element in the array.

- **nbytes**: It returns the total number of bytes consumed by the array's elements.

- **strides**: It returns a tuple indicating the number of bytes to step in each dimension when traversing the array.

- **flags**: It returns an object containing information about memory layout, such as whether the array is writeable, contiguous, etc.

- **real and imag**: For complex arrays, these attributes return the real and imaginary parts of the array, respectively.

- **data**: It returns a buffer object pointing to the start of the array's data.

The code to understand the array attributes is provided as follows:

```
import numpy as np

# Create a 2D array
arr = np.array([[1, 2, 3], [4, 5, 6]])
```

```
# Print array attributes
print("Shape:", arr.shape)
print("Number of Dimensions:", arr.ndim)
print("Size:", arr.size)
print("Data Type:", arr.dtype)
print("Size of Each Element (in bytes):", arr.itemsize)
print("Total Bytes Consumed by the Array:", arr.nbytes)
print("Strides:", arr.strides)
print("Memory Layout Flags:", arr.flags)
print("Real Part of the Array:", arr.real)
print("Imaginary Part of the Array:", arr.imag)
print("Buffer Object:", arr.data)
```

The output is as follows:

```
Shape: (2, 3)
Number of Dimensions: 2
Size: 6
Data Type: int64
Size of Each Element (in bytes): 8
Total Bytes Consumed by the Array: 48
Strides: (24, 8)
Memory Layout Flags:    C_CONTIGUOUS : True
  F_CONTIGUOUS : False
  OWNDATA : True
  WRITEABLE : True
  ALIGNED : True
  WRITEBACKIFCOPY : False
  UPDATEIFCOPY : False
Real Part of the Array: [[1 2 3]
 [4 5 6]]
Imaginary Part of the Array: [[0 0 0]
 [0 0 0]]
Buffer Object: <memory at 0x7faba0777170>
```

NumPy array operations

NumPy offers a wide range of array operations, including arithmetic operations, mathematical functions, array manipulation, logical operations, and more. These operations enable efficient computation and manipulation of arrays, making NumPy a powerful tool for numerical and scientific computing. In this section, we will discuss some of the most commonly used array operations in NumPy.

Arithmetic operations

NumPy arrays support element-wise arithmetic operations such as addition (+), subtraction (-), multiplication (*), division (/), and exponentiation (**). These operations can be performed between arrays of the same shape or between arrays and scalar values. They are helpful in stock market analysis, image processing, weather data analysis, physics simulations, and medical imaging. The code representing the use of arithmetic operations on NumPy arrays is given as follows, and it is self-explanatory:

```
import numpy as np

# Create two arrays
arr1 = np.array([[1, 2, 3], [4, 5, 6]])
arr2 = np.array([[7, 8, 9], [10, 11, 12]])

# Addition
print("Addition:")
print(arr1 + arr2)

# Subtraction
print("\nSubtraction:")
print(arr1 - arr2)

# Multiplication (element-wise)
print("\nMultiplication:")
print(arr1 * arr2)

# Division (element-wise)
print("\nDivision:")
print(arr2 / arr1)

# Exponentiation (element-wise)
print("\nExponentiation:")
print(arr1 ** 2)

# Multiplication with scalar
print("\nMultiplication with scalar:")
print(arr1 * 2)

# Addition with scalar
print("\nAddition with scalar:")
print(arr1 + 10)
```

The output is as follows:

```
Addition:
[[ 8 10 12]
 [14 16 18]]
```

```
Subtraction:
[[-6 -6 -6]
 [-6 -6 -6]]
```

```
Multiplication:
[[ 7 16 27]
 [40 55 72]]
```

```
Division:
[[7.  4.  3. ]
 [2.5 2.2 2. ]]
```

```
Exponentiation:
[[ 1  4  9]
 [16 25 36]]
```

```
Multiplication with scalar:
[[ 2  4  6]
 [ 8 10 12]]
```

```
Addition with scalar:
[[11 12 13]
 [14 15 16]]
```

Mathematical functions

NumPy provides a wide range of mathematical functions that operate element-wise on arrays, such as **np.sin()**, **np.cos()**, **np.exp()**, **np.log()**, **np.sqrt()**, and many more. These functions can be applied to entire arrays or to specific elements. The code representing the use of mathematical functions is given as follows:

```
import numpy as np

# Create an array
arr = np.array([[1, 2, 3], [4, 5, 6]])

# Calculate sine
print("Sine:")
print(np.sin(arr))

# Calculate cosine
print("\nCosine:")
print(np.cos(arr))

# Calculate exponential
print("\nExponential:")
print(np.exp(arr))
```

```
# Calculate natural logarithm
print("\nNatural Logarithm:")
print(np.log(arr))

# Calculate square root
print("\nSquare Root:")
print(np.sqrt(arr))

# Calculate absolute value
print("\nAbsolute Value:")
print(np.abs(arr))
```

The output is as follows:

Sine:
```
[[ 0.84147098  0.90929743  0.14112001]
 [-0.7568025  -0.95892427 -0.2794155 ]]
```

Cosine:
```
[[ 0.54030231 -0.41614684 -0.9899925 ]
 [-0.65364362  0.28366219  0.96017029]]
```

Exponential:
```
[[  2.71828183   7.3890561   20.08553692]
 [ 54.59815003 148.4131591  403.42879349]]
```

Natural Logarithm:
```
[[0.         0.69314718 1.09861229]
 [1.38629436 1.60943791 1.79175947]]
```

Square Root:
```
[[1.         1.41421356 1.73205081]
 [2.         2.23606798 2.44948974]]
```

Absolute Value:
```
[[1 2 3]
 [4 5 6]]
```

Aggregation functions

NumPy offers aggregation functions that compute summary statistics across arrays, such as **np.sum()**, **np.mean()**, **np.median()**, **np.min()**, **np.max()**, **np.std()**, and **np.var()**. These functions can operate along specific axes of multi-dimensional arrays. The code representing aggregation functions is given as follows:

```
import numpy as np

# Create an array
arr = np.array([[1, 2, 3], [4, 5, 6]])
```

```python
# Calculate sum
print("Sum:")
print(np.sum(arr))

# Calculate mean
print("\nMean:")
print(np.mean(arr))

# Calculate median
print("\nMedian:")
print(np.median(arr))

# Calculate minimum
print("\nMinimum:")
print(np.min(arr))

# Calculate maximum
print("\nMaximum:")
print(np.max(arr))

# Calculate standard deviation
print("\nStandard Deviation:")
print(np.std(arr))

# Calculate variance
print("\nVariance:")
print(np.var(arr))
```

The output is as follows:

```
Sum:
21

Mean:
3.5

Median:
3.5

Minimum:
1

Maximum:
6

Standard Deviation:
1.707825127659933
```

```
Variance:
2.9166666666666665
```

Array manipulation functions

NumPy provides functions for reshaping, slicing, concatenating, and splitting arrays. Some commonly used functions include **np.reshape()**, **np.transpose()**, **np.concatenate()**, **np.split()**, **np.vstack()**, and **np.hstack()**. The code representing array manipulation functions are given as under:

```python
import numpy as np
# Create some arrays for manipulation
arr1 = np.array([[1, 2, 3], [4, 5, 6]])
arr2 = np.array([[7, 8, 9], [10, 11, 12]])
arr3 = np.array([13, 14, 15, 16, 17, 18])

# Reshape array
print("Reshape:")
reshaped_arr = np.reshape(arr3, (2, 3))
print(reshaped_arr)

# Transpose array
print("\nTranspose:")
transposed_arr = np.transpose(arr1)
print(transposed_arr)

# Concatenate arrays
print("\nConcatenate:")
concatenated_arr = np.concatenate((arr1, arr2), axis=0)
print(concatenated_arr)

# Split array
print("\nSplit:")
split_arr = np.split(arr3, 3)
for part in split_arr:
    print(part)

# Vertical stack
print("\nVertical Stack:")
vstacked_arr = np.vstack((arr1, arr2))
print(vstacked_arr)

# Horizontal stack
print("\nHorizontal Stack:")
hstacked_arr = np.hstack((arr1, arr2))
print(hstacked_arr)
```

The output is as follows:

```
Reshape:
[[13 14 15]
 [16 17 18]]
```

```
Transpose:
[[1 4]
 [2 5]
 [3 6]]
```

```
Concatenate:
[[ 1  2  3]
 [ 4  5  6]
 [ 7  8  9]
 [10 11 12]]
```

```
Split:
[13 14]
[15 16]
[17 18]
```

```
Vertical Stack:
[[ 1  2  3]
 [ 4  5  6]
 [ 7  8  9]
 [10 11 12]]
```

```
Horizontal Stack:
[[ 1  2  3  7  8  9]
 [ 4  5  6 10 11 12]]
```

NaN values

In NumPy, several array manipulation and statistical functions are sensitive to **not a number** (**NaN**) values, meaning the presence of NaN can affect or invalidate the result. For example:

- `np.mean()`, `np.sum()`, `np.min()`, `np.max()`, and similar functions return NaN if any element in the array is NaN.

- Comparison and logical operations involving NaN typically return **False**, as NaN is not equal to itself (`np.nan == np.nan` is **False**), which can lead to unexpected behavior in filtering or masking.

- Sorting functions, like `np.sort()`, retain NaN values in their original position relative to sorting rules (though behavior may vary slightly by version).

To handle NaN values safely, NumPy provides NaN-aware versions of many functions (e.g., **np.nanmean()**, **np.nansum()**, **np.nanmin()**, etc.) which ignore NaN values during computation. Using these ensures more reliable results when working with datasets containing missing or undefined values.

Logical operations

NumPy supports element-wise logical operations, such as **np.logical_and()**, **np.logical_or()**, **np.logical_not()**, and **np.logical_xor()**. These operations are useful for Boolean array manipulation and conditional filtering. The code representing these functions is given as under:

```python
import numpy as np
# Create two boolean arrays
arr1 = np.array([True, False, True, False])
arr2 = np.array([True, True, False, False])

# Logical AND
logical_and_result = np.logical_and(arr1, arr2)
print("Logical AND:")
print(logical_and_result)

# Logical OR
logical_or_result = np.logical_or(arr1, arr2)
print("\nLogical OR:")
print(logical_or_result)

# Logical NOT
logical_not_result = np.logical_not(arr1)
print("\nLogical NOT:")
print(logical_not_result)

# Logical XOR
logical_xor_result = np.logical_xor(arr1, arr2)
print("\nLogical XOR:")
print(logical_xor_result)
```

The output is as follows:

```
Logical AND:
[ True False False False]
```

```
Logical OR:
[ True  True  True False]
```

```
Logical NOT:
[False  True False  True]
```

Logical XOR:
[False True   True False]

Sorting and searching

NumPy provides functions for sorting arrays (**np.sort()**) and finding elements (**np.where()**, **np.argmax()**, **np.argmin()**) based on specific conditions. These functions facilitate data manipulation and analysis. The code representing these functions is given as under:

```
import numpy as np

# Create an array
arr = np.array([3, 1, 4, 1, 5, 9, 2, 6, 5, 3, 5])

# Sorting array
sorted_arr = np.sort(arr)
print("Sorted Array:")
print(sorted_arr)
# Finding indices where a condition is met
indices_where = np.where(arr == 5)
print("\nIndices where elements are 5:")
print(indices_where)

# Finding the index of the maximum element
index_max = np.argmax(arr)
print("\nIndex of maximum element:")
print(index_max)

# Finding the index of the minimum element
index_min = np.argmin(arr)
print("\nIndex of minimum element:")
print(index_min)
```

The output is as follows:

Sorted Array:
[1 1 2 3 3 4 5 5 5 6 9]

Indices where elements are 5:
(array([4, 8, 10]),)

Index of maximum element:
5

Index of minimum element:
1

Linear algebra operations

NumPy includes a comprehensive set of linear algebra functions for matrix operations, including matrix multiplication (**np.dot()**), matrix inversion (**np.linalg.inv()**), eigenvalue decomposition (**np.linalg.eig()**), singular value decomposition (**np. linalg.svd()**), and more. The code representing the above operations is given as follows:

```python
import numpy as np

# Create an array
arr = np.array([3, 1, 4, 1, 5, 9, 2, 6, 5, 3, 5])

# Sorting array
sorted_arr = np.sort(arr)
print("Sorted Array:")
print(sorted_arr)

# Finding indices where a condition is met
indices_where = np.where(arr == 5)
print("\nIndices where elements are 5:")
print(indices_where)

# Finding the index of the maximum element
index_max = np.argmax(arr)
print("\nIndex of maximum element:")
print(index_max)

# Finding the index of the minimum element
index_min = np.argmin(arr)
print("\nIndex of minimum element:")
print(index_min)
```

The output is as follows:

```
Sorted Array:
[1 1 2 3 3 4 5 5 5 6 9]

Indices where elements are 5:
(array([4, 8, 10]),)

Index of maximum element:
5

Index of minimum element:
1
```

Universal functions

Universal functions, or ufuncs, are a core feature of NumPy that provide efficient element-wise operations on arrays. They operate on **ndarrays** in an element-by-element fashion, supporting a wide range of mathematical operations. Ufuncs are designed to be fast and efficient, taking advantage of NumPy's underlying C implementation to execute operations much faster than Python loops.

Key features of ufuncs

Certain key characteristics of ufuncs are given as follows:

- **Element-wise operations**: Perform operations on each element of an array independently.

- **Broadcasting**: Automatically expand the dimensions of arrays to make their shapes compatible for element-wise operations.

- **Type casting**: Handle different data types and cast them to a common type if necessary.

- **Reduction operations**: Perform operations like sum, product, min, and max across an axis of an array.

- **Aggregation functions**: Include operations like **np.add**, **np.subtract**, **np.multiply**, **np.divide**, **np.power**, and more.

The code demonstrates the use of some common ufuncs in NumPy:

```
import numpy as np

# Create arrays
arr1 = np.array([1, 2, 3, 4, 5])
arr2 = np.array([10, 20, 30, 40, 50])

# Addition (element-wise)
add_result = np.add(arr1, arr2)
print("Addition:")
print(add_result)

# Subtraction (element-wise)
sub_result = np.subtract(arr2, arr1)
print("\nSubtraction:")
print(sub_result)

# Multiplication (element-wise)
mul_result = np.multiply(arr1, arr2)
```

```
print("\nMultiplication:")
print(mul_result)

# Division (element-wise)
div_result = np.divide(arr2, arr1)
print("\nDivision:")
print(div_result)

# Power (element-wise)
power_result = np.power(arr1, 2)
print("\nPower:")
print(power_result)

# Sine (element-wise)
sin_result = np.sin(arr1)
print("\nSine:")
print(sin_result)
```

The output is as follows:

```
[11 22 33 44 55]
[ 9 18 27 36 45]
[ 10  40  90 160 250]
[10. 10. 10. 10. 10.]
[ 1  4  9 16 25]
[ 0.84147098  0.90929743  0.14112001 -0.7568025  -0.95892427]
```

Advantages of using ufuncs

The benefits of using ufuncs are as follows:

- **Speed**: Ufuncs are implemented in C, making them significantly faster than equivalent operations written in pure Python.

- **Convenience**: Ufuncs handle broadcasting and 'type casting automatically, simplifying code and reducing the need for manual shape alignment.

- **Functionality**: Ufuncs provide a comprehensive suite of mathematical operations, making NumPy highly versatile for scientific computing.

Vectorized operations

Vectorized operations in NumPy refer to performing element-wise operations on entire arrays without the need for explicit loops. This leverages the power of NumPy's underlying C implementation to perform operations much faster than Python loops. The Python code demonstrating the use of vectorized operations is as follows:

```
import numpy as np

# Create arrays
arr1 = np.array([1, 2, 3, 4, 5])
arr2 = np.array([10, 20, 30, 40, 50])

# Perform element-wise addition
result_add = arr1 + arr2
print("Element-wise Addition:")
print(result_add)
# Output: [11 22 33 44 55]

# Perform element-wise multiplication
result_mul = arr1 * arr2
print("\nElement-wise Multiplication:")
print(result_mul)
# Output: [ 10  40  90 160 250]

# Perform element-wise square
result_square = arr1 ** 2
print("\nElement-wise Square:")
print(result_square)
# Output: [ 1  4  9 16 25]

# Perform element-wise sine
result_sin = np.sin(arr1)
print("\nElement-wise Sine:")
print(result_sin)
# Output: [ 0.84147098  0.90929743  0.14112001 -0.7568025  -0.95892427]
```

Broadcasting

Broadcasting is a powerful feature in NumPy that allows arithmetic operations on arrays of different shapes. It automatically expands the smaller array to match the shape of the larger array without actually copying the data.

Rules of broadcasting

There are two rules associated with broadcasting:

- **Trailing dimensions match**: If two arrays have different shapes, NumPy compares their shapes element-wise, starting with the trailing dimensions. Two dimensions are compatible if they are equal or if one of them is 1.

- **Broadcasting to a common shape**: NumPy implicitly broadcasts the smaller array to the shape of the larger array.

The code demonstrating broadcasting is given as follows:

```
import numpy as np

# Create a 1D array and a 2D array
arr1 = np.array([1, 2, 3])
arr2 = np.array([[10], [20], [30]])

# Perform element-wise addition with broadcasting
result_add = arr1 + arr2
print("Broadcasting Addition:")
print(result_add)
```

The output is as follows:

```
[[11 12 13]
 [21 22 23]
 [31 32 33]]
```

Element wise multiplication is done with broadcasting as follows:

```
# Create another 1D array
arr3 = np.array([10, 20, 30])

# Perform element-wise multiplication with broadcasting
result_mul = arr1 * arr3[:, np.newaxis]
print("\nBroadcasting Multiplication:")
print(result_mul)
```

The output is as follows:

```
[[10 20 30]
 [20 40 60]
 [30 60 90]]
```

Note: **Vectorized operations perform element-wise operations on arrays efficiently without explicit loops. Broadcasting automatically expands arrays of different shapes to be compatible for element-wise operations.**

Indexing, slicing, and iterating NumPy arrays

Indexing is used to access individual elements of an array using their indices. Slicing extracts subsets of an array using **[start:stop:step]** syntax. Iterating means looping over elements or rows in an array to perform operations on each element.

Indexing

Indexing in NumPy refers to accessing individual elements of an array using their indices. It can be used to access elements of one-dimensional or multi-dimensional arrays. The code to understand indexing is given as follows:

```
import numpy as np
# Create a 1D array
arr1 = np.array([10, 20, 30, 40, 50])
print("Element at index 2:", arr1[2])

# Create a 2D array
arr2 = np.array([[1, 2, 3], [4, 5, 6], [7, 8, 9]])
print("Element at row 1, column 2:", arr2[1, 2])
```

The output is as follows:

```
Element at index 2: 30
Element at row 1, column 2: 6
```

Slicing

Slicing in NumPy allows you to extract a subset of an array. The syntax for slicing is **[start:stop:step]**, where **start** is the index to begin with, **stop** is the index to end before, and **step** is the step size. The following code describes slicing:

```
import numpy as np

# Create a 1D array
arr1 = np.array([10, 20, 30, 40, 50])
print("Slice from index 1 to 4:", arr1[1:4])

# Create a 2D array
arr2 = np.array([[1, 2, 3], [4, 5, 6], [7, 8, 9]])
print("Slice rows 1 and 2, all columns:\n", arr2[1:3, :])

print("Slice all rows, columns 1 and 2:\n", arr2[:, 1:3])
```

The output is as follows:

```
Slice from index 1 to 4: [20 30 40]
Slice rows 1 and 2, all columns:
[[4 5 6]
[7 8 9]]
Slice all rows, columns 1 and 2:
[[2 3]
[5 6]
[8 9]]
```

Iterating

Iterating over NumPy arrays is similar to iterating over lists in Python. You can iterate over individual elements in a 1D array or over rows in a 2D array. The code to understand this is given as follows:

```python
import numpy as np

# Create a 1D array
arr1 = np.array([10, 20, 30, 40, 50])
print("Iterating over 1D array:")
for element in arr1:
    print(element)
```

The output is as follows:

```
10
20
30
40
50
```

The code is as follows:

```python
# Create a 2D array
arr2 = np.array([[1, 2, 3], [4, 5, 6], [7, 8, 9]])
print("\nIterating over 2D array rows:")
for row in arr2:
    print(row)
```

The output is as follows:

```
[1 2 3]
[4 5 6]
[7 8 9]
```

The code is as follows:

```python
# Iterating over each element in a 2D array
print("\nIterating over each element in 2D array:")
for row in arr2:
    for element in row:
        print(element)
```

The output is as follows:

```
1
2
3
4
5
```

6
7
8
9

Boolean indexing and conditional filtering in NumPy

Boolean indexing and conditional filtering allow you to select elements from an array based on specific conditions. This is a powerful feature in NumPy that helps you filter and manipulate data efficiently.

Boolean indexing

Boolean indexing involves creating a Boolean array (an array of **True** and **False** values) that matches the shape of the original array. You can use this Boolean array to index the original array, selecting only the elements where the Boolean array is **True**. The code to demonstrate Boolean indexing is given as follows:

```
import numpy as np

# Create a 1D array
arr = np.array([1, 2, 3, 4, 5, 6, 7, 8, 9, 10])

# Create a boolean array where elements are greater than 5
bool_arr = arr > 5
print("Boolean Array:")
print(bool_arr)
```

The output is as follows:

```
Boolean Array: [False False False False False  True  True  True  True  True]
```

```
# Use the boolean array to index the original array
filtered_arr = arr[bool_arr]
print("Filtered Array (elements > 5):")
print(filtered_arr)
```

Output:

```
Filtered Array (elements > 5): [6  7  8  9 10]
```

Conditional filtering

Conditional filtering allows you to directly use conditions to filter an array without explicitly creating a Boolean array. This is often more concise and readable. The code to represent conditional filtering is given as under:

```
import numpy as np

# Create a 1D array
arr = np.array([1, 2, 3, 4, 5, 6, 7, 8, 9, 10])

# Filter the array to include only elements greater than 5
filtered_arr = arr[arr > 5]
print("Filtered Array (elements > 5):")
print(filtered_arr)
```

The output is as follows:

Filtered Array (elements > 5): [6 7 8 9 10]

The code is as follows:

```
# Filter the array to include only even elements
even_filtered_arr = arr[arr % 2 == 0]
print("Filtered Array (even elements):")
print(even_filtered_arr)
```

The output is as follows:

Filtered Array (even elements): [2 4 6 8 10]

The code is as follows:

```
# Filter the array to include elements between 3 and 7
range_filtered_arr = arr[(arr >= 3) & (arr <= 7)]
print("Filtered Array (elements between 3 and 7):")
print(range_filtered_arr)
```

The output is as follows:

Filtered Array (elements between 3 and 7): [3 4 5 6 7]

Example with 2D arrays

Boolean indexing and conditional filtering also work with multi-dimensional arrays. The code is given as follows:

```
import numpy as np

# Create a 2D array
arr_2d = np.array([[1, 2, 3], [4, 5, 6], [7, 8, 9]])

# Filter the array to include elements greater than 4
filtered_arr_2d = arr_2d[arr_2d > 4]
print("Filtered 2D Array (elements > 4):")
print(filtered_arr_2d)
```

The output is as follows:

```
Filtered 2D Array (elements > 4): [5 6 7 8 9]
```

Fancy indexing in NumPy

Fancy indexing refers to using arrays of integers or Boolean values to index into an array. It allows you to access multiple elements of an array at once, and it is a more powerful and flexible way to index than regular slicing.

Using integer arrays for indexing

With fancy indexing, you can use arrays of integers to index another array. This allows you to pick out arbitrary elements from an array based on the indices specified in the integer array. The role of integer array indexing is shown in the following code:

```python
import numpy as np

# Create a 1D array
arr = np.array([10, 20, 30, 40, 50])

# Use an integer array to select elements at specific indices
index_arr = np.array([0, 2, 4])
selected_elements = arr[index_arr]
print("Selected elements using integer array indexing:")
print(selected_elements)
```

The output is as follows:

```
Selected elements using integer array indexing: [10 30 50]
```

```python
# Create a 2D array
arr_2d = np.array([[1, 2, 3], [4, 5, 6], [7, 8, 9]])

# Use an integer array to select specific rows

row_indices = np.array([0, 2])
selected_rows = arr_2d[row_indices]
print("\nSelected rows using integer array indexing:")
print(selected_rows)
```

The output is as follows:

```
Selected rows using integer array indexing:

[[1 2 3]
 [7 8 9]]
```

```python
# Use an integer array to select specific columns
```

```
col_indices = np.array([0, 2])
selected_cols = arr_2d[:, col_indices]
print("\nSelected columns using integer array indexing:")
print(selected_cols)
```

The output is as follows:

Selected columns using integer array indexing:
```
[[1 3]
[4 6]
[7 9]]
```

Advanced indexing techniques

Advanced indexing techniques combine fancy indexing with other indexing methods to achieve more complex data manipulations. This includes using multiple arrays for indexing, mixing integer arrays with slices, and using Boolean arrays for conditional selection. In NumPy, caution must be taken when using broadcasting or mixed indexing, especially when array shapes do not align. Broadcasting allows operations between arrays of different shapes, but if the shapes are incompatible, it results in a broadcasting mismatch error. Similarly, when using mixed indexing, combining basic indexing (like slices) with advanced indexing (like integer arrays or Boolean masks), you must ensure the index arrays are compatible in shape. Otherwise, it can raise index errors or, worse, produce incorrect results without any error. These issues often occur when trying to apply operations across dimensions that do not align or when index arrays have mismatched lengths, leading to unintended behavior or data corruption. Always check array shapes before performing operations to avoid such issues.

The code to demonstrate the concept is given as follows:

```
import numpy as np

# Create a 2D array
arr_2d = np.array([[1, 2, 3, 4], [5, 6, 7, 8], [9, 10, 11, 12]])

# Select elements at (0,1), (1,2), and (2,3)
row_indices = np.array([0, 1, 2])
col_indices = np.array([1, 2, 3])
selected_elements = arr_2d[row_indices, col_indices]
print("Selected elements using advanced indexing:")
print(selected_elements)
```

The output is as follows:

Selected elements using advanced indexing: [2 7 12]

```
# Use boolean array for conditional selection
```

```
bool_arr = arr_2d > 5
print("\nBoolean array for elements greater than 5:")
print(bool_arr)
```

The output is as follows:

```
Boolean array for elements greater than 5:
[[False False False False]
[False  True  True  True]
[ True  True  True  True]]
```

```
selected_elements = arr_2d[bool_arr]
print("\nElements greater than 5:")
print(selected_elements)
```

The output is as follows:

```
Elements greater than 5: [ 6  7  8  9 10 11 12]
```

```
# Mixing integer arrays with slices
selected_mixed = arr_2d[1, [0, 2, 3]]
print("\nMixed indexing (row 1, columns 0, 2, 3):")
print(selected_mixed)
```

The output is as follows:

```
Mixed indexing (row 1, columns 0, 2, 3): [5 7 8]
```

Reshaping arrays in NumPy

Reshaping arrays is a common operation in NumPy that involves changing the shape of an array without changing its data.

Changing dimensions

You can use **reshape()**, **ravel()**, and **flatten()** to change the shape and dimensionality of arrays. Each of them is explained as follows:

- **reshape()**: It changes the shape of an array to a specified shape without changing its data, as shown in the following code:

  ```
  import numpy as np

  arr = np.array([1, 2, 3, 4, 5, 6])
  reshaped_arr = arr.reshape((2, 3))
  print("Reshaped Array:\n", reshaped_arr)
  ```

     o   The output is as follows:

```
Reshaped Array:
[[1 2 3]
 [4 5 6]]
```

- **ravel()**: It returns a contiguous flattened array (1D) as shown in following code:

```
arr = np.array([[1, 2, 3], [4, 5, 6]])
raveled_arr = arr.ravel()
print("Raveled Array:", raveled_arr)
```

     o   The output is as follows:

```
Raveled Array: [1 2 3 4 5 6]
```

- **flatten()**: It returns a copy of the array collapsed into 1D as shown in the following code:

```
flattened_arr = arr.flatten()
print("Flattened Array:", flattened_arr)
```

     o   The output is as follows:

```
Flattened Array: [1 2 3 4 5 6]
```

Note: Difference between `ravel()` and `flatten` methods is that `ravel()` returns a flattened array, but it does not create a copy if not necessary. If possible, it returns a view of the original array, whereas `flatten()` returns a new array that is a flattened version of the original array. This method always returns a copy of the data. `flatten()` may be slightly slower than `ravel()` due to the copying process.

Adding and removing dimensions

You can use **np.newaxis**, **expand_dims()**, and **squeeze()** to adjust the number of dimensions in arrays. Each of them is explained as follows:

- **np.newaxis**: It adds a new axis to an array, increasing its dimensions as shown in following code:

```
arr = np.array([1, 2, 3])
expanded_arr = arr[:, np.newaxis]
print("Expanded Array with np.newaxis:\n", expanded_arr)
```

     o   The output is as follows:

```
Expanded Array with np.newaxis:
[[1]
 [2]
 [3]]
```

- **expand_dims()**: It adds a new axis at the specified position as shown in the following code:

```
expanded_arr = np.expand_dims(arr, axis=1)
print("Expanded Array with expand_dims:\n", expanded_arr)
```

- o   The output is as follows:

Expanded Array with expand_dims:
```
[[1]
 [2]
 [3]]
```

- **squeeze()**: It removes axes of length 1 from an array as shown in the following code:

```
arr = np.array([[[1], [2], [3]]])
squeezed_arr = np.squeeze(arr)
print("Squeezed Array:\n", squeezed_arr)
```

- o   The output is as follows:

Squeezed Array: [1 2 3]

Combining and splitting NumPy arrays

We can use **np.concatenate()**, **hstack()**, and **vstack()** to join multiple arrays. Each of them is explained as follows:

- **Concatenation**:

  - o   **np.concatenate()**: It joins a sequence of arrays along an existing axis as shown in the following code:

```
arr1 = np.array([[1, 2], [3, 4]])
arr2 = np.array([[5, 6]])
concatenated_arr = np.concatenate((arr1, arr2), axis=0)
print("Concatenated Array:\n", concatenated_arr)
```

Output:
Concatenated Array:
```
[[1 2]
 [3 4]
 [5 6]]
```

  - o   **hstack()**: It stacks arrays in sequence horizontally (column-wise) as shown in the following code:

```
arr1 = np.array([1, 2, 3])
arr2 = np.array([4, 5, 6])
hstacked_arr = np.hstack((arr1, arr2))
print("Horizontally Stacked Array:", hstacked_arr)
```

Output:

```
Horizontally Stacked Array: [1 2 3 4 5 6]
```

o **vstack()**: It stacks arrays in sequence vertically (row-wise) as shown in the following code:

```
vstacked_arr = np.vstack((arr1, arr2))
print("Vertically Stacked Array:\n", vstacked_arr)
```

Output:

```
Vertically Stacked Array:
[[1 2 3]
 [4 5 6]]
```

- **Splitting arrays**: We can use **np.split()**, **hsplit()**, and **vsplit()** to divide arrays into multiple sub-arrays. Each of them is described as under:

  o **np.split()**: It splits an array into multiple sub-arrays along a specified axis as shown in the following code:

```
arr = np.array([[1, 2, 3], [4, 5, 6], [7, 8, 9]])
split_arr = np.split(arr, 3)
print("Split Array:", split_arr)
```

Output:

```
Split Array: [array([[1, 2, 3]]), array([[4, 5, 6]]),
array([[7, 8, 9]])]
```

  o **hsplit()**: It splits an array into multiple sub-arrays horizontally (column-wise) as shown in the following code:

```
hsplit_arr = np.hsplit(arr, 3)
print("Horizontally Split Array:", hsplit_arr)
```

Output:

```
Horizontally Split Array:
[array([[1],
        [4],
        [7]]), array([[2],
                      [5],
                      [8]]), array([[3],
                                    [6],
                                    [9]])]
```

  o **vsplit()**: It splits an array into multiple sub-arrays vertically (row-wise) as shown in the following code:

```
vsplit_arr = np.vsplit(arr, 3)
print("Vertically Split Array:", vsplit_arr)
```

Output:
```
Vertically Split Array:
[array([[1, 2, 3]]), array([[4, 5, 6]]), array([[7, 8, 9]])]
```

Random numbers and simulations in NumPy

NumPy provides extensive capabilities for generating random numbers and performing simulations, which are essential for tasks such as statistical analysis, modeling, and machine learning.

Generating random numbers

np.random module is used for generating random numbers. The following examples display this concept:

- **rand()**: It generates random numbers from a uniform distribution over [0, 1).

```
import numpy as np
random_uniform = np.random.rand(3, 2)
print("Random numbers from a uniform distribution [0, 1):\n",
random_uniform)
```

  o The output is as follows:

```
Random numbers from a uniform distribution [0, 1): [[0.15171257
0.89364036]
 [0.36098089 0.93872435]
 [0.13982056 0.6110147 ]]
```

- **randn()**: It generates random numbers from the standard normal distribution (mean=0, variance=1).

```
random_normal = np.random.randn(3, 2)
print("Random numbers from a standard normal distribution:\n",
random_normal)
```

  o The output is as follows:

```
Random numbers from a standard normal distribution:
 [[-0.25383554  1.05323299]
 [-1.11469577  0.07825761]
 [ 0.82416024  0.16877336]]
```

- **randint()**: It generates random integers from a specified range.

```
random_integers = np.random.randint(1, 10, size=(3, 2))
print("Random integers from 1 to 9:\n", random_integers)
```

  o The output is as follows:

```
Random integers from 1 to 9:
[[3 4]
[5 2]
[1 6]]
```

- **choice()**: It generates a random sample from a given 1D array.

```
sample_array = np.array([10, 20, 30, 40, 50])
random_sample = np.random.choice(sample_array, size=3)
print("Random sample from the array [10, 20, 30, 40, 50]:", random_
sample)
```

  o The output is as follows:

```
Random sample from the array [10, 20, 30, 40, 50]: [30 20 40]
Statistical Distributions
```

- **normal()**: It generates samples from a normal (Gaussian) distribution.

```
normal_samples = np.random.normal(loc=0, scale=1, size=(3, 2))
print("Samples from a normal distribution (mean=0, std=1):\n",
normal_samples)
```

  o The output is as follows:

```
Samples from a normal distribution (mean=0, std=1):
[[-0.47211286  0.9056904 ]
[ 1.24497555  0.15488953]
[ 0.06604319 -1.05578585]]
```

- **uniform()**: It generates samples from a uniform distribution over [low, high).

```
uniform_samples = np.random.uniform(low=0, high=10, size=(3, 2))
print("Samples from a uniform distribution [0, 10):\n", uniform_
samples)
```

  o The output is as follows:

```
Samples from a uniform distribution [0, 10): [[7.16566386
4.48232734]
[6.26972914 0.69273363]
[0.52703126 9.59008009]]
```

- **binomial()**: It generates samples from a binomial distribution.

```
binomial_samples = np.random.binomial(n=10, p=0.5, size=5)
print("Samples from a binomial distribution (n=10, p=0.5):",
binomial_samples)
```

  o The output is as follows:

```
Samples from a binomial distribution (n=10, p=0.5): [3 6 4 5 3]
```

Input and output in NumPy

NumPy provides a variety of methods for reading from and writing to both text and binary files. These methods allow for efficient data storage and retrieval, which is crucial for handling large datasets in scientific computing and data analysis. The following NumPy methods are used for reading and writing text files:

- **Reading and writing text files**: Three main methods are given as follows:
    - **np.loadtxt()**: For reading well structured text files without missing values.
    - **np.genfromtxt()**: For reading text files with missing values.
    - **np.savetxt()**: For writing arrays to text files.

- **Binary data handling**: The main methods are explained as follows:
    - **np.save()**: For saving arrays to binary **.npy** files.
    - **np.load()**: For loading arrays from binary files.
    - **npz files**: For storing multiple arrays efficiently using **np.savez()** and **np.load()**.

These methods provide robust and efficient ways to handle data input and output in NumPy, making it easier to manage and manipulate large datasets.

- **Reading and writing text files**: Data can be written and read by using various NumPy methods, explained in detail as follows:
    - **Reading data with np.loadtxt()**: **np.loadtxt()** is used to read data from a text file. It is best suited for well-structured data without missing values. You can specify the delimiter and other parameters to customize the reading process. The code is given as under:

      ```
      import numpy as np

      # Save a sample text file for reading
      sample_data = np.array([[1.0, 2.0, 3.0], [4.0, 5.0, 6.0]])
      np.savetxt( sample.txt , sample_data, delimiter= , )

      # Read the text file using np.loadtxt
      loaded_data = np.loadtxt( sample.txt , delimiter= , )
      print("Data read using np.loadtxt:\n", loaded_data)
      ```

      Output:
      ```
      Data read using np.loadtxt:
      [[1. 2. 3.]
       [4. 5. 6.]]
      ```

○ **Reading data with np.genfromtxt():** `np.genfromtxt()` is more flexible than **np.loadtxt()** and can handle missing values, which it replaces with NaN by default. This function is useful when dealing with incomplete or irregular datasets.

```
# Save a sample text file with missing values for reading
sample_data_with_nan = np.array([[1.0, 2.0, np.nan], [4.0, 5.0,
6.0]])
np.savetxt( sample_with_nan.txt , sample_data_with_nan,
delimiter= , )

# Read the text file using np.genfromtxt
loaded_data_with_nan = np.genfromtxt( sample_with_nan.txt ,
delimiter= , )
print("Data read using np.genfromtxt:\n", loaded_data_with_nan)
```

Output:

```
Data read using np.genfromtxt:
    [[ 1.   2.  nan]
     [ 4.   5.   6.]]
```

○ **Writing data with np.savetxt():** `np.savetxt()` is used to write data to a text file. You can specify the delimiter and other formatting options. This method is useful for exporting arrays to a text format for sharing or further analysis. The code is given as follows:

```
data_to_save = np.array([[7.0, 8.0, 9.0], [10.0, 11.0, 12.0]])
np.savetxt( saved_data.txt , data_to_save, delimiter= , )

# Verify by reading the saved file
verified_data = np.loadtxt( saved_data.txt , delimiter= , )
print("Data written and read back using np.savetxt:\n",
verified_data)
```

Output:

```
Data written and read back using np.savetxt:
[[ 7.   8.   9.]
 [10. 11.  12.]]
```

Binary data handling

Binary data can also be handled using NumPy by two prominent methods as explained as follows:

• **Saving and loading arrays with np.save() and np.load():** `np.save()` is used to save an array to a binary file with a `.npy` extension, and **np.load()** is used to load the array from the file. This method is efficient for saving large datasets as it preserves the data type and structure. See the following code for more understanding:

```
binary_data = np.array([[13.0, 14.0, 15.0], [16.0, 17.0, 18.0]])
np.save( binary_data.npy , binary_data)

# Load the binary file
loaded_binary_data = np.load( binary_data.npy )
print("Data saved and loaded using np.save and np.load:\n", loaded_
binary_data)
```

Output:

```
Data saved and loaded using np.save and np.load:
[[13. 14. 15.]
 [16. 17. 18.]]
```

- **Working with .npy and .npz files**: **.npy** files store single arrays, while **.npz** files can store multiple arrays in a compressed format. **np.savez()** is used to save multiple arrays into a single **.npz** file, and **np.load()** can be used to retrieve them. This is useful for complex datasets involving multiple arrays.

```
# Save multiple arrays into a single .npz file
array1 = np.array([1, 2, 3])
array2 = np.array([4, 5, 6])
np.savez( multiple_arrays.npz , array1=array1, array2=array2)

# Load the .npz file
loaded_npz = np.load( multiple_arrays.npz )
print("Array1 from .npz file:", loaded_npz[ array1 ])
print("Array2 from .npz file:", loaded_npz[ array2 ])
```

Output:

```
Array1 from .npz file: [1 2 3]
Array2 from .npz file: [4 5 6]
```

Performance and optimization in NumPy

One of the key strengths of NumPy is its performance. NumPy is highly optimized for numerical operations and is significantly faster than native Python code that uses lists or loops for similar tasks.

This performance boost comes from several factors:

- **Vectorization**: NumPy operations are vectorized, which means they operate on entire arrays at once, without explicit Python loops.

- **Internal implementation**: NumPy is implemented in C and uses optimized libraries (like BLAS and LAPACK) under the hood.

- **Broadcasting**: NumPy avoids memory-intensive copying of data by using broadcasting rules to perform operations on arrays of different shapes.

- **Memory efficiency**: NumPy arrays use less memory than Python lists and provide options to set specific data types for more control.

Optimization tips in NumPy are provided as follows:

- Use **vectorized operations** instead of loops.

- Choose appropriate **data types** (e.g., float32 instead of float64 if precision is not critical).

- Use **in-place operations** (e.g., `a += b`) to save memory.

- Use **broadcasting** instead of duplicating data for operations on different shapes.

- Profile your code using tools like **`%timeit`** in Jupyter or cProfile.

Conclusion

In this chapter, we explored the powerful capabilities of NumPy, the foundational library for numerical computing in Python. We began by understanding its core concepts and features, such as its efficiency, speed, and ability to handle large multi-dimensional arrays and matrices. We learned how to create NumPy arrays using different methods, including manual creation, conversion from lists, and using built-in functions like zeros(), ones(), and arange().

We covered input and output operations, including reading and writing data from text and binary files, which is crucial for handling real-world datasets. Operations in NumPy, such as arithmetic computations, statistical functions, and universal functions (ufuncs), showcased the library's ability to perform fast, vectorized operations without explicit loops.

Indexing, slicing, and iterating allowed us to access and manipulate array data efficiently, while techniques like splitting and reshaping gave us control over array structure. The random module introduced ways to generate random numbers, useful for simulations and machine learning tasks.

Finally, we explored advanced topics like handling binary data, broadcasting rules, and performance and optimization techniques that make NumPy indispensable in scientific and analytical applications.

In the subsequent chapter, we will discuss Pandas in detail, which will make you understand data science in more depth.

Multiple choice questions

1. **What does NumPy stand for?**

    a. Numerical Python

    b. Number Python

    c. Numerical Py

    d. Number Py

2. **Which of the following is the correct way to import NumPy?**

    a. import numpy as np

    b. import numpy

    c. include numpy

    d. import NumPy

3. **What is the main object in NumPy?**

    a. List

    b. Tuple

    c. ndarray

    d. Series

4. **How do you create a 1D NumPy array?**

    a. np.array([1, 2, 3])

    b. np.array(1, 2, 3)

    c. np.array(1; 2; 3)

    d. np.array([1;2;3])

5. **Which function creates an array filled with zeros?**

    a. np.zeros()

    b. np.empty()

    c. np.ones()

    d. np.fill(0)

6. **What does np.arange(0, 10, 2) return?**

    a. [0 1 2 3 4 5 6 7 8 9]

    b. [0 2 4 6 8]

    c. [2 4 6 8 10]

    d. [1 3 5 7 9]

7. **How do you find the shape of a NumPy array?**

   a. array.length()

   b. len(array)

   c. array.shape

   d. array.size()

8. **Which function returns the number of dimensions in an array?**

   a. array.shape()

   b. array.ndim

   c. array.dim()

   d. array.len()

9. **What will np.ones((2,3)) produce?**

   a. 1D array of 6 ones

   b. 3x2 matrix of ones

   c. 2x3 matrix of ones

   d. Error

10. **How can you reshape a 1D array into a 2D array?**

    a. array.flatten()

    b. array.resize()

    c. array.reshape()

    d. array.split()

11. **What does np.linspace(0, 1, 5) return?**

    a. [0. 0.2 0.4 0.6 0.8]

    b. [0. 0.25 0.5 0.75 1.]

    c. [0. 0.2 0.4 0.6 0.8 1.]

    d. [0. 0.25 0.5 0.75 1.]

12. **Which function is used to create an identity matrix?**

    a. np.eye()

    b. np.identity()

    c. np.ones()

    d. np.diagonal()

13. **What is the output of np.array([1, 2, 3]) + 5?**

    a. [6 7 8]

    b. [1 2 3 5]

    c. [1 2 3]

    d. Error

14. **What is broadcasting in NumPy?**

    a. Sending arrays over the network

    b. Performing element-wise operations on arrays of different shapes

    c. Copying arrays

    d. Slicing arrays

15. **What will np.mean(np.array([1, 2, 3, 4])) return?**

    a. 10

    b. 2.5

    c. 2

    d. 3

16. **How do you stack arrays vertically?**

    a. np.hstack()

    b. np.vstack()

    c. np.stack(axis=1)

    d. np.concat()

17. **Which function returns the standard deviation?**

    a. np.var()

    b. np.std()

    c. np.mean()

    d. np.average()

18. **How do you generate a random number between 0 and 1 in NumPy?**

    a. np.rand()

    b. np.random()

    c. np.random.rand()

    d. random.rand()

19. **What is the use of np.copy()?**

    a. Creates a view of an array

    b. Copies elements from another array

    c. Creates a deep copy of the array

    d. None of the above

20. **Which function converts an array into a 1D array?**

    a. array.flatten()

    b. array.resize()

    c. array.shape()

    d. array.reshape(1)

21. **What does np.random.randint(1, 10) return?**

    a. A float between 1 and 10

    b. An array of integers

    c. A random integer from 1 to 10 (excluding 10)

    d. An error

22. **How can you reverse a NumPy array arr?**

    a. arr.reverse()

    b. arr[::-1]

    c. np.flip(arr, axis=1)

    d. arr.reverse(axis=0)

23. **What is the output of np.array([1, 2, 3]) * np.array([4, 5, 6])?**

    a. [4, 10, 18]

    b. [5, 7, 9]

    c. [1, 2, 3, 4, 5, 6]

    d. Error

24. **Which function returns cumulative sum of array elements?**

    a. np.sum()

    b. np.accumulate()

    c. np.cumsum()

    d. np.add()

25. **Which of the following functions can be used to concatenate two arrays?**

    a. np.combine()

    b. np.concat()

    c. np.concatenate()

    d. np.append()

26. **What does the axis parameter in NumPy functions control?**

    a. Shape

    b. Memory location

    c. Direction of operation

    d. Speed

27. **What is the output of np.array([[1,2],[3,4]]).T?**

    a. Transposed array

    b. Inverted values

    c. Same as input

    d. Error

28. **Which of the following methods returns a flattened copy of an array?**

    a. array.flatten()

    b. array.ravel()

    c. array.reshape(1, -1)

    d. array.reshape(-1)

29. **Which of these will give a view, not a copy, of the array?**

    a. arr.copy()

    b. arr[:]

    c. np.copy(arr)

    d. arr + 0

30. **What does np.unique() do?**

    a. Removes duplicates and sorts

    b. Sorts the array

    c. Reverses the array

    d. Adds random elements

31. **What is the use of np.where()?**

    a. Locates index of a value

    b. Returns conditionally selected elements

    c. Moves data in array

    d. Creates random values

32. **What does np.all() return?**

    a. True if any element is true

    b. True if all elements are true

    c. Returns all elements

    d. Filters odd numbers

33. **How can you check for NaN values in NumPy?**

    a. np.isnan()

    b. np.isnull()

    c. np.check_nan()

    d. np.has_nan()

34. **What is the result of np.dot(a, b)?**

    a. Element-wise product

    b. Cross product

    c. Matrix multiplication

    d. Outer product

35. **What does np.argsort() return?**

    a. Sorted array

    b. Indices that would sort the array

    c. Sorted unique values

    d. Sorted reversed array

36. **Which method fills an array with a scalar value?**

    a. arr.fill(x)

    b. arr.set(x)

    c. arr.put(x)

    d. arr.value(x)

37. **Which of the following returns the largest value in the array?**

    a. arr.max()

    b. arr.maximum()

    c. arr.argmax()

    d. np.high(arr)

38. **What does np.empty((2,3)) return?**

    a. 2x3 matrix of zeros

    b. 2x3 matrix of ones

    c. 2x3 matrix with uninitialized values

    d. Error

39. **Which NumPy function checks the memory size of an array element?**

    a. arr.size

    b. arr.dtype

    c. arr.itemsize

    d. arr.shape

40. **Which NumPy function creates a copy with a different data type?**

    a. astype()

    b. copy()

    c. dtype()

    d. convert()

Answers

1. a
2. a
3. c
4. a
5. a
6. b
7. c
8. b
9. c
10. c

11. d
12. a
13. a
14. b
15. b
16. b
17. b
18. c
19. c
20. a
21. c
22. b
23. a
24. c
25. c
26. c
27. a
28. a
29. b
30. a
31. b
32. b
33. a
34. c
35. b
36. a
37. a
38. c
39. c
40. a

Questions

1. What is NumPy and why is it used in Python?
2. How do you create a NumPy array from a Python list?
3. What is the difference between np.array() and np.asarray()?
4. How can you generate a range of numbers in NumPy?
5. What is the difference between np.zeros() and np.empty()?
6. How do you check the shape and data type of a NumPy array?
7. How do you reshape a 1D array into a 2D array?
8. How do you perform element-wise operations on arrays?
9. How do broadcasting rules work in NumPy?
10. How do you access rows, columns, or specific elements in a NumPy array?
11. How do you stack two arrays vertically and horizontally?
12. How do you find the maximum, minimum, and mean of a NumPy array?
13. What is the difference between np.copy() and simple assignment (=)?
14. How do you filter or select elements based on conditions?
15. How do you generate random numbers using NumPy?
16. What is the purpose of np.linspace() and how is it different from np.arange()?
17. How do you compute the dot product and matrix multiplication in NumPy?
18. How do you handle NaN values in NumPy arrays?
19. How do you sort a NumPy array by row or column?
20. How do you save and load NumPy arrays to and from disk?

Programming exercises

1. How do you flatten a multi-dimensional array in NumPy?
2. What does np.where() do and how can it be used?
3. How can you find the unique elements in a NumPy array?
4. What are structured arrays in NumPy and when would you use them?
5. How do you compute the inverse or determinant of a matrix using NumPy?
6. What is the difference between np.dot(), np.matmul(), and the @ operator?
7. How can you convert a NumPy array to a different data type?
8. What is the difference between np.all() and np.any()?

9. How do you perform set operations (like union, intersection) using NumPy?

10. How do you create a Boolean mask and use it to index an array?

11. How can you normalize a NumPy array to a 0–1 scale?

12. How do you compute moving averages using NumPy?

13. How do you remove outliers from a NumPy array using statistical thresholds?

14. How can you apply a custom function element-wise to a NumPy array?

15. How do you replace all NaNs in a NumPy array with the mean of that array?

16. How do you create a 2D grid of coordinates using NumPy?

17. How can you use NumPy to simulate rolling a die 1000 times and analyze the result?

18. How can you create one-hot encoded vectors using NumPy?

19. How do you calculate cosine similarity between two vectors using NumPy?

20. How do you generate a correlation matrix from a 2D NumPy array?

Join our Discord space

Join our Discord workspace for latest updates, offers, tech happenings around the world, new releases, and sessions with the authors:

https://discord.bpbonline.com

CHAPTER 3
Pandas

Introduction

Pandas is a powerful, open-source Python library designed for data analysis and manipulation. It offers two main data structures: Series (one-dimensional) and DataFrame (two-dimensional), which facilitate efficient handling of structured data. Pandas simplifies data loading from various sources like CSV, Excel, and SQL databases into DataFrames for easy manipulation. In data analysis, Pandas is essential for cleaning, transforming, and visualizing data. It provides tools for filtering, merging, reshaping, and aggregating data. It also effectively handles missing data, enabling identification, filling, or removal of missing values. Pandas' group-by functionality is crucial for split-apply-combine operations on large datasets. For time series data, Pandas supports date parsing, indexing, resampling, and rolling window calculations. Its integration with visualization libraries like Matplotlib and Seaborn allows for creating informative plots. In finance, it is used for time series analysis and stock market predictions. In healthcare, Pandas helps analyze patient records and clinical trial data. In retail and e-commerce, it supports customer behavior analysis, inventory management, and sales forecasting. Pandas is also essential in data preprocessing for machine learning models, reporting, and automating repetitive data tasks, making it a vital tool across data-driven industries. Overall, Pandas transforms raw data into meaningful insights efficiently and effectively.

Structure

The chapter covers the following topics:

- Key features of Pandas
- Pandas basics
- Series
- DataFrame

Objectives

This chapter aims to provide a practical and comprehensive introduction to the Pandas library, focusing on its two primary data structures: Series and DataFrames. The readers are expected to gain a clear understanding of the Series as a one-dimensional labeled array capable of holding various data types, and the DataFrame as a two-dimensional, tabular structure that supports heterogeneous data across columns. Through step-by-step examples, the chapter aims to build proficiency in essential data manipulation tasks such as selecting and filtering data, handling missing values using functions like **fillna()** and **dropna()**, sorting, and indexing. It also covers how to create, modify, and delete columns or rows, as well as how to perform more advanced operations like grouping, aggregation, merging, joining, and reshaping data using pivot tables. By applying these techniques to real-world scenarios, the chapter helps readers develop the ability to clean, transform, and analyze datasets effectively. Ultimately, the goal is to equip readers with a solid foundation in Pandas, enabling them to handle diverse data tasks with confidence and prepare data for further analysis or visualization in data science and analytics workflows.

Key features of Pandas

Pandas is a versatile and powerful tool that significantly enhances productivity and efficiency in data analysis and manipulation tasks. Some key features and benefits of using Pandas are as follows:

- **Data structures**: Pandas can handle two types of data structures:
    - ○ **Series**: A one-dimensional labeled array capable of holding any data type.
    - ○ **DataFrame**: A two-dimensional labeled data structure with columns of potentially different types, like a spreadsheet or SQL table.

- **Data alignment and indexing**: Pandas are capable of automatic and explicit data alignment and hold powerful indexing capabilities for selecting, filtering, and modifying data. The difference between implicit and explicit alignment operations is given as follows:

```python
import pandas as pd
# Create two Series with different indexes
s1 = pd.Series([10, 20, 30], index=['a', 'b', 'c'])
s2 = pd.Series([1, 2, 3], index=['b', 'c', 'd'])

# ◈ Implicit alignment (automatically aligns by index)
print("Implicit Alignment:")
print(s1 + s2)

# ◈ Explicit alignment (manual reindexing before operation)
print("\nExplicit Alignment:")
s2_aligned = s2.reindex(s1.index, fill_value=0)  # Fill missing with
0
print(s1 + s2_aligned)
```

o **Output**:

```
Implicit Alignment:
a     NaN
b     21.0
c     32.0
d     NaN
dtype: float64

Explicit Alignment:
a     10
b     21
c     32
dtype: int64
```

- **Data cleaning and handling**: Pandas has a large set of functions for handling missing data by filling or dropping them. It also handles data type conversion and transformation capabilities.

- **Data manipulation**: Pandas has advanced data reshaping and pivoting capabilities, along with GroupBy functionality for split-apply-combine operations on datasets.

- **IO tools**: Pandas has functions to read from and write to various file formats like CSV, Excel, SQL databases, JSON, etc.

- **Time series support**: Pandas has robust support for working with time series data, including date range generation, frequency conversion, and moving window statistics.

- **Merge and join**: Pandas has functions for combining data from multiple DataFrames using database-style joins and merges.

- **Visualization**: Pandas has built-in integration with Matplotlib for quick and easy plotting.

Benefits of Pandas

Pandas exhibit a huge set of benefits. Some of them are given as follows:

- **Ease of use**: Intuitive and user-friendly API that aligns well with the mental model of working with structured data, making it easy to learn and use. The Pandas API resembles spreadsheet operations with features like column selection, filtering, sorting, and aggregations, similar to Excel. This familiarity helps Excel users quickly adapt to Pandas for more powerful data analysis.

- **Efficiency**: Optimized for performance, allowing for efficient data manipulation and analysis on large datasets.

- **Flexibility**: Handles a wide range of data types and formats, providing versatility in data analysis tasks.

- **Integration**: Seamless integration with other data science libraries and tools in the Python ecosystem, such as NumPy, Matplotlib, and SciPy.

- **Productivity**: Rich functionality that reduces the need for writing extensive custom code for common data operations, thus speeding up the data analysis process.

- **Community and documentation**: Extensive documentation and a large, active community provide ample resources for learning and troubleshooting.

- **Real-world applications**: Widely used in various industries for tasks like financial analysis, data science, machine learning, and more due to its reliability and efficiency.

Pandas basics

Pandas is an open-source library built on top of NumPy. It provides easy-to-use data structures and data analysis tools, especially for working with tabular data (like spreadsheets or SQL tables). The core data structures of Pandas are explained as follows:

- **Series**: A **Series** is a one-dimensional labeled array and is created as follows:

```
import pandas as pd

s = pd.Series([10, 20, 30])
print(s)
```

  - **Output**:
    ```
    0    10
    1    20
    2    30
    dtype: int64
    ```

Each item has an **index** and a **value**.

- **DataFrame**: A **DataFrame** is a two-dimensional labeled data structure (like a table or spreadsheet) and can be created as follows:

```
import pandas as pd

data = {
    'Name': ['Romil', 'Tom'],
    'Age': [25, 30]
}
df = pd.DataFrame(data)
print(df)
```

  o **Output**:

```
       Name  Age
0     Romil   25
1       Tom   30
```

Certain common operations on Pandas are explained as follows; their description is given in comments alongside the code:

- **Reading data**: The code is as follows:

```
df = pd.read_csv('data.csv')        # Read CSV file
```

- **Viewing data**: The code is as follows:

```
df.head()          # First 5 rows
df.tail(3)         # Last 3 rows
df.info()          # Summary info
df.describe()      # Statistical summary
```

- **Selecting data**: The code is as follows:

```
df['Name']                 # Select column
df[['Name', 'Age']]        # Multiple columns
df.loc[0]                  # Row by label/index
df.iloc[0]                 # Row by position
```

- **Filtering and conditions**: The code is as follows:

```
df[df['Age'] > 25]      # Rows where Age > 25
```

- **Modifying data**: The code is as follows:

```
df['Age'] = df['Age'] + 1    # Update values
```

- **Adding new columns**: The code is as follows:

```
df['New'] = df['Age'] * 2
```

- **Removing columns and rows**: The code is as follows:

```
df.drop('New', axis=1)       # Drop column
df.drop(0, axis=0)           # Drop row
```

- **Aggregation and grouping**: The code is as follows:

```
df.groupby('Name').mean()    # Group by Name and average
```

- **Saving data**: The code is as follows:

```
df.to_csv('output.csv', index=False)
```

Series

In Pandas, a Series is a one-dimensional labeled array that can hold data of any type (integers, strings, floats, Python objects, etc.). Think of it as a column in a spreadsheet or a single column in a DataFrame.

Key features of a series

The main features of the series include the following:

- **Labeled index**: Each element has an associated label (called an index), which allows for intuitive and flexible data selection.

- **Homogeneous data**: All elements in a series are of the same data type.

- **Size immutable**: Once created, the size of a Series cannot be changed directly.

The following code shows how to create a **Series** in **pandas**:

```
import pandas as pd

# From a list
s = pd.Series([10, 20, 30, 40])
print(s)
```

The output is as follows:

```
0    10
1    20
2    30
3    40
dtype: int64
```

We can also define the custom index labels as follows:

```
s = pd.Series([10, 20, 30], index=['a', 'b', 'c'])
print(s)
```

The output is as follows:

```
a    10
b    20
c    30
dtype: int64
```

We can access the data as follows:

```
print(s['a'])    # Output: 10
print(s[0])      # Output: 10
```

The useful attributes and methods associated with series are as follows:

- **s.index**: Returns the index (labels)
- **s.values**: Returns the underlying data
- **s.mean()**: Romputes the mean
- **s.sum()**: Romputes the sum
- **s.head(n)**: Returns the first n items
- **s.tail(n)**: Returns the last n items

Now we will understand the use of series through a real-world scenario. Suppose you are managing a small e-commerce store and you want to analyze daily sales over a week, including some missing days (e.g., no sales recorded) as described in the following steps:

1. **Create a Series with dates and sales as follows:**

   ```
   import pandas as pd
   import numpy as np

   # Sales data for some days (with a missing day)
   sales_data = [200, 220, np.nan, 250, 300, 270, 310]
   dates = pd.date_range(start='2024-07-01', periods=7)

   # Create Series with date as index
   sales_series = pd.Series(sales_data, index=dates)
   print(sales_series)
   ```

   The output is as follows:

   ```
   2024-07-01    200.0
   2024-07-02    220.0
   2024-07-03      NaN
   2024-07-04    250.0
   2024-07-05    300.0
   2024-07-06    270.0
   2024-07-07    310.0
   Freq: D, dtype: float64
   ```

2. **Detect missing data as follows:**

   ```
   print(sales_series.isna())
   ```

The output is as follows:

```
2024-07-01    False
2024-07-02    False
2024-07-03     True
2024-07-04    False
2024-07-05    False
2024-07-06    False
2024-07-07    False
Freq: D, dtype: bool
```

3. **Fill the missing value (forward fill) as follows:**

```
sales_series_filled = sales_series.ffill()
print(sales_series_filled)
```

The output is as follows:

```
2024-07-01    200.0
2024-07-02    220.0
2024-07-03    220.0
2024-07-04    250.0
2024-07-05    300.0
2024-07-06    270.0
2024-07-07    310.0
Freq: D, dtype: float64
```

4. **Total weekly sales are as follows:**

```
total_sales = sales_series_filled.sum()
print("Total sales:", total_sales)
```

The output is as follows:

```
Total sales: 1770.0
```

5. **Days with high sales (> 250) are as follows:**

```
high_sales = sales_series_filled[sales_series_filled > 250]
print(high_sales)
```

The output is as follows:

```
2024-07-05    300.0
2024-07-06    270.0
2024-07-07    310.0
Freq: D, dtype: float64
```

6. **Slice dates between July 3 and July 5 as follows:**

```
print(sales_series_filled['2024-07-03':'2024-07-05'])
```

The output is as follows:

```
2024-07-03    220.0
2024-07-04    250.0
2024-07-05    300.0
Freq: D, dtype: float64
```

The above complete example shows how Series can handle:

- Missing data (NaN)
- Date-based indexing
- Easy filtering and slicing
- Aggregations like `.sum()`

DataFrame

A DataFrame in Pandas is a two-dimensional, labeled, and tabular data structure, similar to a spreadsheet, SQL table, or a dictionary of Series objects. It is one of the most commonly used data structures in data analysis and manipulation with Python. At its core:

- A DataFrame is like a table with rows and columns.
- Each column is a Series and can have a different data type (e.g., numbers, strings, Booleans).
- Rows and columns have labels (index for rows, and column names).

Creating a DataFrame

DataFrames can be created a various ways. Some of them are explained as follows:

- **Creating a DataFrame from a dictionary**: The code is given as follows:

```python
import pandas as pd

data = {
    'Name': ['Romil', 'Tom', 'Richard'],
    'Age': [25, 30, 35],
    'City': ['New York', 'Paris', 'London']
}
df = pd.DataFrame(data)
print(df)
```

The output is as follows:

```
      Name  Age      City
0    Romil   25  New York
1      Tom   30     Paris
2  Richard   35    London
```

- **Creating a DataFrame with a custom index**: The code is given as follows:

```
df = pd.DataFrame(data, index=['A', 'B', 'C'])
print(df)
```

The output is as follows:

```
     Name  Age      City
A    Romil   25  New York
B      Tom   30     Paris
C  Richard   35    London
```

- **Creating a DataFrame from a list of dictionaries**: The code is given as follows:

```
data = [
    {'Name': 'Romil', 'Age': 25},
    {'Name': 'Tom', 'Age': 30, 'City': 'Paris'}
]

df = pd.DataFrame(data)
print(df)
```

The output is as follows:

```
    Name  Age   City
0  Romil   25    NaN
1    Tom   30  Paris
```

Common operations on DataFrames

We can perform various operations on DataFrames like accessing column(s), accessing certain rows, positions, adding or dropping a column, and accessing a value based on a condition. All of these operations are explained through the following set of codes:

- **Accessing columns**:

```
print(df['Name'])        # A Series
print(df[['Name', 'Age']])  # Another DataFrame
```

- **Access rows (by position or label)**:

```
print(df.iloc[0])      # First row (by integer position)
print(df.loc['A'])     # Row 'A' (by label)
```

- **Add a new column**:

```
df['Country'] = ['USA', 'France', 'UK']
```

- **Drop a column or row**:

```
df.drop('City', axis=1, inplace=True)     # Drop column
df.drop('A', axis=0, inplace=True)        # Drop row
```

- **Filter rows (condition)**:
  ```
  df[df['Age'] > 30]
  ```

- **Handling missing data**:
  ```
  df.isnull()              # Detect missing values
  df.fillna('Unknown')     # Replace NaN with a default value
  df.dropna()              # Remove rows with NaN
  ```

- **Aggregation and grouping**:
  ```
  df['Age'].mean()           # Average age
  df.groupby('City').mean()  # Group by city
  ```

Now, let us create a DataFrame pertaining to an e-commerce business and infer customer spending. The code is given as follows:

```
data = {
    'OrderID': [1001, 1002, 1003],
    'Customer': ['Romil', 'Tom', 'Romil'],
    'Amount': [250, 400, 150],
    'Date': pd.to_datetime(['2024-04-01', '2024-04-02', '2024-04-03'])
}

orders = pd.DataFrame(data)
print(orders)
```

The output is as follows:

```
   OrderID Customer  Amount        Date
0     1001    Romil     250  2024-04-01
1     1002      Tom     400  2024-04-02
2     1003    Romil     150  2024-04-03
```

Analyzing total spent by each customer: To determine the expenses of each customer following code is used:

```
orders.groupby('Customer')['Amount'].sum()
```

The output is as follows:

```
Customer
Romil    400
Tom      400
Name: Amount, dtype: int64
```

Note: The `ffill()` method in Pandas is used to forward-fill missing values with the last known non-null value.

Combining multiple DataFrames

Combining multiple DataFrames is a core task in data analysis, think of it as merging tables in SQL or stacking spreadsheets together. There are three main ways to combine DataFrames in Pandas:

- **Concatenation (stacking)**: It is used to stack DataFrames vertically or horizontally, like appending or joining along an axis. Let us take an example of appending sales data for different weeks as shown in the following code, and we can see in the output that all six days are combined in a single DataFrame:

```python
import pandas as pd

# Week 1 sales
week1 = pd.DataFrame({
    'Day': ['Mon', 'Tue', 'Wed'],
    'Sales': [200, 220, 250]
})

# Week 2 sales
week2 = pd.DataFrame({
    'Day': ['Thu', 'Fri', 'Sat'],
    'Sales': [270, 300, 310]
})

# Combine vertically (axis=0)
combined = pd.concat([week1, week2], ignore_index=True)
print(combined)
```

The output is as follows:

```
    Day  Sales
0   Mon    200
1   Tue    220
2   Wed    250
3   Thu    270
4   Fri    300
5   Sat    310
```

- **Merge (SQL-style joins)**: Merging is used when you want to combine data based on a common key (like a database join). You can understand through the following code, where we combine customer information with orders, and in the output, we can see that **OrderID**, **Amount**, and **Name** can be merged based on **CustomerID**:

```python
customers = pd.DataFrame({
    'CustomerID': [1, 2, 3],
    'Name': ['Romil', 'Tom', 'Richard']
```

```
})

orders = pd.DataFrame({
    'OrderID': [101, 102, 103],
    'CustomerID': [1, 2, 1],
    'Amount': [250, 400, 150]
})

# Merge on CustomerID
merged = pd.merge(orders, customers, on='CustomerID')
print(merged)
```

The output is as follows:

```
   OrderID  CustomerID  Amount    Name
0      101           1     250   Romil
1      103           1           150   Romil
2      102           2           400       Tom
```

- **Join (on index)**: It is used when your index is meaningful and you want to join based on the index. For example, we want to join two DataFrames, one containing product info and the other containing prices by index as presented in the following code, where output represents that both the DataFrames are joined based on their indices:

```
products = pd.DataFrame({
    'Name': ['T-shirt', 'Shoes'],
    'Category': ['Clothing', 'Footwear']
}, index=['A', 'B'])

prices = pd.DataFrame({
    'Price': [20, 50]
}, index=['A', 'B'])

# Join on index
joined = products.join(prices)
print(joined)
```

The output is as follows:

```
      Name  Category  Price
A  T-shirt  Clothing     20
B    Shoes  Footwear     50
```

Note: Use lists of dicts when each item represents a record with named fields (ideal for row-wise operations). Prefer dicts of lists when you need fast access to data by field (column-wise operations), like in DataFrames.

Reshaping DataFrames

We can also reshape DataFrames using the pivot table. The code is as follows:

```python
import pandas as pd

data = {
    'Name': ['Asher', 'Tom', 'Charles', 'Diana', 'Eve'],
    'Age': [25, 30, 35, None, 29],
    'City': ['New York', 'Paris', 'London', 'Paris', 'New York'],
    'Income': [50000, 60000, 55000, 52000, None]
}

df = pd.DataFrame(data)

#reshaping with Pivot tables
# Average income by city and senior status

pivot = df.pivot_table(values='Income', index='City', columns='Senior',
aggfunc='mean')
print(pivot)
```

The output is as follows:

```
Senior       False     True
City
London         NaN   55000.0
New York   50000.0      NaN
Paris      60000.0      NaN
```

Conclusion

In this chapter, we explored the core components of the Pandas library, Series and DataFrames, and their essential operations for effective data manipulation and analysis in Python. We began with the Series, a one-dimensional labeled array capable of storing various data types, and saw how it can be used for indexing, slicing, handling missing values, and performing vectorized operations. We then expanded to the DataFrame, a two-dimensional, table-like data structure that is central to most Pandas workflows. It allows storage of heterogeneous data across columns and provides powerful functionality for accessing, filtering, and transforming data. Key operations discussed included selecting specific rows and columns, applying conditions to filter data, and managing missing values using methods like fillna() and dropna(). We also demonstrated how to add new columns, rename them, drop unwanted data, and sort entries based on one or more columns. Advanced techniques such as grouping (groupby()), aggregating, merging multiple DataFrames (merge()), and reshaping data using pivot tables (pivot_table()) were introduced to show how Pandas can adapt to various analytical needs. Through practical examples, we showed how Pandas simplifies real-world data tasks such as sales reporting, customer analysis, and dataset merging. By mastering these tools, users can handle diverse datasets more efficiently and prepare them for further analysis or visualization. Overall, this chapter provides a solid foundation in Pandas, equipping you with the skills necessary to clean, analyze, and transform data, a critical step in any data science or analytics workflow.

In the next chapter, we will learn about data pre-processing, which pertains to data gathering and preparation, where we will also learn about data manipulation.

Multiple choice questions

1. **What is a DataFrame in Pandas?**

   a. A one-dimensional array

   b. A two-dimensional table of data

   c. A list of values

   d. A dictionary of lists

2. **What method is used to read a CSV file into a Pandas DataFrame?**

   a. read_csv()

   b. import_csv()

   c. read()

   d. load_csv()

3. **How can you access the first row of a DataFrame df?**

   a. df.iloc[0]

   b. df.loc[0]

   c. df.head(1)

   d. All of the above

4. **How do you select the column Age from the DataFrame df?**

   a. df['Age']

   b. df.Age

   c. df.loc['Age']

   d. Both a and b

5. **Which method is used to drop missing values from a DataFrame?**

   a. remove_na()

   b. dropna()

   c. fillna()

   d. del_na()

6. **Which of the following is used to merge two DataFrames, df1 and df2, on a common column?**

   a. merge()

   b. concat()

   c. join()

   d. append()

7. **How do you filter rows based on a condition in Pandas?**

   a. df.select('column_name')

   b. df[df['column'] > value]

   c. df.filter('column_name')

   d. df.column > value

8. **Which of the following methods is used to sort data in a DataFrame?**

   a. order()

   b. sort_values()

   c. sort()

   d. rank()

9. **How can you fill missing values in a DataFrame?**

   a. df.fillna()

   b. df.replace_na()

   c. df.impute()

   d. df.dropna()

10. **Which of the following functions can be used to group data in Pandas?**

   a. group()

   b. groupby()

   c. aggregate()

   d. partition()

11. **What function would you use to check for missing data in a DataFrame?**

   a. isnull()

   b. missing()

    c. has_null()

    d. null()

12. **Which of the following is used to add a new column to a DataFrame?**

    a. df.append()

    b. df.insert()

    c. df['new_column'] = value

    d. df.add_column()

13. **How do you concatenate two DataFrames vertically in Pandas?**

    a. df.merge()

    b. df.append()

    c. df.concat()

    d. df.concatenate()

14. **Which of the following methods is used to read an Excel file into Pandas?**

    a. read_excel()

    b. read_spreadsheet()

    c. import_excel()

    d. load_excel()

15. **How can you display the first five rows of a DataFrame?**

    a. df.first()

    b. df.head()

    c. df.begin()

    d. df.show()

16. **What does the axis=0 parameter do in Pandas functions like drop() and sum()?**

    a. It refers to operations on rows

    b. It refers to operations on columns

    c. It specifies the data type

    d. It does nothing

17. **What is the purpose of pivot_table() in Pandas?**

    a. To group data by index

    b. To reshape and aggregate data

    c. To merge two DataFrames

    d. To sort data

18. **Which method would you use to check the type of an object in Pandas?**
    a. df.type()
    b. type(df)
    c. df.object()
    d. df.info()

19. **How do you remove duplicate rows from a DataFrame in Pandas?**
    a. df.drop_duplicates()
    b. df.remove_duplicates()
    c. df.unique()
    d. df.distinct()

20. **What method would you use to convert a Pandas Series to a list?**
    a. series.to_list()
    b. list(series)
    c. series.tolist()
    d. Both b and c

Answers

1. b
2. a
3. d
4. d
5. b
6. a
7. b
8. b
9. a
10. b
11. a
12. c
13. b
14. a
15. b
16. a

17. b

18. b

19. a

20. d

Questions

1. What is the difference between a Series and a DataFrame in Pandas?

2. How can you create a Series from a list of values in Pandas?

3. How can you select a specific column in a DataFrame?

4. How can you filter rows based on a condition in a DataFrame?

5. What are the common methods to handle missing data in Pandas?

6. How would you rename a column in a DataFrame?

7. What is the purpose of the groupby() method in Pandas, and how is it used?

8. How can you add a new column to an existing DataFrame based on a condition?

9. How do you concatenate two or more DataFrames vertically and horizontally in Pandas?

10. What is the difference between merge() and join() in Pandas?

11. How can you sort a DataFrame based on one or more columns?

12. What is a pivot table in Pandas, and how can it be created?

13. How can you drop rows or columns in Pandas?

14. How can you check if there are any missing values in a DataFrame?

15. How would you calculate the mean, sum, or other aggregations for a specific column in a DataFrame?

Programming exercises

1. **Create a Pandas DataFrame from the following dictionary**:

```
data = {
    'Product': ['Laptop', 'Phone', 'Tablet', 'Monitor'],
    'Price': [1200, 800, 300, 150],
    'Stock': [50, 150, 200, 80]
}
```

   a. Display the DataFrame.

   b. Add a column for Total Value (Price * Stock)

2. **Create a DataFrame of the following student data:**

```
data = {
    'Name': ['Asher', 'Tom', 'Charles', 'Diana', 'Eve'],
    'Age': [23, 21, 22, 24, 23],
    'Grade': ['A', 'B', 'C', 'A', 'B']
}
```

    a.   Filter and display students who are older than 22 and have Grade 'A'.

3. **Create the following DataFrame:**

```
data = {
    'Name': ['Asher', 'Tom', 'Charles', 'Diana'],
    'Age': [25, None, 30, 35],
    'Salary': [50000, 55000, None, 60000]
}
```

    a.   Find all rows with missing values.

    b.   Fill the missing values in the Age column with the average age.

    c.   Fill the missing values in the Salary column with the median salary.

4. **Create the following DataFrame for sales data:**

```
data = {
    'Product': ['A', 'B', 'A', 'C', 'B', 'A', 'C'],
    'Amount': [200, 150, 250, 300, 100, 350, 200],
    'Region': ['North', 'South', 'North', 'East', 'South', 'North',
'East']
}
```

    a.   Group the data by Product and calculate the total Amount for each product.

5. **Create two DataFrames:**

```
# DataFrame 1: Customer info
df1 = pd.DataFrame({
    'CustomerID': [1, 2, 3],
    'Name': ['Asher', 'Tom', 'Charles']
})

# DataFrame 2: Order details
df2 = pd.DataFrame({
    'OrderID': [101, 102, 103],
    'CustomerID': [1, 2, 1],
    'Amount': [250, 400, 150]
})
```

    a.   Merge the two DataFrames on CustomerID and display the result.

6. **Create the following DataFrame:**

```
data = {
    'Date': ['2024-04-01', '2024-04-02', '2024-04-01', '2024-04-03'],
    'Product': ['A', 'B', 'A', 'B'],
    'Sales': [150, 200, 250, 300]
}
```

    a.   Create a pivot table that shows the total Sales for each Product by Date.

7. **Create the following DataFrame:**

```
python
CopyEdit
data = {
    'Product': ['Laptop', 'Phone', 'Tablet', 'Monitor'],
    'Price': [1200, 800, 300, 150],
    'Stock': [50, 150, 200, 80]
}
```

    a.   Sort the products by Price in descending order.

    b.   Sort the products by Stock in ascending order.

8. **Create a DataFrame with duplicate rows:**

```
data = {
    'Product': ['Laptop', 'Phone', 'Laptop', 'Tablet'],
    'Price': [1200, 800, 1200, 300]
}
```

    a.   Remove duplicate rows from the DataFrame and display the result.

9. **Create the following DataFrame:**

```
data = {
    'Name': ['Asher', 'Tom', 'Charles'],
    'Salary': [55000, 60000, 75000]
}
```

    a.   Write a function to apply a 10% salary increase, and apply this function to the Salary column.

10. **Create a DataFrame with time series data:**

```
data = {
    'Date': pd.date_range('2024-01-01', periods=5, freq='D'),
    'Sales': [100, 150, 200, 250, 300]
}
```

    a.   Set the Date column as the index of the DataFrame.

    b.   Calculate the rolling sum of Sales with a window of 3 days.

Join our Discord space

Join our Discord workspace for latest updates, offers, tech happenings around the world, new releases, and sessions with the authors:

https://discord.bpbonline.com

## CHAPTER 4

Data Collection and Data Preprocessing

Introduction

Data collection and data preprocessing are foundational steps in the data science process, crucial for ensuring the quality and usability of data for analysis.

Data collection involves gathering raw data from various sources such as databases, web scraping, sensors, surveys, or APIs. This data can come in different formats, including structured data like databases and spreadsheets, or unstructured data like text, images, and videos. The goal is to obtain relevant and sufficient data that accurately represents the phenomenon under study, which will form the basis for analysis and modeling.

Data preprocessing is the subsequent step that prepares the collected data for analysis by cleaning and transforming it. This process includes handling missing values, removing duplicates, and correcting errors to ensure data quality. It also involves normalizing or standardizing data to ensure consistency, encoding categorical variables, and sometimes reducing dimensionality to simplify the dataset without losing essential information. Effective preprocessing helps mitigate issues that could skew analysis, improve the performance of machine learning models, and ensure that the data is suitable for extracting meaningful insights. Together, these steps form the critical foundation for any data-driven project, ensuring the reliability and validity of the subsequent analysis.

Structure

The chapter covers the following topics:

- Types of data
- Data collection
- Datasets
- Data formats
- Data parsing
- Data transformation
- Real-time issues in data transformation

Objectives

The objective of this chapter is to provide a comprehensive understanding of the fundamental components involved in data handling within data science. It begins by exploring the various types of data, structured, semi-structured, and unstructured, followed by an overview of different datasets commonly used in analytical and machine learning applications. The chapter then explores the process of data parsing, which involves converting raw or semi-structured data into a structured format for further processing. It also covers essential techniques in data transformation, such as normalization and feature extraction, like aggregation, which are crucial for preparing data for analysis. Finally, the chapter discusses real-time challenges in data gathering, including data quality issues, inconsistencies, latency, and integration difficulties, highlighting practical considerations when working with data in real-world environments.

Types of data

In data science, data can be categorized into several types based on various criteria such as structure, source, and nature. Here are the primary types of data commonly encountered in data science:

- **Based on structure**: It can be divided into three main categories as follows:
  - **Structured data**: It is highly organized and easily searchable data with a defined format for databases, spreadsheets, and CSV files. Its characteristics include that it is stored in tables with rows and columns, follows a predefined schema, easily accessible using SQL.
  - **Unstructured data**: In this type, the data is without a predefined structure, often diverse and complex. Examples include text documents, images, videos, audio files, and social media posts. It lacks a consistent format, requires specialized tools for processing and analysis.

o **Semi-structured data**: The data that does not conform to a strict structure but contains tags or markers to separate elements. Its examples include JSON, XML, and HTML files. It contains elements of both structured and unstructured data, somewhat organized but flexible.

- **Based on source**: It is divided into two main categories as follows:

  o **Primary data**: Data collected firsthand for a specific purpose. Examples are surveys, experiments, and sensor readings. It is directly obtained from original sources, tailored to specific research needs.

  o **Secondary data**: The data that has been previously collected and is available for reuse. Examples include public databases, research reports, and historical records. It is collected by someone else for a different purpose, and often needs validation for the current use.

- **Based on nature**: It is divided into two main categories as follows:

  o **Quantitative data**: The data that can be measured and expressed numerically. Examples include sales figures, temperature readings, and test scores. It allows for mathematical and statistical analysis, includes discrete and continuous data.

  o **Qualitative data**: It is descriptive data that cannot be measured numerically. Examples include interview transcripts, open-ended survey responses, and images. It provides context and insights through descriptions, requires textual or thematic analysis.

- **Based on time**: It is divided into two main categories as follows:

  o **Time-series data**: Time-based classifications include time-series data, collected at specific intervals like stock prices and weather data, useful for trend analysis and forecasting.

  o **Cross-sectional data**: It is collected at a single point in time, such as census data, providing a snapshot for comparison. Collection methods distinguish observational data, gathered without intervention, like sensor data, reflecting natural occurrences but potentially subject to observer bias, from experimental data, obtained through controlled experiments like clinical trials, which allow for determining causality.

- **Based on the collection method**: It is divided into two main categories as follows:

  o **Observational data**: This data was collected through observation without intervention. Examples include Behavioral observations, sensor data. It reflects natural occurrences, can be subject to observer bias.

  o **Experimental data**: The data collected through controlled experiments. Examples include clinical trial results, lab experiment data. Used for controlled conditions, allows for causality determination.

- **Based on accessibility**: Regarding accessibility, open data is freely available to the public, such as government datasets and public research data, often licensed for reuse. In contrast, proprietary data is owned by organizations or individuals and is not publicly accessible, including company sales data and private research findings, typically protected by intellectual property laws. Understanding these data types helps data scientists select appropriate methods for data collection, preprocessing, analysis, and interpretation, leading to more accurate and meaningful insights.

Note: **Understanding these different types of data helps data scientists choose appropriate methods for data collection, preprocessing, analysis, and interpretation, ultimately leading to more accurate and meaningful insights.**

Structured vs. unstructured data

Among all the types of data described above, the most important is to understand structured and unstructured data. In this section, we describe structured and unstructured data in detail.

Structured data

Structured data is highly organized and formatted in a way that is easily searchable in databases. This data adheres to a predefined schema and is often stored in tabular formats, such as rows and columns. The further details are provided as follows:

- **Characteristics**: It has the following characteristics:
  - **Format**: Stored in relational databases, spreadsheets, and data tables.
  - **Schema**: Follows a fixed schema with defined data types for each field (e.g., integer, string, date).
  - **Accessibility**: Easily queried using **structured query language** (**SQL**).
  - **Consistency**: High consistency and integrity due to the rigid structure.
- **Examples**: Examples include the following:
  - Customer databases with fields like name, age, address, and purchase history.
  - Financial records, such as transaction logs or account balances.
  - Inventory management systems track product IDs, quantities, and locations.
- **Advantages**:
  - **Ease of use**: Simplifies data entry, retrieval, and analysis due to its organized format.
  - **Performance**: Efficient for queries and transactions in databases.
  - **Reliability**: Ensures data integrity and consistency.

- **Disadvantages**:
  - o **Flexibility**: Limited in handling complex or diverse data types.
  - o **Scalability**: Can become challenging to scale with very large datasets or varied data sources.

Unstructured data

Unstructured data lacks a predefined format or schema, making it more flexible but also more challenging to manage and analyze. This data is often rich in information but not easily searchable in traditional databases. The details are as follows:

- **Characteristics**:
  - o **Format**: Includes text files, images, videos, audio recordings, emails, social media posts, and sensor data.
  - o **Schema**: Does not conform to a fixed schema, often stored in raw formats.
  - o **Accessibility**: Requires specialized tools and techniques to process and analyze (e.g., natural language processing, image recognition).
  - o **Diversity**: Highly varied in nature and format.
- **Examples**: Text documents, such as emails, reports, and social media posts. Multimedia files, including photos, videos, and audio recordings. Sensor data from IoT devices without a predefined structure.
- **Advantages**:
  - o **Richness**: Captures a wide array of data types, providing more comprehensive insights.
  - o **Flexibility**: Can handle diverse and complex data sources without a predefined structure.
  - o **Volume**: Suitable for large-scale data generated from various sources.
- **Disadvantages**:
  - o **Complexity**: Requires more advanced processing and analysis techniques.
  - o **Performance**: Can be slower to query and analyze due to a lack of structure.
  - o **Management**: More challenging to store, manage, and ensure data quality

Key differences between structured and unstructured data

The comparison is based on three parameters described as follows:

- **Organization**:
  - **Structured data**: Organized in rows and columns with a predefined schema.
  - **Unstructured data**: Lacks a predefined structure and can be stored in various formats.

- **Accessibility**:
  - **Structured data**: Easily queried with SQL.
  - **Unstructured data**: Requires specialized tools and techniques for processing.

- **Analysis**:
  - **Structured data**: Suitable for traditional statistical analysis and reporting.
  - **Unstructured data**: Needs advanced analytics like machine learning, natural language processing, and image recognition.

It can be better understood through *Table 4.1:*

Aspect	Structured data	Unstructured data	Case study example
Definition	Data organized in rows and columns	Data without predefined format or structure	Customer feedback analysis
Format	Tables, databases (SQL, Excel)	Text, images, videos, audio	Structured: Customer records in a CRM
Ease of analysis	Easy to analyze using traditional tools	Requires specialized tools (e.g., NLP, CV)	Unstructured: Product reviews or comments
Storage	Relational databases	Data lakes, NoSQL databases	Structured stored in MySQL
Tools used	SQL, Excel, Pandas	NLP libraries, image processing tools, NoSQL	Unstructured analyzed using sentiment analysis tools
Examples	Employee records, Sales data	Emails, social media posts, customer call recordings	

Table 4.1: The comparison of structured vs. unstructured data with examples

Note: **In data science, both structured and unstructured data play vital roles. Structured data is crucial for traditional analytics and reporting, while unstructured data provides deeper insights through advanced analytics techniques, enabling organizations to harness the full potential of their data.**

Data collection

There are various methods of data collection, which offer unique advantages and are chosen based on the specific requirements of the data science project, including the type of data needed, the scale of data collection, and the available resources. Combining multiple methods often provides the most comprehensive datasets, enabling more robust analysis and insights. We describe different data collection methods as follows:

- **Web scraping**: It is a technique used to extract large amounts of data from websites. This process involves programmatically retrieving web pages and parsing the HTML to extract the desired information. Web scraping tools and libraries, such as BeautifulSoup and Scrapy in Python, can automate this process, making it efficient to gather data on product prices, reviews, social media interactions, and more. While powerful, web scraping must be conducted responsibly, adhering to the website's terms of service and avoiding overloading servers with too many requests.

- **Application programming interfaces**: They provide a structured way to access data from various services and platforms. **Application programming interfaces** (**APIs**) allow applications to communicate with each other, enabling data exchange. For instance, social media platforms like *Twitter* and *Facebook* offer APIs that allow developers to access user data, posts, and trends. APIs often return data in structured formats such as JSON or XML, making it easier to integrate and analyze. They are essential for accessing real-time data and services provided by third-party platforms without the need to directly scrape web pages.

- **Databases**: They are organized collections of data that can be easily accessed, managed, and updated. They are crucial for storing large volumes of structured data, which can be queried using languages like SQL. Relational databases (e.g., MySQL, PostgreSQL) organize data into tables, while NoSQL databases (e.g., MongoDB, Cassandra) handle unstructured or semi-structured data more flexibly. Databases are central to many business operations, providing reliable storage for transactional data, customer information, inventory management, and more.

- **Sensors**: They are devices that detect and respond to various types of inputs from the physical environment, such as temperature, humidity, motion, and pressure. Data from sensors is crucial in fields like the **Internet of Things** (**IoT**), where real-time monitoring and data collection are essential. For example, sensors in smart homes can monitor energy usage, while environmental sensors track air quality and weather conditions. The data collected by sensors is often streamed continuously and can be used for real-time analysis and decision-making in various applications, including industrial automation, healthcare, and environmental monitoring.

- **Surveys and questionnaires**: These are traditional but effective methods of primary data collection, especially useful for gathering qualitative data and insights directly from individuals. Surveys can be conducted online, via phone, or in person, allowing researchers to collect responses to specific questions tailored to their research objectives. They are commonly used in market research, customer feedback, and social science studies. Well-designed surveys can provide valuable insights into consumer behavior, preferences, and opinions, which can be analyzed to inform business strategies and decisions.

- **Logs and event tracking**: Logs and event tracking are methods used to collect data about user interactions and system events. This approach is prevalent in web and application analytics, where every action taken by a user, such as clicks, page views, and transactions, is recorded in log files. These logs provide a detailed record of user behavior, system performance, and error events. Tools like Google Analytics, Mixpanel, and custom logging solutions help aggregate and analyze this data to understand user engagement, improve user experience, and optimize system performance.

- **Manual data entry**: Manual data entry involves human operators inputting data into systems, often from paper-based sources or other non-digital formats. This method is labor-intensive and time-consuming, but can be necessary for digitizing records, especially historical data or data collected through non-digital means. It is crucial in situations where automated data collection is not feasible. Ensuring accuracy and minimizing human error through double-entry or verification processes is essential to maintain data integrity.

- **Crowdsourcing**: Crowdsourcing involves collecting data from a large group of people, typically through the internet. Platforms like Amazon Mechanical Turk and CrowdFlower (now Figure Eight) facilitate this by allowing organizations to post tasks that users complete for a fee. Crowdsourcing can be used for a wide range of data collection activities, including data labeling, image recognition, and sentiment analysis. This method is beneficial for obtaining large volumes of data quickly and for tasks that require human judgment.

- **Mobile data collection**: Mobile data collection utilizes mobile devices such as smartphones and tablets to gather data. This method is particularly effective for field research, remote surveys, and on-the-go data capture. Mobile data collection apps like **Open Data Kit (ODK)** and SurveyCTO enable users to collect data offline, which is then synced to a central database when connectivity is available. This approach is valuable in areas with limited internet access and for capturing real-time data in diverse environments.

- **Wearables and IoT devices**: Wearables and IoT devices are increasingly used for data collection in real-time and continuous monitoring. Wearable devices like fitness trackers and smartwatches collect data on physical activity, heart rate, sleep patterns, and more. IoT devices, embedded in smart home systems, industrial equipment, and environmental sensors, collect vast amounts of data on temperature, humidity, machinery performance, and other metrics. This data is crucial for health monitoring, predictive maintenance, and smart city applications.

- **Satellite and remote sensing**: Satellite and remote sensing involve collecting data from satellite imagery and remote sensors to monitor large-scale environmental and geographic phenomena. This method is essential for applications in agriculture, forestry, disaster management, and urban planning. For example, satellite imagery can track deforestation, monitor crop health, and assess natural disaster impacts. Remote sensing technologies provide high-resolution, real-time data that is invaluable for **geographic information systems (GIS)** and environmental studies.

Datasets

In data science, datasets are fundamental for training models, validating hypotheses, and deriving insights. Different types of datasets are used based on the domain, problem type, and data availability. The following section provides a detailed explanation of various types of datasets used in data science.

Based on source and availability

These are categorized as follows:

- **Open datasets**
  - Freely available for public use.
  - Often used for learning, benchmarking, and prototyping.
  - **Examples**:
    - **UCI Machine Learning Repository: https://archive.ics.uci.edu/**
    - **Kaggle Datasets: https://www.kaggle.com/datasets**
    - **Google Dataset Search: https://datasetsearch.research.google.com/**
    - **AWS Open Data: https://registry.opendata.aws/**

- **Proprietary datasets**:
  - Owned by companies or institutions.
  - May require purchase or permission to access.
  - Used in commercial or sensitive projects (e.g., customer data, medical records).

- **Simulated datasets**:
  - Artificially generated data is used when real data is scarce or restricted.
  - Useful in algorithm testing and validation.

Based on data type

These are categorized as follows:

- **Structured datasets**:
  - Data is organized in tabular form with rows and columns (like Excel or SQL).
  - Each column has a specific data type (e.g., integer, float, string).
  - **Examples**:
    - Financial transactions
    - Sales records
    - Customer databases

- **Unstructured datasets**:
  - Data is not organized in a pre-defined format.
  - Requires significant preprocessing.
  - **Examples**:
    - Text (emails, tweets, reviews)
    - Images (photos, medical scans)
    - Audio (recordings, speech)
    - Video

- **Semi-structured datasets**:
  - Mix of structured and unstructured formats.
  - Often found in formats like JSON, XML, or NoSQL databases.
  - **Examples**:
    - Web logs
    - API responses
    - Social media posts with metadata

Based on domain

These are categorized as follows:

- **Image datasets**:
  - Used in computer vision tasks (e.g., classification, detection).
  - **Examples**:
    - **MNIST**: Handwritten digits

- **CIFAR-10/100**: Object classification
- **ImageNet**: Large-scale object classification
- **COCO**: Object detection, segmentation

- **Text datasets**:
  - Used in **natural language processing (NLP)**.
  - **Examples**:
    - **IMDB reviews**: Sentiment analysis
    - **20 Newsgroups**: Document classification
    - **SQuA**: Question answering
    - **Wikipedia Dumps**: Language modeling

- **Time-series datasets**:
  - Sequential data indexed by time.
  - Used in forecasting and anomaly detection.
  - **Examples**:
    - Stock prices
    - Weather data
    - IoT sensor readings

- **Audio datasets**:
  - Used in speech recognition, audio classification.
  - **Examples**:
    - **LibriSpeech**: Speech recognition
    - **UrbanSound8K**: Environmental sounds
    - **Common Voice**: Multilingual speech

- **Video datasets**:
  - Sequence of images with or without audio.
  - Used in activity recognition, video classification.
  - **Examples**:
    - **UCF101**: Human action recognition
    - **Kinetics**: Video understanding

- **Graph datasets**:
  - Represent relationships between entities.

- o   Used in social network analysis, recommendation systems.
- o   **Examples:**
  - **Cora**: Citation network
  - **Facebook Graph**: Friend connections
  - **Open Graph Benchmark (OGB)**

Based on machine learning task

These are categorized as follows:

- **Classification datasets:**
  - o   Target variable is categorical.
  - o   **Examples:**
    - Breast cancer detection (benign/malignant)
    - Email spam detection
- **Regression datasets:**
  - o   Target variable is continuous.
  - o   **Examples:**
    - House price prediction
    - Sales forecasting
- **Clustering datasets:**
  - o   No labels; used to find natural groupings.
  - o   **Examples:**
    - Customer segmentation
    - Genetic data
- **Reinforcement learning datasets:**
  - o   Contain environment states, actions, and rewards.
  - o   **Examples:**
    - OpenAI Gym
    - D4RL (offline reinforcement learning)
- **Anomaly detection datasets:**
  - o   Identify outliers or unusual patterns.

o **Examples:**

- Network intrusion detection
- Fraud detection

Real-world examples by domain

Some of the real-world examples of datasets in various sectors, such as education, finance, and healthcare, are summarized in *Table 4.2*:

Domain	Dataset example	Purpose
Healthcare	MIMIC-III	Clinical patient data
Finance	Yahoo Finance	Stock data
E-commerce	Amazon Reviews	Sentiment analysis, product ranking
Education	MOOCs (KDD Cup)	Dropout prediction
Transportation	NYC Taxi Trips	Route optimization, demand forecast

Table 4.2: Some of the real-world datasets

Note: **While choosing a dataset, the following points must be taken care of:**

- **Consider data quality, size, format, and licensing.**
- **Understand the goal: training a model, benchmarking, or real-time deployment.**
- **Always check ethical considerations, especially with sensitive data (e.g., healthcare, facial images).**

Data formats

Data analysis involves various formats of data, depending on the type of analysis, tools, and industry. Here are the key formats used in data analysis:

- **Structured data formats**: These formats are highly organized and easily stored in relational databases.

   o **Comma-separated values (CSV)**: Plain text format where values are separated by commas.

   o **Tab-separated values (TSV)**: Similar to CSV but uses tabs as delimiters.

   o **XLS/XLSX (Microsoft Excel)**: Used in spreadsheets, supports formulas, charts, and formatting.

   o **SQL Databases**: Stores data in relational tables (MySQL, PostgreSQL, SQLite).

   o **Parquet**: Columnar storage format optimized for large-scale data processing (Apache Parquet).

- **Semi-structured data formats**: These formats contain some structure but are more flexible than relational databases.

  o **JavaScript Object Notation (JSON)**: Widely used in APIs and web applications, stores data in key-value pairs.

  o **Extensible Markup Language (XML)**: Used in web services, config files, and document storage.

  o **Yet Another Markup Language (YAML)**: Human-readable, used for configuration files.

  o **Avro**: Schema-based format used in big data applications.

- **Unstructured data formats**: These formats do not have a predefined structure and require processing to extract insights.

  o **TXT (Plain Text)**: Contains raw data with no structure.

  o **Portable Document Format (PDF)**: Often used for reports and documents.

  o **DOC/DOCX (Microsoft Word)**: Text documents that may include tables and charts.

  o **Log files**: System-generated records of events or actions.

  o **Hypertext Markup Language (HTML)**: Used for web data extraction.

- **Big data and binary formats**: These formats are optimized for large-scale data storage and processing.

  o **Hierarchical Data Format 5 (HDF5)**: Used in scientific computing and machine learning.

  o **Optimized Row Columnar (ORC)**: Columnar format for high-performance big data analytics.

  o **Feather**: Fast and lightweight format for data frames (used with Python and R).

  o **Pickle (Python)**: Serialized binary format for Python objects.

- **Geospatial data formats**: Used for location-based data analysis.

  o **GeoJSON**: JSON-based format for storing geographical data.

  o **Shapefiles (.shp)**: Used in GIS applications for mapping.

  o **Keyhole Markup Language (KML)**: Used in Google Earth and mapping tools.

- **Image, audio, and video formats**: For AI and multimedia analytics.

  o **PNG, JPEG, TIFF**: Image formats used in computer vision.

    o   **WAV, MP3**: Audio formats for speech and sound analysis.

    o   **MP4, AVI**: Video formats for motion analysis and AI-based recognition.

Various sorts of data formats are summarized in *Table 4.3*:

Format	Type	Best for	Schema enforcement*
CSV	Tabular	Simple, structured data	No
JSON	Semi-structured	APIs, nested records	No
Parquet	Columnar	Big data, Spark	Yes
HDF5	Scientific	Large-scale numeric data	Yes
SQL/SQLite	Database	Relational structured data	Yes
TXT	Unstructured	Raw text, NLP	No
JPEG/PNG	Image	Computer vision	No
MP3/WAV	Audio	Speech/audio processing	No
MP4	Video	Video analytics	No

Table 4.3: Summary of various data formats

*****Schema**: A schema defines the structure of data, including fields, data types, and relationships. It ensures consistency and validation in how data is stored and accessed.

Benefits of data format types

With data format types being in place, it becomes easy for the user to carry out multiple operations and make the most of them. Some of the benefits of having data format types have been listed as follows:

- **Calculations**: Calculations have never been easy before the introduction of data format types. With these formats, all you have to do is punch in the values, and within no time, all the calculation is done and at your disposal.

- **Formatted**: The data, if kept well formatted and organized, is presentable and understandable by the users. Thus, individuals referring to such data can make the most of it. If a user has to make a similar presentation at different points in time, they can simply pick up a format and keep using it for drafting presentations.

- **Consistency**: Data types help users to have variables that are consistent throughout the program. So, you can simply rely on the variable to make presentations or calculations.

- **Readable**: The data is readable and accessible to users all the time without any hassle. Hence, any job can be done at the earliest with maximum output produced.

Data parsing

Data parsing is the process of converting raw data into a structured, readable, and usable format. It involves analyzing a data stream (like text, JSON, XML, CSV, HTML, etc.) and transforming it into a format that a program or a database can understand and process. Data parsing typically follows these steps:

1. **Input data**: The process starts with input data, which can come from various sources like:

   - Web scraping (HTML pages)
   - APIs (JSON, XML responses)
   - Logs (server logs, error logs)
   - Files (CSV, TXT, Excel, etc.)

2. **Lexical analysis (Tokenization)**: The data is broken down into smaller components (tokens), which are individual elements like words, numbers, or symbols.

3. **Syntax analysis (Parsing rules applied)**: The parser applies predefined rules to check the structure of the data and organizes it into a hierarchical or tabular format.

4. **Data extraction and transformation**:

   - Irrelevant data is filtered out.
   - Important fields are extracted.
   - Data may be transformed into a structured format (e.g., a table or database).

5. **Output data**: The parsed data is stored or processed further, such as:

   - Saving in a database
   - Using in software applications
   - Analyzing for insights

The summary of common tools used for parsing is given in *Table 4.4*:

Format	Tools/Libraries	Language
CSV	`csv, pandas`	Python
JSON	`json, pandas`	Python
XML	`ElementTree, lxml`	Python
HTML	`BeautifulSoup, Selenium, Scrapy`	Python
Logs	`Regex, logstash`	Various

Table 4.4: Commonly used parsing tools

Types of data parsers

Data parsing is a crucial step in data processing that extracts meaningful information from raw or semi-structured data. It involves identifying and separating different data components such as fields, records, and tokens to understand the structure and content of the data. Once parsed, the data is converted into usable formats or objects, such as Python dictionaries, tables, or other structured representations, that make it suitable for analysis, transformation, or storage in databases. Different parsers are designed for different data formats:

- **JSON parser**: It is used to parse JSON data (common in APIs) as shown in the following example:

```
{
  "name": "Raghav",
  "age": 25,
  "city": "New York"
}
```

  JSON parsers extract and organize this data for use in applications.

- **XML parser**: It is used for parsing XML data, often seen in web services, as given in the following example:

```
<user>
  <name>Raghav</name>
  <age>25</age>
  <city>New York</city>
</user>
```

- **HTML parser**: It is used for extracting data from web pages. Libraries like **BeautifulSoup** (Python) or **Cheerio** (JavaScript) help parse HTML.

- **CSV parser**: It parses CSV files into structured tables, given as follows:

```
Name, Age, City
Raghav, 25, New York
```

- **Log file parser**: It extracts and analyzes log files for system monitoring or debugging.

  Let us consider the following **data.csv**, **data.json**, and **data.xml** files with attributes name, age, and city:

Name	Age	City
Raghav	30	New York
Sunny	25	Los Angeles

- **data.csv:**

  ```
  [
      {"name": "Charu", "age": 35, "city": "Chicago"},
      {"name": "Dhruv", "age": 40, "city": "Houston"}
  ]
  ```

- **data.json:**

  ```
  <root>
  <person>
  <name>Harry</name>
  <age>28</age>
  <city>Miami</city>
  </person>
  <person>
  <name>Jiansh</name>
  <age>33</age>
  <city>Seattle</city>
  </person>
  </root>
  ```

- **data.xml**: The following code represents the conversion of CSV, JSON, and XML files into the same format, where **data.csv**, **data.json**, and **data. xml** files are stored in the DPA directory, where Jupyter is installed, and their data is given as under:

  ```python
  import csv
  import json
  import xml.etree.ElementTree as ET

  # Function to parse a CSV file and return a list of
  dictionariesdef parse_csv(file_path):
      with open("DPA/data.csv", mode='r', encoding='utf-8') as
  file:
          reader = csv.DictReader(file)
          data = [row for row in reader]
      return data

  # Function to parse a JSON file and return the loaded data
  structure (usually a dict or list)
  def parse_json(file_path):
      with open("DPA/data.json", mode='r', encoding='utf-8') as
  file:
          data = json.load(file)
      return data
  ```

```
# Function to parse an XML file and return data as a list of
dictionaries
def parse_xml(file_path):
    tree = ET.parse("DPA/data.xml")
    root = tree.getroot()
    data = [] #empty list
    for child in root:
        data.append({elem.tag: elem.text for elem in child})
    return data
# Main block to execute functions if script is run directly
if __name__ == "__main__":
    csv_data = parse_csv("data1.csv")
    print("CSV Data:", csv_data)

    json_data = parse_json("data.json")
    print("JSON Data:", json_data)

    xml_data = parse_xml("data.xml")
    print("XML Data:", xml_data)
```

The output is as follows:

```
CSV Data: [{'name': 'Raghav', 'age': '30', 'city': 'New York'},
{'name': 'Sunny', 'age': '25', 'city': 'Los Angeles'}]
JSON Data: [{'name': 'Charu', 'age': 35, 'city': 'Chicago'},
{'name': 'Dhruv', 'age': 40, 'city': 'Houston'}]
XML Data: [{'name': 'Harry', 'age': '28', 'city': 'Miami'},
{'name': 'Jiansh', 'age': '33', 'city': 'Seattle'}]
```

Types of data parsing

Data parsing takes two approaches when it comes to the semantic analysis of text, namely grammar-driven data parsing and data-driven data parsing. An important aspect of parsing is to capture information from data in a way that it fits contextual structures. Here is how these two approaches work:

- **Grammar-driven data parsing**: Grammar-driven data parsing means the parser uses a set of formal grammar rules for the parsing process. The way this works is that sentences from unstructured data get fragmented and transformed into a structured format. The problem with grammar-driven data parsing is that models lack robustness. This is overcome by relaxing the grammatical constraints so that sentences outside the scope of grammar rules can be ruled out for later analysis. Text parsing is a subset of grammar parsing and assigns a number of analyses to a given string. It resolves disambiguation problems faced by traditional methods of parsing as well.

- **Data-driven data parsing**: Data-driven data parsing uses a probabilistic model and bypasses deductive approaches of text analysis, often used by grammar-driven models. In this type of parsing, the parsing program applies rule-based techniques, semantic equations, and **natural language processing** (**NLP**) for sentence structuring and analysis. Unlike grammar-based parsing, data-driven data parsing employs statistical parsers and modern treebanks for obtaining broad coverage from languages. Parsing conversational languages and sentences that require precision with domain-specific unlabeled data fall under the scope of data-driven data parsing.

Data parser use cases

What does a parser do? It extracts data from documents, gives structure to it, and filters details.

Data parsing is used by different industry verticals to convert information from documents into electronic formats. The following are the most popular use cases of parsing in industries:

- **Business workflow optimization**: Data parsers are used by companies to structure unstructured datasets into usable information. Businesses use data parsing for optimizing their workflows related to data extraction. Parsing is used in the fields of investment analysis, marketing, social media management, and other business applications.

- **Finance and accounting**: Banks and NBFCs use data parsing to scrape through billions of customer data, and extract key information from applications. Data parsing is used for analyzing credit reports, investment portfolios, income verification, and deriving better insights about customers. Finance firms use parsing for determining interest rates and loan repayment periods post-data extraction.

- **Shipping and logistics**: Businesses that deliver products/services online use data parsers to extract billing and shipping details. Parsers are used for arranging shipping labels and ensuring the formatting of data is correct.

- **Real estate industry**: Lead data is extracted from real estate emails by property owners and builders. Parsing technologies are used for extracting data for CRM platforms and process documentation in order to forward it to real estate agents. From contact details, property addresses, cash flow data, and lead sources, parsers are very beneficial for real estate companies when it comes to making purchases, rentals, and sales.

Data transformation

Data transformation is the process of converting data from one format, structure, or value system into another. This process is essential in data analysis, data integration, and machine learning, ensuring that data is clean, consistent, and suitable for processing.

Steps in data transformation

The following are the steps of transforming data into a useful form:

1. **Data extraction**: Retrieve data from sources like databases, APIs, or files.

2. **Data cleansing**: Fix inconsistencies, remove duplicates, and handle missing values.

3. **Data normalization**: Convert data into a common format (e.g., standardizing date formats).

4. **Data aggregation**: Summarize or group data (e.g., calculating totals, averages).

5. **Data enrichment**: Add additional information (e.g., joining data from multiple sources).

6. **Data encoding**: Convert categorical data into numerical form for analysis.

7. **Data formatting**: Change file formats (e.g., CSV to JSON, XML to SQL).

8. **Data loading**: Store transformed data into a target system (e.g., database, data warehouse).

The types of data transformation are as follows:

- **Structural transformation**:
  - **Changing data formats** (e.g., JSON l SV, SQL|Parquet)
  - **Rearranging columns** (e.g., moving Date from last to first column)
  - **Splitting and merging data** (e.g., splitting Full Name into First Name and Last Name)

- **Data cleaning and standardization**:
  - Removing duplicates
  - Handling missing values (e.g., replacing NULL with Unknown)
  - Standardizing units (e.g., converting inches to cm)

- **Data aggregation and summarization**:
  - Grouping data by category (e.g., total sales per region)
  - Computing averages, sums, and counts

- **Data normalization and scaling**:
  - Converting values to a standard range (e.g., 0 to 1 for machine learning)
  - Standardizing dates (e.g., YYYY-MM-DD format)

- **Data encoding**:
  - Converting categorical variables into numerical form (e.g., Male = 0, Female = 1)
  - Encoding text for machine learning models

Example of data transformation

Consider a **salary.csv** file, as given below, we will transform the data of this file by normalizing the values of the (Age, Salary, and Score) columns:

Name	Age	Salary	Score
Raghav	25	50000	85
Sunny	30	60000	78
Charu	35	70000	92
Dhruv	40	80000	88
Eve	28	55000	81

The following code represents the transformation by using **MinMaxScaler**, where the values of columns with number datatype (**Age**, **Salary**, and **Score**) of **salary.csv** file are normalized to new values that can be seen in the output of the code. The normalization helps avoid the outliers in the data and gives better results in analysis.

```python
import pandas as pd
from sklearn.preprocessing import MinMaxScaler

def normalize_data(file_path):
    try:
        # Load data
        df = pd.read_csv(file_path)

        # Initialize scaler
        scaler = MinMaxScaler()

        # Normalize numeric columns only
        numeric_cols = df.select_dtypes(include=['float64', 'int64']).columns
        df[numeric_cols] = scaler.fit_transform(df[numeric_cols])

        return df
    except Exception as e:
        return f"Error: {str(e)}"

if __name__ == "__main__":
    file_path = input("Enter CSV file path: ")
    normalized_df = normalize_data(file_path)
    print("Normalized Data:")
    print(normalized_df)
```

The output is as follows:

```
Enter CSV file path: DPA/salary.csv
Normalized Data:
```

	Name	Age	Salary	Score
0	Raghav	0.000000	0.000000	0.500000
1	Sunny	0.333333	0.333333	0.000000
2	Charu	0.666667	0.666667	1.000000
3	Dhruv	1.000000	1.000000	0.714286
4	Eve	0.200000	0.166667	0.214286

In the same way, the following code aggregates the values of **Age**, **Salary**, and **Score**, columns of the **salary.csv** file:

```python
import pandas as pd

def aggregate_data(file_path):
    try:
        # Load data
        df = pd.read_csv(file_path)

        # Perform aggregation: calculate the mean of Age, Salary, and Score
        aggregated_df = df.agg({'Age': 'mean', 'Salary': 'mean', 'Score':
'mean'})

        return aggregated_df
    except Exception as e:
        return f"Error: {str(e)}"

if __name__ == "__main__":
    file_path = input("Enter CSV file path: ")
    aggregated_df = aggregate_data(file_path)
    print("Aggregated Data:")
    print(aggregated_df)
```

The output is as follows:

```
Enter CSV file path: DPA/salary.csv
Aggregated Data:
Age            31.6
Salary      63000.0
Score          84.8
dtype: float64
```

Real-time issues in data transformation

Real-time data gathering involves collecting and processing data as it is generated. While this provides timely insights, there are several challenges and issues associated with it:

- **Data latency**:
    - Delay in data collection, transmission, and processing can hinder real-time performance.

- o Network congestion, hardware limitations, or inefficient algorithms can cause delays.

- **Data accuracy and quality**:
  - o Sensors and devices may provide noisy, incomplete, or erroneous data.
  - o Synchronization issues between different data sources can compromise data accuracy.

- **High volume of data (big data)**:
  - o Real-time systems often deal with massive streams of data.
  - o Storing, processing, and analyzing such high volumes can be resource-intensive.

- **Limited bandwidth**:
  - o Data transmission in real-time systems, especially in remote areas, can be limited by available network bandwidth.
  - o This may result in data loss, delays, or the need for data compression.

- **Scalability**:
  - o As the number of data sources or data volume increases, systems must scale efficiently.
  - o Inadequate system architecture can result in bottlenecks and performance degradation.

- **Security and privacy concerns**:
  - o Real-time data gathering often involves sensitive information.
  - o Ensuring data encryption, secure transmission, and user privacy is crucial.

- **Data redundancy**:
  - o Continuous data streaming may lead to redundant or duplicate data being collected.
  - o Efficient mechanisms are needed to filter and manage such data.

- **Hardware and sensor failures**:
  - o Real-time systems depend heavily on hardware like sensors and IoT devices.
  - o Failures or malfunctions can disrupt data flow and affect system reliability.

- **Cost issues**:
  - o Maintaining infrastructure for real-time data collection, processing, and storage can be costly.
  - o Balancing performance and cost is a challenge for many organizations.

- **Complexity in integration**:
    - Integrating real-time data gathering with existing systems, databases, and software platforms can be complex.
    - Compatibility issues and software bugs may arise.

Conclusion

In conclusion, this chapter has laid the groundwork for understanding the foundational aspects of working with data in data science. We examined the different types of data and datasets, emphasizing their characteristics and relevance in various analytical contexts. The chapter also explained the importance of data parsing in transforming raw or semi-structured information into formats suitable for processing, and how data transformation techniques are essential in preparing data for meaningful analysis. Lastly, we addressed real-time issues in data gathering, such as inconsistencies, latency, and integration challenges, which are critical considerations in practical data-driven environments. Together, these concepts form the essential first steps in any data science workflow, ensuring that data is accurate, consistent, and ready for deeper analysis and modeling.

In the subsequent chapter, we will study data cleaning techniques in detail.

Multiple choice questions

1. **Which of the following is an example of structured data?**
    a. A scanned image
    b. A JSON file
    c. A table in a relational database
    d. A video file

2. **Semi-structured data is best represented by**:
    a. MP4 files
    b. XML or JSON formats
    c. Plain text documents
    d. SQL tables

3. **Which of these is not an example of a dataset?**
    a. Weather records in a CSV file
    b. A table of employee salaries
    c. A paragraph in a novel
    d. A collection of images with labels

4. **Unstructured data typically includes:**

   a. Database tables

   b. Spreadsheets

   c. Sensor logs in CSV format

   d. Social media posts

5. **What is the primary goal of data parsing?**

   a. To store data in the cloud

   b. To convert raw data into a usable structure

   c. To visualize data

   d. To encrypt data

6. **In Python, which module is commonly used to parse JSON data?**

   a. xml

   b. json

   c. csv

   d. sql

7. **Data transformation is used to:**

   a. Compress files

   b. Convert data formats and values

   c. Generate charts

   d. Backup data

8. **Which of the following is a data transformation technique?**

   a. Normalization

   b. Compression

   c. Compilation

   d. Encryption

9. **Which file format is best suited for storing structured tabular data?**

   a. .mp3

   b. .csv

   c. .png

   d. .json

10. **What kind of issue is most common in real-time data collection?**

    a. Compilation error

    b. High latency and missing values

    c. High CPU usage

    d. Encryption failure

11. **Which of these is an example of real-time data?**

    a. A scanned newspaper

    b. Social media feed updates

    c. An archived weather report

    d. A saved PDF report

12. **Which tool is commonly used to parse HTML data in Python?**

    a. pandas

    b. numpy

    c. BeautifulSoup

    d. matplotlib

13. **A dataset that contains multiple categories of labeled images is an example of:**

    a. Unstructured data

    b. Semi-structured data

    c. Structured data

    d. Static data

14. **Which of the following is an issue commonly faced during data transformation?**

    a. Increased internet speed

    b. Data loss due to improper mapping

    c. Battery drainage

    d. Software licensing

15. **Which method is used to scale numerical data into a fixed range, like 0 to 1?**

    a. Data parsing

    b. Normalization

    c. Tokenization

    d. Serialization

16. **A dataset used for model testing is usually called:**

    a. Training data

    b. Production data

    c. Testing data

    d. Raw data

17. **The process of identifying different fields or tokens in a text file is part of:**

    a. Data modeling

    b. Data visualization

    c. Data parsing

    d. Data storage

18. **Which of the following is a cause of data inconsistency in real-time systems?**

    a. Regular updates

    b. Simultaneous data entry from multiple sources

    c. Data encryption

    d. Data compression

19. **An API typically returns data in which of the following formats?**

    a. DOCX

    b. PDF

    c. JSON

    d. CSV only

20. **What does real-time data imply?**

    a. Data stored in backup

    b. Data from simulations only

    c. Data collected and processed instantly

    d. Data gathered from historical archives

Answers

1. c
2. b
3. c
4. d
5. b

6. b

7. b

8. a

9. b

10. b

11. b

12. c

13. c

14. b

15. b

16. c

17. c

18. b

19. c

20. c

Questions

1. What are the main types of data used in data science? Provide examples of each.

2. Differentiate between structured, semi-structured, and unstructured data.

3. What is a dataset? How do open datasets differ from proprietary datasets?

4. Explain the purpose of data parsing in a data processing pipeline.

5. What are common tools or libraries used for parsing JSON and CSV data?

6. Define data transformation. Why is it important in data preprocessing?

7. List and briefly describe three common data transformation techniques.

8. What challenges might occur when gathering real-time data from multiple sources?

9. How can data inconsistencies affect the accuracy of real-time analytics?

10. What strategies can be used to handle missing or delayed data in real-time systems?

11. Suppose you receive daily CSV logs from different sources with different formats. How would you design a system to parse and standardize the data?

12. Explain how data normalization and encoding are used in machine learning pipelines. Provide examples.

13. You are working with sensor data in real-time. Describe the challenges you might face with data quality and how you would address them.

14. Discuss a real-world scenario where real-time data transformation is critical (e.g., fraud detection, traffic monitoring).

Programming exercises

1. Load a CSV file and print the data types of each column.

2. Read a .json file and extract specific fields.

3. Extract product names and prices from a sample HTML page.

4. Generate a dummy dataset and normalize numerical columns between 0 and 1.

5. Parse a list of dictionaries (e.g., from an API) into a DataFrame.

6. Write a script that summarizes the dataset.

7. Write a function to clean data entries as they are received.

Join our Discord space

Join our Discord workspace for latest updates, offers, tech happenings around the world, new releases, and sessions with the authors:

https://discord.bpbonline.com

CHAPTER 5
Data Cleaning

Introduction

Data cleaning (also known as **data cleansing** or **data scrubbing**) is the process of identifying and correcting (or removing) errors, inconsistencies, inaccuracies, or incomplete information from a dataset to improve its quality. In the data science workflow, data cleaning is a critical early step that directly impacts the accuracy and reliability of any subsequent analysis or model building. It ensures that the data used for statistical analysis, machine learning, or decision-making is accurate, complete, and consistent. Data cleaning is crucial in data science because it directly influences the accuracy, reliability, and usefulness of the insights derived from data. Improving data quality ensures that errors such as duplicates, missing values, and inconsistencies are corrected, leading to more accurate and meaningful analyses. Clean data enhances the performance of machine learning models and statistical methods, resulting in better predictions and insights. It also saves time and resources by preventing the need for reanalysis due to flawed data. Moreover, clean data supports informed decision-making by providing a trustworthy foundation for analysis. In regulated industries like healthcare and finance, data cleaning also plays a key role in maintaining data integrity and ensuring compliance with legal and ethical standards. Overall, data cleaning is a vital step that ensures the success and reliability of any data-driven project.

Structure

The chapter covers the following topics:

- Data consistency
- Heterogeneous data
- Missing data
- Data transformation
- Data segmentation

Objectives

The objective of this chapter is to equip readers with the knowledge and practical skills necessary for effective data cleaning, a critical step in preparing data for analysis. It aims to help readers understand and ensure data consistency by identifying and resolving inconsistencies in formats, values, and structures. The chapter also focuses on maintaining heterogeneous data types across datasets to ensure uniformity. It addresses various types of missing data and demonstrates how to handle them using strategies such as deletion, imputation, or substitution, all illustrated through Python code. Additionally, the chapter covers essential data transformation techniques, including normalization, standardization, and encoding of categorical variables, to improve data quality and compatibility with analytical tools. Finally, it introduces data segmentation as a method to partition datasets into meaningful subsets for more focused analysis. Practical examples and code snippets using Python libraries like Pandas and NumPy are provided throughout to help readers apply these techniques effectively in real-world scenarios.

Data consistency

Data consistency in data cleaning is crucial for accurate, reliable, and efficient data usage. By ensuring that data remains uniform across a dataset, organizations can improve data quality, streamline analytics, and make better business decisions. Data consistency refers to ensuring that all data across a dataset (or multiple datasets) follows the same format, values, and logical relationships. It ensures that the same data point is represented uniformly across all records and prevents contradictions in the dataset. Let us consider the following examples to understand it:

- A customer's birth date should not be recorded as both 01/01/1990 and 1990-01-01 in the same dataset.

- A product price should not be $50 in one record and $49.99 in another for the same product.

- A person's name should not be recorded as *John Doe* in one table and *J. Doe* in another.

Data consistency is crucial in maintaining data integrity, preventing duplication, and ensuring reliability in data analysis.

Causes of data inconsistency

Inconsistencies in data can arise due to various reasons, such as:

- **Human errors**: Manual data entry mistakes (e.g., typos, misformatted data).

- **Multiple data sources**: Different data formats from various sources (e.g., CRM vs. ERP systems).

- **Data migration issues**: Moving data between systems without proper validation.

- **Lack of standardization**: Inconsistent formats (e.g., different date formats, varying units of measurement).

- **Data duplication**: The same data is entered multiple times in different ways.

Importance of data consistency

Data consistency is essential for:

- **Accurate decision-making**: Inconsistent data can lead to incorrect business insights.

- **Data integration**: Combining datasets from multiple sources requires uniformity in data representation.

- **Error reduction**: Eliminating inconsistencies helps reduce errors in reporting and analytics.

- **Compliance and standards**: Many industries (e.g., finance, healthcare) require strict data consistency for regulatory compliance.

Methods to ensure data consistency

To maintain consistency in a dataset, data cleaning techniques such as the following are applied:

- **Standardization of data formats**: It ensures uniform formats for dates, phone numbers, currency, etc. **Example**: Converting all dates to YYYY-MM-DD instead of mixing MM/DD/YYYY and DD-MM-YYYY.

- **Removing duplicates**: It uses algorithms to detect and remove duplicate records. **Example**: If *John Smith* appears multiple times with the same email but different spellings, merge them into a single record.

- **Validation and error detection**: It applies validation rules to identify incorrect or inconsistent values. **Example**: Checking for age values under 0 or above 120 in a customer dataset.

- **Enforcing referential integrity**: It ensures relationships between different data tables remain correct. **Example**: If a customer order exists, their corresponding customer ID must be present in the customer database.

- **Consistent naming conventions**: It standardizes column names, categories, and labels across datasets. **Example**: Using Product_ID instead of sometimes PID and other times ProductID.

- **Handling missing or conflicting data**: It fills missing data using appropriate imputation methods (e.g., mean, mode). It resolves conflicts by establishing a single source of truth.

- **Use of data cleaning tools**: Tools like OpenRefine, Trifacta, and Pandas (in Python) can help automate data cleaning and consistency checks.

Data consistency issues

Here, we will discuss certain real-world issues of data consistency. Imagine an e-commerce business analyzing customer purchase data across different platforms (website, mobile app, and in-store purchases). If the following instances occur:

- The mobile app records state names as abbreviations (e.g., CA for California).

- The website uses full names (e.g., California).

- The in-store system uses numeric codes (e.g., 06 for California).

Then, analyzing customer behavior by state becomes difficult. A data consistency process would standardize all entries to one format (e.g., using full state names).

The following code demonstrates how to fix common data inconsistencies using Pandas. This includes:

1. Standardizing date formats.
2. Normalizing categorical values (e.g., 'Male', 'male', 'M' → 'Male').
3. Removing duplicate rows.

```
import pandas as pd

# Sample data with inconsistencies
data = {
    'CustomerID': [101, 102, 103, 104, 105, 105],
    'Name': ['Ansh', 'Bobby', 'Harry', 'Dhruvi', 'Eve', 'Eve'],
    'Gender': ['Male', 'male', 'M', 'Female', 'F', 'FEMALE'],
    'SignupDate': ['01-05-2023', '2023/05/01', 'May 1, 2023', '2023-05-01',
'01-May-2023', '2023-05-01']
}

df = pd.DataFrame(data)
```

```
print("Original DataFrame:\n", df)

# -------------------------------
# 1. Fixing date format inconsistencies
#df['SignupDate'] = pd.to_datetime(df['SignupDate'], errors='coerce',
dayfirst=True)# Converts to datetime, handles mixed formats

# ----------- Fix SignupDate with format parsing -----------
from dateutil import parser

def parse_date(val):
    try:
        return parser.parse(val, dayfirst=True)
    except Exception:
        return pd.NaT

df['SignupDate'] = df['SignupDate'].apply(parse_date)
# -------------------------------
# 2. Standardizing categorical values (Gender column)
def standardize_gender(val):
    val = str(val).strip().lower()
    if val in ['male', 'm']:
        return 'Male'
    elif val in ['female', 'f']:
        return 'Female'
    else:
        return 'Other'

df['Gender'] = df['Gender'].apply(standardize_gender)

# -------------------------------
# 3. Removing duplicate rows (if any)
df = df.drop_duplicates()

print("\nCleaned DataFrame:\n", df)
```

The output is as follows:

Original DataFrame:

	CustomerID	Name	Gender	SignupDate
0	101	Ansh	Male	01-05-2023
1	102	Bobby	male	2023/05/01
2	103	Harry	M	May 1, 2023
3	104	Dhruvi	Female	2023-05-01
4	105	Eve	F	01-May-2023
5	105	Eve	Female	2023-05-01

```
Cleaned DataFrame:
```

	CustomerID	Name	Gender	SignupDate
0	101	Ansh	Male	2023-05-01
1	102	Bobby	Male	2023-05-01
2	103	Harry	Male	2023-05-01
3	104	Dhruvi	Female	2023-05-01
4	105	Eve	Female	2023-05-01

Heterogeneous data

Both heterogeneous and missing data pose challenges in data cleaning, requiring structured approaches to standardization, transformation, and imputation. Proper handling improves the accuracy, consistency, and usability of data for analysis. Heterogeneous data refers to data that comes from multiple sources, formats, or structures, making it difficult to integrate and analyze. It can have differences in:

- **Data types** (numeric, text, images, etc.)
- **Formats** (dates in different formats, varying measurement units)
- **Sources** (databases, APIs, web scraping, spreadsheets)
- **Granularity** (some records have detailed information, while others lack specifics)

Examples of heterogeneous data:

- A company collects customer information from:
    - Website sign-ups (email and phone number).
    - Social media interactions (username and engagement data).
    - Call center logs (voice recordings and text transcripts).
    - In-store transactions (purchase history and receipts).

Each source provides different data types and structures, leading to heterogeneity.

Challenges of heterogeneous data

The heterogeneous data face certain challenges as described as follows:

- **Data integration issues**: Merging different formats and structures is complex.
- **Inconsistent data representation**: A product price might be recorded as $50 in one system and 50 USD in another.
- **Scalability problems**: Large-scale heterogeneous datasets require more processing power.

- **Difficulty in data cleaning**: Different formats and structures make automated cleaning harder.

How to handle heterogeneous data

There are various ways to handle heterogeneous data, which are given as follows:

- **Standardization**: It converts all dates to a uniform format (e.g., YYYY-MM-DD) and ensures consistent measurement units (e.g., converting all distances to kilometers).

- **Data transformation**: It converts unstructured data (like text or images) into structured formats where possible and uses data mapping techniques to align different field names and formats.

- **Schema matching**: It aligns columns with the same meaning (e.g., Customer_ID in one system and UserID in another).

- **Data integration tools**: It uses **extract, transform, load** (**ETL**) tools like Apache NiFi, Talend, or Pandas in Python.

The following code represents how to identify and remove heterogeneous data in columns:

```python
import pandas as pd

# Sample data with heterogeneous entries
data = {
    'Age': [25, '30', 'unknown', 45, None],
    'Salary': [50000, 60000, 'N/A', 70000, 80000],
    'Active': [True, 'Yes', 'No', False, 'True']
}

df = pd.DataFrame(data)

print("Original DataFrame:\n", df)

# ----------- Step 1: Convert to appropriate types and coerce errors ------
------
df['Age'] = pd.to_numeric(df['Age'], errors='coerce')
df['Salary'] = pd.to_numeric(df['Salary'], errors='coerce')

# For 'Active', let's map all truthy variations to boolean
def normalize_active(val):
    if str(val).strip().lower() in ['true', 'yes', '1']:
        return True
    elif str(val).strip().lower() in ['false', 'no', '0']:
        return False
    else:
```

```
        return None  # Mark invalids for removal
df['Active'] = df['Active'].apply(normalize_active)

# ----------- Step 2: Drop rows with remaining invalid (NaN) entries ------
------
df_clean = df.dropna()

print("\nCleaned DataFrame:\n", df_clean)
```

The output is as follows:

```
Original DataFrame:
       Age Salary Active
0       25  50000   True
1       30  60000    Yes
2  unknown    N/A     No
3       45  70000  False
4     None  80000   True

Cleaned DataFrame:
    Age  Salary  Active
0  25.0   50000    True
1  30.0   60000    True
3  45.0   70000   False
```

We can see from the code and output that the original DataFrame contains heterogeneous values like unknown, N/A, and none values. Such heterogeneous response values are removed from the updated DataFrame. One can also add an additional column in the original DataFrame as is heterogeneous, which will take values as True or False rather than removing all those rows which contain heterogenous values. This can be done by adding the following code to the existing code:

```python
import pandas as pd

# Sample data with heterogeneous entries
data = {
    'Age': [25, '30', 'unknown', 45, None],
    'Salary': [50000, 60000, 'N/A', 70000, 80000],
    'Active': [True, 'Yes', 'No', False, 'True']
}

df = pd.DataFrame(data)

# Step 1: Attempt to convert columns to expected types
df['Age_clean'] = pd.to_numeric(df['Age'], errors='coerce')
df['Salary_clean'] = pd.to_numeric(df['Salary'], errors='coerce')

def normalize_active(val):
```

```
      val = str(val).strip().lower()
      if val in ['true', 'yes', '1']:
          return True
      elif val in ['false', 'no', '0']:
          return False
      else:
          return None

df['Active_clean'] = df['Active'].apply(normalize_active)

# Step 2: Identify rows with any NaN in cleaned columns
df['IsHeterogeneous'] = df[['Age_clean', 'Salary_clean', 'Active_clean']].
isna().any(axis=1)

# Step 3: Optional - drop intermediate clean columns
df_final = df.drop(columns=['Age_clean', 'Salary_clean', 'Active_clean'])

print(df_final)
```

The output is as follows:

```
       Age  Salary  Active   IsHeterogeneous
0       25   50000    True            False
1       30   60000     Yes            False
2  unknown     N/A      No             True
3       45   70000   False            False
4     None   80000    True             True
```

Missing data

Missing data occurs when expected values in a dataset are absent, leading to gaps that can affect analysis and decision-making.

Types of missing data

There are three main types of missing data, which are described as follows:

- **Missing completely at random (MCAR)**:
    - The absence of data has no relationship with other data.
    - **Example**: A sensor randomly fails to record temperature readings.
- **Missing at random (MAR)**:
    - The missingness depends on other known variables.
    - **Example**: High-income individuals might be less likely to disclose their salary in a survey.

- **Missing not at random (MNAR)**:
  - The missing values depend on the value itself.
  - **Example**: Patients with severe health conditions might not respond to certain medical surveys.

Causes of missing data

Due to certain reasons, data goes missing in the dataset, which are given as follows:

- **Human errors**: Data entry mistakes or skipped fields.
- **Technical issues**: Software crashes, sensor failures.
- **Data collection limitations**: Some users may choose not to provide certain information.
- **Merging datasets**: Some datasets might lack fields present in others.

Handling missing data

Data cleaning can be performed in different ways, which are described as follows:

- **Deletion methods**:
  - **Listwise deletion**: Remove entire rows with missing values (only if the missing data is minimal).
  - **Pairwise deletion**: Use available data for analysis without deleting rows.
- **Imputation techniques**:
  - **Mean/median/mode imputation**: Fill missing numerical data with the column's mean, median, or mode.
  - **Forward or backward fill**: Use previous or next values to fill missing data (e.g., time series data).
  - **Predictive imputation**: Use machine learning models (e.g., regression, k-NN) to estimate missing values.
- **Using default or placeholder values**: Assign placeholders like Unknown or N/A for categorical data.
- **Dropping unnecessary columns**: If a column has too many missing values (e.g., 80% missing), it may be better to drop it.
- **Flagging missing data**: Add a binary column to indicate missing values for further analysis.

The following file represents a CSV file called **sample_data.csv**, which is demonstrated as follows:

id	name	age	gender	salary	joining_date	department
1	Alice	25	Female	50000	15-01-2020	HR
2	Bob	30	Male	60000	23-06-2019	IT
3	Charlie		Male	55000	01-07-2021	Finance
4		40	Female		15-03-2018	IT
5	Eve	35		70000	09-08-2022	HR
6	Frank	29	Male	65000		Finance
7	Grace	50	Female	72000	25-09-2017	HR
8	Henry	60	Male	80000	30-11-2016	IT
9	Isaac		Female	75000	20-05-2015	Finance
10	Jack	45	Male		10-12-2023	

Table 5.1: sample_data.csv file

As we can see that certain cell values are missing in columns viz, name, age, gender, salary, joining_date, and department. By applying missing value imputation as presented in the following code, we get all values filled as shown in the new output file **cleaned_data. csv**:

```
import pandas as pd
import numpy as np

def clean_data(df):
    # Drop duplicates
    df = df.drop_duplicates()

    # Identify column types
    categorical_cols df.select_dtypes(include=['object']).columns.tolist()
    numerical_cols = df.select_dtypes(include=['number']).columns.tolist()
    datetime_cols = [col for col in df.columns if 'date' in col.lower()]

    # Handle missing values
    for col in numerical_cols:
        df[col].fillna(df[col].median(), inplace=True)  # Use median for
robustness

    for col in categorical_cols:
        df[col].fillna(df[col].mode()[0], inplace=True)

    for col in datetime_cols:
        df[col] = pd.to_datetime(df[col], errors='coerce')
        df[col].fillna(pd.Timestamp('2000-01-01'), inplace=True)  # Default
fallback date
```

```
    # Standardize text data
    for col in categorical_cols:
        df[col] = df[col].astype(str).str.lower().str.strip()

    # Handle outliers in numerical columns using IQR method
    for col in numerical_cols:
        Q1 = df[col].quantile(0.25)
        Q3 = df[col].quantile(0.75)
        IQR = Q3 - Q1
        lower_bound = Q1 - 1.5 * IQR
        upper_bound = Q3 + 1.5 * IQR
        df[col] = np.where((df[col] < lower_bound) | (df[col] > upper_
bound), df[col].median(), df[col])

    return df

# Load data from CSV
file_path = "sample_data.csv"  # Update with actual file path
df = pd.read_csv(file_path)

# Clean the data with the updated function
cleaned_df = clean_data(df)

# Save the cleaned dataset
cleaned_file_path = "cleaned_data.csv"  # Update as needed
cleaned_df.to_csv(cleaned_file_path, index=False)

print(f"Cleaned data saved to {cleaned_file_path}")
```

The output is as follows:

id	name	Age	gender	salary	joining_date	department
1	alice	25	female	50000	15-01-2020	hr
2	bob	30	male	60000	23-06-2019	It
3	charlie	37.5	male	55000	01-07-2021	Finance
4	alice	40	female	67500	15-03-2018	It
5	eve	35	male	70000	09-08-2022	Hr
6	frank	29	male	65000	20-05-2015	Finance
7	grace	50	female	72000	25-09-2017	Hr
8	henry	60	male	80000	30-11-2016	It
9	isaac	37.5	female	75000	20-05-2015	Finance
10	jack	45	male	67500	10-12-2023	Finance

The above code is self-explanatory, where **sample_data** is the input CSV file with missing values. Initially, all column data types are determined; thereafter, numerical columns are imputed with the median value, categorical columns are imputed with the mode value, and date and time columns are standardized to a similar format. All categorical columns are set to lower case, and outliers in numerical values, if any removed by the **interquartile range (IQR)** method.

Data transformation

Data transformation is the process of converting raw data into a clean, consistent, and usable format for analysis. It involves changing data structure, format, or values to ensure uniformity across datasets. The importance of data transformation is given as follows:

- Improves data quality by resolving inconsistencies.
- Standardizes different data sources into a common format.
- Enables efficient data integration and analysis.
- Helps in feature engineering for machine learning models.

Types of data transformation

Data transformation can be performed in multiple ways, which are described as follows:

- **Format standardization**: It ensures all data follows a uniform format. You can understand through the following examples:
    - **Dates**: Convert 02/15/2025, 15-02-2025 → 2025-02-15 (YYYY-MM-DD).
    - **Phone numbers**: Convert +1 (123) 456-7890 → +11234567890.

- **Data type conversion**: It converts one data type into another to ensure consistency. You can understand through the following examples:
    - Converting the string 100 to the integer 100.
    - Converting TRUE to Boolean True.

- **Normalization and scaling**: It rescales numerical data to a common range, usually between 0 and 1. You can understand through the following example:
    - Convert income values ranging from $20,000 to $500,000 into a scale of 0 to 1.

- **Standardization**: It converts data into a normal distribution with a mean of 0 and a standard deviation of 1. You can understand through the following examples:
    - Standardizing exam scores from different schools to compare fairly.

- **Data aggregation**: It summarizes detailed data into a higher-level view. You can understand through the following example:
    - Converting hourly sales data into daily, weekly, or monthly sales totals.

- **Encoding categorical data**: It converts text-based categorical data into numerical values. You can understand through the following examples:

  o Male → 1, Female → 0 (Binary encoding).

  o Red, Blue, Green → [1,0,0], [0,1,0], [0,0,1] (One-hot encoding).

- **Feature engineering**: It includes creating new meaningful variables from existing data. You can understand through the following example:

  o From the Date of Birth, generate a new Age column.

- **Handling outliers**: It detects and transforms extreme values that can skew analysis. You can understand through the following example:

  o Log transformation: Converts a skewed distribution into a normal one.

- **Data merging and splitting**: Merging combines multiple datasets based on a key field. For example: Joining customer details with their transaction history and splitting separates a dataset into multiple columns or files, for example, includes the splitting of Full Name into First Name and Last Name.

Note:

- **Standardization is used when data follows a Gaussian (normal) distribution and you want to center the data around the mean (mean = 0, standard deviation = 1). It is ideal for algorithms like SVM, logistic regression, and linear regression.**

- **Normalization is used when you want to scale data to a fixed range (typically 0 to 1), especially when the distribution is not normal. It is preferred for distance-based models like KNN and neural networks.**

Data segmentation

Data segmentation is the process of dividing a dataset into smaller, meaningful groups based on common characteristics. It helps in targeted analysis, decision-making, and personalized data handling. The importance of data segmentation is given as follows:

- Enhances targeted analysis for marketing, customer insights, and predictive modeling.
- Reduces computational complexity by working on specific data segments.
- Improves personalization by grouping data based on behavioral patterns.

Types of data segmentation

Data segmentation is categorized into six types as follows:

- **Demographic segmentation**: It groups data based on demographic factors such as age, gender, income, and location; for example, Customer dataset is segmented into different age groups for targeted advertising.

- **Behavioral segmentation**: It groups data based on user actions, such as purchase history, website visits, or engagement levels, for example, segregating customers into frequent buyers vs one-time buyers.

- **Geographic segmentation**: It divides data based on location-related attributes (e.g., country, city, zip code). For example, a retail business segments customers based on urban and rural locations.

- **Psychographic segmentation**: It categorizes data based on values, lifestyle, and interests. For example, social media users are grouped based on their preferred content type.

- **Time-based segmentation**: It divides data based on time intervals, such as daily, weekly, or seasonal trends. For example, analyzing e-commerce traffic segmented by weekdays vs. weekends.

- **Predictive segmentation**: It uses machine learning to segment data based on predicted behavior. For example, identifying customers likely to churn based on past purchasing patterns.

Consider the CSV file **sample_transformation_data.csv** given in *Table 5.2*:

Name	Age	Salary	Department
Roshan	25	50000	HR
Ajay	30	60000	IT
Meena	35	70000	Finance
Pinky	40	80000	Marketing
Riya	28	55000	IT
Heena	50	90000	Finance

Table 5.2: CSV file sample

We will execute the following code to transform the columns and perform segmentation on this datafile:

```
import pandas as pd
from sklearn.preprocessing import MinMaxScaler, LabelEncoder

def transform_data(df):
    # Normalize numerical columns (Scaling Salary)
    scaler = MinMaxScaler()
    df['Salary_Scaled'] = scaler.fit_transform(df[['Salary']])

    # Encode categorical columns (Label Encoding Department)
    encoder = LabelEncoder()
    df['Department_Encoded'] = encoder.fit_transform(df['Department'])
```

```python
    # Create a new column (Age Group)
    df['Age_Group'] = pd.cut(df['Age'], bins=[20, 30, 40, 50, 60],
labels=['Young', 'Middle-Aged', 'Senior', 'Very Senior'])

    return df

def segment_data(df):
    # Segment based on Salary
    df['Salary_Segment'] = pd.cut(df['Salary'], bins=[0, 60000, 80000,
100000], labels=['Low', 'Medium', 'High'])

    # Segment based on Department
    department_groups = df.groupby('Department')['Salary'].mean()
    df['Department_Segment'] = df['Department'].map(department_groups)

    return df

# Example usage
if __name__ == "__main__":
    # Load sample data
    input_csv = "sample_transformation_data.csv"
    df = pd.read_csv(input_csv)

    # Transform and segment the data
    transformed_df = transform_data(df)
    segmented_df = segment_data(transformed_df)

    # Save segmented data to a new CSV file
    segmented_csv = "segmented_data.csv"
    segmented_df.to_csv(segmented_csv, index=False)

    print(f"Segmented data saved to {segmented_data.csv}")
```

The output is as follows:

Name	Age	Salary	Department	Salary Scaled	Department Encoded	Age Group	Salary Segment	Department Segment
Roshan	25	50000	HR	0	1	Young	Low	50000
Ajay	30	60000	IT	0.25	2	Young	Low	57500
Meena	35	70000	Finance	0.5	0	Middle-Aged	Medium	80000
Pinky	40	80000	Marketing	0.75	3	Middle-Aged	Medium	80000
Riya	28	55000	IT	0.125	2	Young	Low	57500
Heena	50	90000	Finance	1	0	Senior	High	80000

Figure 5.1: segmented_data.csv

From the output of the above code, we can see that new columns are added to the existing file named **Salary_Scaled**, **Department_Encoded**, **Age_Group**, **Salary_Segment**, and **Department_Segment**. The data transformation is done as salary of employees is normalized between 0 and 1 and department names are encoded as 0, 1, 2, 3. On the other hand, segmentation is applied to age, salary, and department columns, where age is categorized into groups as young, middle-aged, and senior. Salary is categorized as low, medium, and high, and departments are also segmented based on the mean salary offered by the department.

Therefore, from the above code, we can see how data is transformed and segmented in order to obtain better analysis and insights from the existing data.

Data transformation vs. data segmentation

The key differences between data transformation and data segmentation are summarized in the following table:

Aspect	Data transformation	Data segmentation
Definition	Modifies and standardizes data to ensure consistency	Divides data into meaningful groups
Purpose	Prepares data for analysis, storage, or integration	Helps in targeted analysis and decision-making
Techniques	Standardization, normalization, aggregation, encoding	Demographic, behavioral, geographic, time-based segmentation
Example	Converting all date formats to YYYY-MM-DD	Segmenting customers into high spenders and low spenders

Table 5.3: Differences between data transformation and data segmentation

Conclusion

This chapter provides a comprehensive guide to data cleaning, a crucial step in the data preprocessing pipeline. It begins by emphasizing the importance of data consistency, ensuring uniformity in formats, values, and structure across datasets. Readers learn to detect and resolve inconsistencies such as varied date formats or mismatched categories. The chapter then explores heterogeneous data, focusing on aligning data types and units to maintain coherence throughout the dataset. Techniques for handling missing data are discussed in depth, including deletion, imputation, and the use of placeholder values, with practical code examples in Python using libraries like Pandas. The section on data transformation highlights normalization, standardization, and encoding categorical variables to prepare data for analysis or machine learning. Finally, data segmentation is introduced as a method for partitioning data based on logical conditions or clusters to facilitate targeted analysis. Each concept is accompanied by illustrative code snippets, making the chapter both theoretical and hands-on. By the end, readers gain a solid understanding of how to clean and prepare data effectively, laying a strong foundation for accurate and insightful analysis.

In the next chapter, we will study exploratory data analysis, which statistics, clustering, association and hypothesis generation

Multiple choice questions

1. **Which of the following indicates data inconsistency?**

    a. All phone numbers have the same format

    b. Dates recorded as both 12/31/2023 and 31-12-2023

    c. All age values are numeric

    d. Gender column has only Male and Female entries

2. **Inconsistent data can lead to**:

    a. Easier data analysis

    b. Misleading results

    c. Improved accuracy

    d. Faster queries

3. **Which method helps in resolving data inconsistency?**

    a. Dropping all data

    b. Standardizing formats and values

    c. Ignoring inconsistencies

    d. Increasing dataset size

4. **If a dataset contains USA, usa, and U.S.A in the country column, what is this an example of?**

    a. Missing data

    b. Data inconsistency

    c. Heterogeneous data

    d. Data transformation

5. **Which tool can help detect inconsistencies in large datasets?**

    a. Pandas unique() method

    b. SQL SELECT

    c. Excel SUM formula

    d. Text editor

6. **What is heterogeneous data in a dataset?**

    a. Data having uniform types

    b. Data having mixed types in one column

    c. Missing values in the data

    d. Data that is normalized

7. **Which of the following is an example of heterogeneous data?**

    a. Column with only integers

    b. Column with strings and integers mixed

    c. Column with all null values

    d. Column with standardized float values

8. **Why is heterogeneous data problematic?**

    a. It simplifies calculations

    b. It prevents statistical analysis and modeling

    c. It reduces storage space

    d. It automatically normalizes the data

9. **What is a common way to handle heterogeneous data in numeric columns?**

    a. Replace all with zero

    b. Convert non-numeric to NaN and handle them

    c. Convert all values to strings

    d. Ignore the heterogeneous entries

10. **Which Pandas function helps convert columns to numeric, coercing errors to NaN?**

    a. astype()

    b. to_numeric(errors='coerce')

    c. fillna()

    d. drop_duplicates()

11. **What does missing data refer to?**

    a. Extra values in a dataset

    b. Absence of values in a dataset

    c. Incorrect data types

    d. Duplicate rows

12. **Which is not a technique to handle missing data?**

    a. Imputation with mean or median

    b. Dropping missing values

    c. Encoding missing as a separate category

    d. Ignoring data type conversion

13. **In Pandas, which function removes rows with missing data?**

    a. fillna()

    b. dropna()

    c. isnull()

    d. unique()

14. **Imputation means**:

    a. Removing data

    b. Replacing missing data with estimated values

    c. Marking data as missing

    d. Changing data types

15. **Which of the following can cause missing data?**

    a. Data entry errors

    b. Sensor failures

    c. Data corruption

    d. All of the above

16. **What is the purpose of data transformation?**

    a. To create missing values

    b. To convert data into a suitable format for analysis

    c. To remove duplicates

    d. To delete irrelevant data

17. **Which technique scales data to a range between 0 and 1?**

    a. Z-score standardization

    b. Normalization (Min-Max scaling)

    c. Binning

    d. Label encoding

18. **What does one-hot encoding do?**

    a. Replaces missing values

    b. Converts categorical variables into binary columns

    c. Normalizes numeric data

    d. Clusters data points

19. **Which method is suitable for handling normally distributed data?**

    a. Min-max scaling

    b. Log transformation

    c. Z-score standardization

    d. Removing outliers

20. **What is the effect of data binning?**

    a. Converting continuous data into categorical bins

    b. Encoding text to numbers

    c. Filling missing values

    d. Removing inconsistent data

21. **Data segmentation helps in:**

    a. Combining all the data into one group

    b. Dividing data into meaningful subgroups

    c. Removing outliers

    d. Filling missing values

22. **Which of the following is an example of segmentation?**

    a. Normalizing age values

    b. Grouping customers by spending behavior

    c. Dropping duplicate rows

    d. Converting categorical data to numbers

23. **Clustering algorithms are often used for:**

    a. Data cleaning

    b. Data segmentation

    c. Data normalization

    d. Missing value imputation

24. **Which segmentation method splits data based on predefined rules?**

    a. K-means clustering

    b. Rule-based segmentation

    c. PCA

    d. Label encoding

25. **Which of the following is not a benefit of data segmentation?**

    a. Better targeted marketing

    b. Enhanced model performance

    c. Increased missing data

    d. Improved customer insights

Answers

1. B,
2. B
3. B
4. B
5. A
6. B
7. B
8. B
9. B
10. B
11. B
12. D
13. B
14. B
15. D
12. B
17. B
18. B
19. C
20. A

21. B

22. B

23. B

24. B

25. C

Questions

1. Define data inconsistency and give an example.

2. Explain heterogeneous data and why it is problematic in a dataset.

3. What are the common causes of missing data in datasets?

4. Describe the purpose of data transformation in data preprocessing.

5. What is data segmentation, and why is it important?

6. How can you detect data inconsistency in a dataset?

7. Describe one common approach to handling heterogeneous data.

8. List three techniques to handle missing data.

9. What is normalization, and when should it be used?

10. Explain how clustering can be used for data segmentation.

11. Why is it important to standardize data formats in a dataset?

12. How does converting non-numeric values to NaN help with heterogeneous data?

13. What is imputation, and how does it help with missing data?

14. Compare normalization and standardization in data transformation.

15. What are the benefits of segmenting customer data in marketing?

16. Describe a scenario where data inconsistency can lead to incorrect analysis.

17. What role does data type conversion play in handling heterogeneous data?

18. Explain how dropping rows with missing data might affect a dataset.

19. What is one-hot encoding, and why is it used?

20. How does rule-based segmentation differ from clustering-based segmentation?

Programming exercises

1. You have a dataset with a Date column containing dates in mixed formats like 2023/01/15, 15-01-2023, and January 15, 2023. Write Python code to standardize all dates to the format YYYY-MM-DD.

2. Given a DataFrame column that contains numbers and some strings mixed together (e.g., [10, '20', 'thirty', 40]), write code to convert all valid numeric entries to floats and replace non-numeric values with NaN.

3. Given a dataset with missing values, write Python code to:

   a. Count the number of missing values per column

   b. Fill missing numeric values with the column mean

   c. Drop rows where more than 50% of values are missing

4. Load a dataset with numeric features. Perform min-max normalization to scale all numeric columns between 0 and 1, and then apply one-hot encoding on a categorical column named Category.

5. Given a dataset of customer spending patterns, use K-means clustering to segment customers into three groups based on their Annual Income and Spending Score. Visualize the clusters using a scatter plot.

Join our Discord space

Join our Discord workspace for latest updates, offers, tech happenings around the world, new releases, and sessions with the authors:

https://discord.bpbonline.com

CHAPTER 6
Exploratory Data Analysis

Introduction

Exploratory data analysis (EDA) is a fundamental step in the data analysis process that involves investigating datasets to summarize their main characteristics, often using visual methods. The goal of EDA is to understand the underlying structure of the data, detect patterns, spot anomalies, test assumptions, and check for missing values or outliers before applying more formal modeling techniques. Through various statistical graphics, plots, and information tables, EDA provides insights that guide the selection of appropriate tools and methods for deeper analysis. Techniques commonly used in EDA include histograms, box plots, scatter plots, and correlation matrices. These tools help analysts assess data distributions, relationships among variables, and trends over time. EDA can be both qualitative and quantitative, depending on the context and nature of the dataset. It is particularly important in fields such as data science, machine learning, and business analytics, where a strong understanding of data can influence model performance and decision-making. By enabling a deeper understanding of data, EDA reduces the risk of incorrect conclusions and enhances the quality of insights. In short, EDA acts as a bridge between raw data and predictive analytics, ensuring that the data is well-understood and prepared for further analysis.

Structure

The chapter covers the following topics:

- Descriptive statistics
- Comparative statistics
- Clustering
- Association
- Hypothesis generation

Objectives

The chapter aims to equip readers with the knowledge and tools needed to summarize, visualize, and interpret data in order to uncover underlying patterns, relationships, and trends. It begins with descriptive statistics to offer foundational insights through measures of central tendency and dispersion. Comparative statistics, including t-tests, F-tests, and **analysis of variance** (**ANOVA**), are introduced to evaluate differences between groups and validate assumptions. The chapter also covers correlation and regression techniques to examine relationships between variables and predict outcomes. Advanced methods such as clustering and association rule mining are explored to identify hidden structures and frequent patterns within data. Additionally, the chapter emphasizes hypothesis generation, guiding readers to form testable questions based on observed data characteristics. By the end, learners will be able to apply EDA techniques to enhance data-driven decision-making and prepare for more complex analytical modeling.

Descriptive statistics

In data science, features are individual measurable properties or characteristics of the data used to make predictions or classifications. They serve as input variables that help machine learning models identify patterns and make decisions. Different statistics are used to improve features. Descriptive statistics is a branch of statistics that focuses on summarizing and organizing data in a meaningful way. It involves methods for presenting the main features of a dataset through numerical measures and visual representations. The primary goal of descriptive statistics is to provide a clear and simple overview of the data, helping analysts understand its general structure and patterns without making any predictions or inferences.

Key measures in descriptive statistics include central tendency (mean, median, and mode), which describe the center of a dataset, and dispersion (range, variance, and standard deviation), which indicate the spread or variability of the data. Additionally, frequency distributions, percentiles, and quartiles help describe how data values are distributed. Data can also be presented visually using tools such as histograms, bar charts, pie charts, and box plots, making it easier to spot trends and outliers.

Descriptive statistics is essential in both research and practical applications, as it lays the groundwork for further statistical analysis. It is commonly used in various fields, including business, healthcare, social sciences, and education, to summarize survey results, monitor performance, and make data-driven decisions. Unlike inferential statistics, descriptive statistics does not involve generalizing findings beyond the given data. In the following, we will understand the central tendency, dispersion, distributions, percentiles, and quartiles.

Measures of central tendency

In data science, mean, median, and mode are measures of central tendency that help summarize a dataset by identifying a typical or central value. These three measures help describe data distributions and guide data preprocessing, feature engineering, and model selection:

- **Mean** (or average) is calculated by summing all the values in a dataset and dividing by the number of values. It is useful for understanding the overall level of the data, but it can be sensitive to extreme values or outliers. For example, in salary data, a few very high salaries can skew the mean upward.

- **Median** is the middle value when the data is arranged in ascending or descending order. If the number of values is even, the median is the average of the two middle numbers. The median is more robust than the mean in the presence of outliers or skewed data, making it useful when the data distribution is not symmetrical.

- **Mode** is the value that appears most frequently in a dataset. It is useful for categorical data where we want to identify the most common category. A dataset may have one mode (unimodal), more than one (bimodal or multimodal), or none if all values are unique.

Measures of dispersion

Range, variance, and standard deviation are statistical measures used to describe the spread or dispersion of data values in a dataset. They help us understand how much the data varies from the center or average:

- **Range** is the simplest measure of dispersion. It is calculated as the difference between the maximum and minimum values in the dataset. While easy to compute, it only considers two values and is highly sensitive to outliers, making it less reliable for understanding overall variability.

- **Variance** measures the average squared deviation of each data point from the mean. It gives a sense of how spread out the data points are. A higher variance indicates that the data points are more spread out, while a lower variance means they are closer to the mean. Variance is useful, but not in the same units as the original data (it is in squared units).

- **Standard deviation** is the square root of the variance and provides a measure of spread in the same units as the original data. It is widely used in data analysis to assess how much individual data points deviate from the mean on average.

Together, these measures help data scientists assess consistency, identify outliers, and compare the variability of different datasets.

Statistical tools

Frequency distributions, percentiles, and quartiles are statistical tools used to describe how data is distributed, making it easier to interpret and analyze large datasets in data science:

- **Frequency distribution** is a summary that shows how often each value or range of values occurs in a dataset. It can be represented as a table or a graph (like a histogram). For example, a frequency table may show how many students scored within specific score ranges on a test. This helps in quickly identifying patterns, such as clustering of values or the presence of outliers.

- **Percentiles** divide a dataset into 100 equal parts and indicate the relative standing of a value within the dataset. The nth percentile represents the value below which **n%** of the data falls. For instance, the 90th percentile of test scores means 90% of the scores are below that value. Percentiles are widely used in standardized testing, health indicators, and performance benchmarking.

- **Quartiles** are a type of percentile that divide the data into four equal parts:

  o **Q1 (first quartile)**: 25th percentile

  o **Q2 (second quartile or median)**: 50th percentile

  o **Q3 (third quartile)**: 75th percentile

These help identify the spread and skewness of the data and are useful in visual tools like box plots for detecting outliers and variability.

Note: A fashion store records the heights of its customers and calculates the average height as 5'6, with a standard deviation of 2 inches. This is a descriptive summary of the data.

In the following program, for a banking system, descriptive statistics mean, median, mode, range, variance, and standard deviation of the amount column of the dataset:

```
import numpy as np
import pandas as pd
from scipy import stats
import matplotlib.pyplot as plt
import seaborn as sns
```

```python
# Create a sample banking dataset with 30 entries
np.random.seed(42)
account_numbers = np.arange(1001, 1031)
names = [f'Customer_{i}' for i in range(1, 31)]
amounts = np.random.randint(1000, 50000, 30)

df = pd.DataFrame({
    'Account_Number': account_numbers,
    'Customer_Name': names,
    'Amount': amounts
})

# Save to CSV file
df.to_csv('banking_data.csv', index=False)
print("Sample banking data saved to 'banking_data.csv'")

# Read data from CSV file
data_from_csv = pd.read_csv('banking_data.csv')['Amount']

# Calculate descriptive statistics
mean_value = np.mean(data_from_csv)
median_value = np.median(data_from_csv)
mode_value = stats.mode(data_from_csv, keepdims=True).mode[0]
range_value = np.max(data_from_csv) - np.min(data_from_csv)
variance_value = np.var(data_from_csv)
std_deviation_value = np.std(data_from_csv)

# Display results
print(f"\nMean Amount: {mean_value}")
print(f"Median Amount: {median_value}")
print(f"Mode Amount: {mode_value}")
print(f"Range Amount: {range_value}")
print(f"Variance of Amount: {variance_value}")
print(f"Standard Deviation of Amount: {std_deviation_value}")

# Visualization
plt.figure(figsize=(8, 6))
sns.histplot(data_from_csv, kde=True, color='blue')
plt.axvline(mean_value, color='red', linestyle='--', label=f'Mean: {mean_value:.2f}')
plt.axvline(median_value, color='green', linestyle='--', label=f'Median: {median_value:.2f}')
plt.axvline(mode_value, color='purple', linestyle='--', label=f'Mode:
```

```
{mode_value}')
plt.title('Amount Distribution with Mean, Median, and Mode')
plt.xlabel('Amount')
plt.ylabel('Frequency')
plt.legend()
plt.show()
```

Output:

Sample banking data saved to 'banking_data.csv'

Mean Amount: 22201.566666666666

Median Amount: 19686.5

Mode Amount: 1189

Range Amount: 47002

Variance of Amount: 235380626.5788889

Standard Deviation of Amount: 15342.119363989086

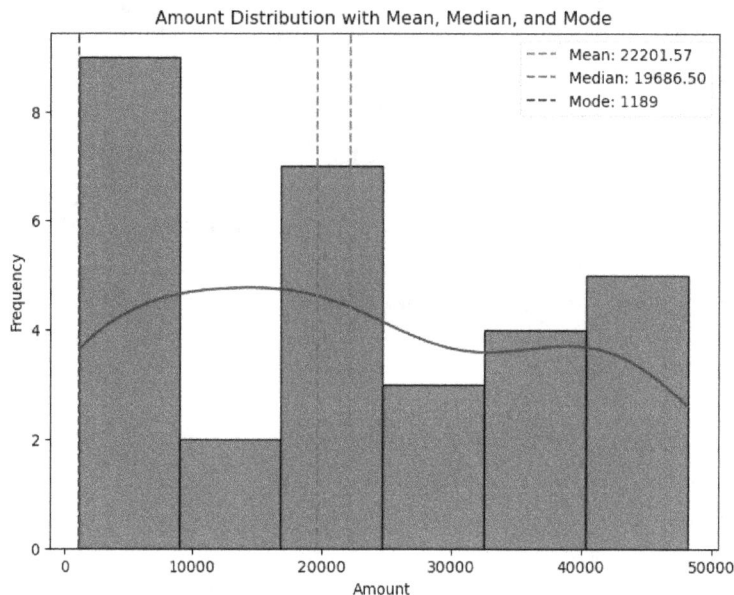

Figure 6.1: Visualization of banking data in terms of mean, median, mode

The banking data is randomly generated by the above code and saved in a csv file, which contains 30 entries. Some of the entries of this file are given in *Table 6.1*. Thereafter, mean, median, mode, range, variance, and standard deviation are computed (given in output). Similarly, the mean, median, and mode are also visualized by using Matplotlib as displayed in *Figure 6.1*:

Account_Number	Customer_Name	Amount
1001	Customer_1	16795
1002	Customer_2	1860
1003	Customer_3	39158
1004	Customer_4	45732
1005	Customer_5	12284
1006	Customer_6	7265
1007	Customer_7	17850
1008	Customer_8	38194
1009	Customer_9	22962
1010	Customer_10	48191

Table 6.1: Sample of Banking_data

Use of descriptive statistics

Descriptive statistics is used in various situations where the goal is to summarize, organize, and present data in a clear and meaningful way. It helps in understanding the basic features of the data and provides simple summaries without drawing conclusions or making predictions.

Here are some common scenarios where descriptive statistics are used:

- **Understanding and exploring data**: Before performing any complex analysis, descriptive statistics are used to explore and get an overview of the dataset. It helps to identify trends, patterns, or errors in the data.

    o **Example**: A fashion store analyzes customer data to find the average purchase value and the most frequently sold item.

- **Reporting and presentation**: Descriptive statistics are used in business reports, academic research, and presentations to summarize data effectively. Visual tools like histograms, bar charts, and pie charts are often used.

    o **Example**: A clothing website displays the average time users spend on the site or the distribution of product ratings.

- **Quality control and monitoring**: Businesses use descriptive statistics to monitor and maintain product quality.

    o **Example**: A garment manufacturer tracks the average size deviations from the standard size to ensure quality control.

- **Survey and market research analysis**: After collecting survey data, descriptive statistics summarize the responses for initial insights.

- o **Example**: A fashion company surveys customers to find the most preferred clothing style. The percentage of respondents choosing each style is calculated and displayed using a pie chart.

- **Comparing performance over time**: Descriptive statistics help in tracking trends and patterns over different time periods.

  - o **Example**: A fashion brand compares average monthly sales to identify which months perform best.

- **Identifying data errors or outliers**: Descriptive statistics can highlight anomalies in the data by checking for unusually high or low values.

  - o **Example**: A business notices an unusually high return rate for a particular clothing item using outlier detection through descriptive statistics.

Comparative statistics

Comparative statistics is a method in data analysis used to compare two or more groups, datasets, or variables to identify similarities, differences, trends, or patterns. It helps researchers and data scientists understand how different conditions, treatments, or categories influence outcomes. This type of analysis is essential in decision-making, policy evaluation, and experimental research.

There are several ways to conduct comparative statistics, depending on the type of data and the research question. For numerical data, measures such as means, medians, ranges, and standard deviations are compared between groups. For example, comparing the average test scores of two different classes can show the effectiveness of different teaching methods. For categorical data, proportions and frequencies are often compared using tools like cross-tabulations or chi-square tests.

Comparative statistics also includes hypothesis testing, such as t-tests (for comparing two means), ANOVA (for comparing more than two groups), and non-parametric tests when data does not meet normality assumptions. Visualization techniques like bar charts, box plots, and line graphs are commonly used to support and illustrate comparisons.

Basically, comparative statistics plays a critical role in exploring relationships and making informed conclusions about differences between groups in various fields such as healthcare, economics, business, and social sciences. Types of comparative analysis are provided as follows:

- **Comparing averages (means)**:
  - o **t-test**: Compares means of two groups (e.g., customer spending in two different stores).
  - o **ANOVA**: Compares means across more than two groups.

- **Comparing variability**:
  - ○ **F-test**: Compares the variances of two datasets.
- **Relationship between variables**:
  - ○ **Correlation (e.g., Pearson's correlation)**: Measures the strength and direction of the relationship between two variables.
  - ○ **Regression analysis**: Predicts the effect of one variable on another (e.g., the effect of price on sales).

Note: A clothing website compares average sales in summer vs. winter using a t-test. If the test finds a significant difference, it suggests seasonal variation in sales.

In the following program, the t-test is used to compare the means of customer spending between the two stores to determine whether there is a statistically significant difference between them.

Role of t-test

The detailed role of the t-test is described as follows:

- **Hypothesis testing**: The t-test evaluates whether the difference in the average spending between store 1 and store 2 is significant or if it occurred by chance.

- **Null hypothesis (H_0)**: There is no significant difference in the average spending between the two stores.

- **Alternative hypothesis (H_1)**: There is a significant difference in the average spending between the two stores.

- **T-statistic**: It measures the size of the difference relative to the variation in the sample data. A higher absolute t-value suggests a greater difference.

- **P-value**: The p-value indicates the probability of obtaining the observed difference (or a more extreme one) if the null hypothesis is true.

If p-value < 0.05 (assuming a 5% significance level), you reject the null hypothesis, meaning the difference is statistically significant.

If p-value ≥ 0.05, you fail to reject the null hypothesis, meaning no significant difference was found.

Since comparative statistics is used to compare values of two or more groups, the following code is used to see the sales difference of two stores, **store1** and **store2**. The code is given as follows:

```
import numpy as np
import pandas as pd
```

```
from scipy import stats
import matplotlib.pyplot as plt
import seaborn as sns

# Generate sample data for two stores with 30 entries each
np.random.seed(42)
store1_amounts = np.random.randint(1000, 50000, 30)
store2_amounts = np.random.randint(1000, 50000, 30)

store1_df = pd.DataFrame({'Customer_ID': range(1, 31), 'Amount': store1_
amounts})
store2_df = pd.DataFrame({'Customer_ID': range(1, 31), 'Amount': store2_
amounts})

# Save data to CSV files
store1_df.to_csv('store1_data.csv', index=False)
store2_df.to_csv('store2_data.csv', index=False)
print("CSV files created: store1_data.csv and store2_data.csv")

# Read data from CSV files
store1_data = pd.read_csv('store1_data.csv')['Amount']
store2_data = pd.read_csv('store2_data.csv')['Amount']

# Perform independent t-test
t_stat, p_value = stats.ttest_ind(store1_data, store2_data)

# Display results
print(f"T-Statistic: {t_stat}")
print(f"P-Value: {p_value}")

# Visualization
plt.figure(figsize=(8, 6))
sns.histplot(store1_data, kde=True, color='blue', label='Store 1')
sns.histplot(store2_data, kde=True, color='orange', label='Store 2')
plt.title('Customer Spending Comparison Between Two Stores')
plt.xlabel('Amount Spent')
plt.ylabel('Frequency')
plt.legend()
plt.show()
```

Output:

CSV files created: store1_data.csv and store2_data.csv
T-Statistic: -0.24406471416223935
P-Value: 0.8080419960854888

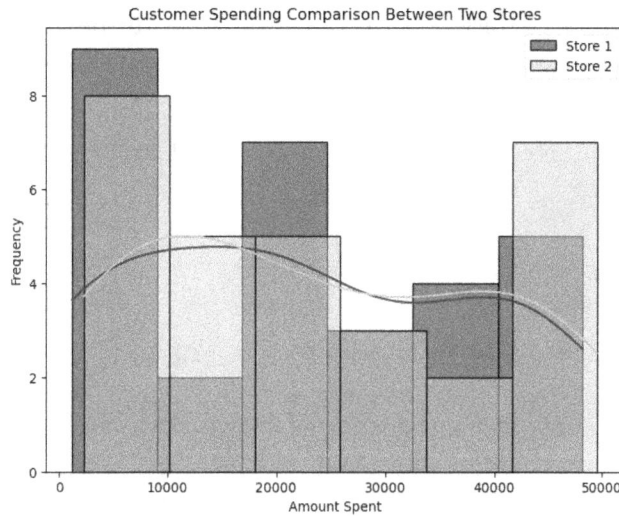

Figure 6.2: *The plot represents no variation between the sales of Store 1 and Store 2*

The above results are given in the output and *Figure 6.2*. They depict that **no** significant variation is found in the sales of two stores, Store 1 and Store 2, due to the negative value of the T-statistic and p-value > 0.05.

Similarly, in the following code, the ANOVA test is used to determine whether there are statistically significant differences in the average customer spending among the three banks. The details of the ANOVA test are given as follows:

- **Role of ANOVA test**: Comparing multiple groups: ANOVA is particularly useful when comparing the means of three or more independent groups (in this case, Bank 1, Bank 2, and Bank 3) to see if there is a significant difference.

- **Hypothesis testing**: The ANOVA test uses the following hypotheses:

  o **Null hypothesis (H$_0$)**: The means of customer spending across all three banks are equal (no significant difference).

  o **Alternative hypothesis (H$_1$)**: At least one bank has a significantly different mean customer spending.

- **F-statistic**: ANOVA calculates an F-statistic, which measures the ratio of variation between the group means to the variation within each group. A higher F-statistic indicates a larger difference between group means.

- **P-value**: The p-value indicates the probability of observing the differences by random chance.

- If p-value < 0.05 (assuming a 5% significance level), the null hypothesis is rejected, meaning a significant difference exists.

If p-value ≥ 0.05, the null hypothesis is not rejected, indicating no significant difference.

Note: If the ANOVA test detects a significant difference, further analysis (like post hoc tests) can be performed to identify which specific banks differ in customer spending.

The test provides valuable insights for bank management to understand customer spending patterns and implement appropriate financial strategies. The code is given as follows:

```python
import numpy as np
import pandas as pd
from scipy import stats

# Generate sample data for three banks with 30 entries each
np.random.seed(42)
bank1_amounts = np.random.randint(1000, 50000, 30)
bank2_amounts = np.random.randint(1000, 50000, 30)
bank3_amounts = np.random.randint(1000, 50000, 30)

bank1_df = pd.DataFrame({'Customer_ID': range(1, 31), 'Amount': bank1_
amounts})
bank2_df = pd.DataFrame({'Customer_ID': range(1, 31), 'Amount': bank2_
amounts})
bank3_df = pd.DataFrame({'Customer_ID': range(1, 31), 'Amount': bank3_
amounts})

# Save data to CSV files
bank1_df.to_csv('bank1_data.csv', index=False)
bank2_df.to_csv('bank2_data.csv', index=False)
bank3_df.to_csv('bank3_data.csv', index=False)
print("CSV files created: bank1_data.csv, bank2_data.csv, and bank3_data.
csv")

# Read data from CSV files
bank1_data = pd.read_csv('bank1_data.csv')['Amount']
bank2_data = pd.read_csv('bank2_data.csv')['Amount']
bank3_data = pd.read_csv('bank3_data.csv')['Amount']

# Perform one-way ANOVA test
f_stat, p_value = stats.f_oneway(bank1_data, bank2_data, bank3_data)

# Display results
print(f"F-Statistic: {f_stat}")
print(f"P-Value: {p_value}")

# Conclusion
if p_value < 0.05:
    print("There is a significant difference in customer spending among the
three banks.")
```

```
else:
    print("There is no significant difference in customer spending among the
three banks.")
```

Output:

```
CSV files created: bank1_data.csv, bank2_data.csv, and bank3_data.csv
F-Statistic: 0.09223185733231277
P-Value: 0.911982737757062
There is no significant difference in customer spending among the three banks.
```

Therefore, from the above code and output, we see that there is no significant difference in customer spending among the three banks by watching the F-statistic and the p-value.

In the following code, the F-test is used to compare the variances of customer spending between the two banks.

Role of the F-test: It is described as follows:

- **Variance comparison**: The F-test checks whether the variances (a measure of spread) of the two datasets are significantly different. It is commonly used to test the assumption of equal variances, which is often a requirement for other statistical tests like the t-test.

- **Hypothesis testing**: The F-test follows these hypotheses:

  o **Null hypothesis (H_0)**: The variances of customer spending between Bank 1 and Bank 2 are equal.

  o **Alternative hypothesis (H_1)**: The variances of customer spending between Bank 1 and Bank 2 are significantly different.

  o If the F-statistic is significantly greater or smaller than 1, it suggests unequal variances.

- **P-value interpretation**:

  o If p-value < 0.05 (assuming a 5% significance level), the null hypothesis is rejected, meaning there is a significant difference in the variances.

  o If p-value ≥ 0.05, the null hypothesis is not rejected, indicating no significant difference in the variances. Note the following:

    ▪ The F-test in this program helps assess whether the spread of customer spending is consistent between the two banks.

    ▪ If a significant difference is found, it may indicate varying spending behaviors or differences in the customer base between the banks.

Let us dive into the code as follows:

```python
import numpy as np
import pandas as pd
from scipy import stats

# Generate sample data for two banks with 30 entries each
np.random.seed(42)
bank1_amounts = np.random.randint(1000, 50000, 30)
bank2_amounts = np.random.randint(1000, 50000, 30)

bank1_df = pd.DataFrame({'Customer_ID': range(1, 31), 'Amount': bank1_
amounts})
bank2_df = pd.DataFrame({'Customer_ID': range(1, 31), 'Amount': bank2_
amounts})

# Save data to CSV files
bank1_df.to_csv('bank1_data.csv', index=False)
bank2_df.to_csv('bank2_data.csv', index=False)
print("CSV files created: bank1_data.csv and bank2_data.csv")

# Read data from CSV files
bank1_data = pd.read_csv('bank1_data.csv')['Amount']
bank2_data = pd.read_csv('bank2_data.csv')['Amount']

# Perform F-Test to compare variances
f_stat = np.var(bank1_data, ddof=1) / np.var(bank2_data, ddof=1)
df1 = len(bank1_data) - 1
df2 = len(bank2_data) - 1
p_value = stats.f.cdf(f_stat, df1, df2)

# Display results
print(f"F-Statistic: {f_stat}")
print(f"P-Value: {2 * min(p_value, 1 - p_value)}")

# Conclusion
if p_value < 0.05:
    print("There is a significant difference in variances between the two
banks.")
else:
    print("There is no significant difference in variances between the two
banks.")
```

Output:

CSV files created: bank1_data.csv and bank2_data.csv
F-Statistic: 1.0014091394705356

```
P-Value: 0.9970007475951235
```
There is no significant difference in variances between the two banks.

Therefore, from the above code and output, we see that there is no significant difference in customer spending between the two banks by watching the F-statistic and the p-value.

In the following code, the correlation coefficient measures the strength and direction of the linear relationship between the **Product_Price** and **Discount** columns.

Role of correlation coefficient: Quantifies relationship: It provides a numerical value (ranging from -1 to +1) that quantifies how closely the two variables are related. The details are as follows:

- **Interpretation**:
  - **+1**: Perfect positive correlation (when one variable increases, the other increases).
  - **-1**: Perfect negative correlation (when one variable increases, the other decreases).
  - **0**: No correlation (no linear relationship between the variables).

- **Decision-making insight**:
  - A positive correlation indicates that higher-priced products tend to have higher discounts.
  - A negative correlation means higher-priced products tend to have lower discounts.
  - A near-zero correlation suggests no meaningful relationship between product price and discount.

- **Visualization support**: The scatter plot and the regression line (red line) visually support the correlation result, making it easier to interpret the relationship between the two variables.

In short, the correlation coefficient helps in understanding pricing strategies and discount patterns in the dataset. Let us understand through code as follows:

```python
import numpy as np
import pandas as pd
import matplotlib.pyplot as plt
import seaborn as sns

# Generate sample data for sales dataset with Product Price and Discount
np.random.seed(42)
product_price = np.random.randint(100, 1000, 50)
discount = np.random.randint(5, 100, 50)
```

```python
sales_df = pd.DataFrame({
    'Product_Price': product_price,
    'Discount': discount
})

# Save data to CSV file
sales_df.to_csv('sales_data.csv', index=False)
print("CSV file created: sales_data.csv")

# Read data from CSV file
data = pd.read_csv('sales_data.csv')

# Perform correlation analysis
correlation_coefficient = data['Product_Price'].corr(data['Discount'])

# Display result
print(f"Correlation Coefficient between Product Price and Discount:
{correlation_coefficient}")

# Conclusion
if correlation_coefficient > 0:
    print("There is a positive correlation between Product Price and
Discount.")
elif correlation_coefficient < 0:
    print("There is a negative correlation between Product Price and
Discount.")
else:
    print("There is no correlation between Product Price and Discount.")

# Visualization using scatter plot
plt.figure(figsize=(8, 6))
sns.scatterplot(x='Product_Price', y='Discount', data=data)
sns.regplot(x='Product_Price', y='Discount', data=data, scatter=False,
color='red')
plt.title(f'Scatter Plot with Correlation Coefficient: {correlation_
coefficient:.2f}')
plt.xlabel('Product Price')
plt.ylabel('Discount')
plt.grid(True)
plt.show()
```

Output:

```
CSV file created: sales_data.csv
Correlation Coefficient between Product Price and Discount: 0.23108767840437763
There is a positive correlation between Product Price and Discount.
```

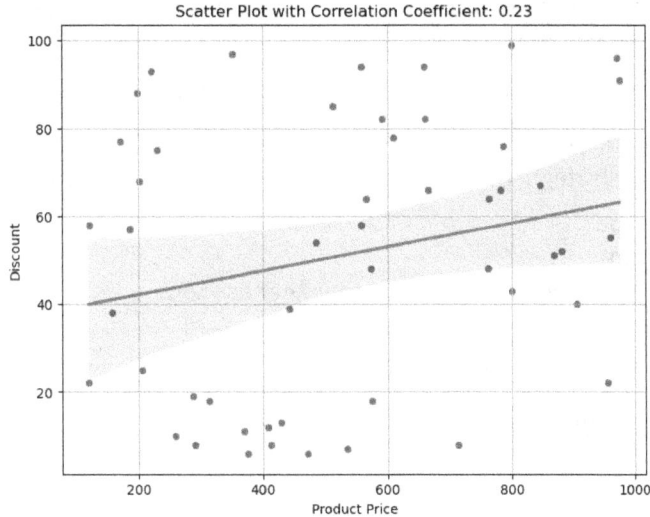

Figure 6.3: *Plot represents positive correlation between product price and discount*

From the above output results and plot shown in *Figure 6.3*, we see that there exists a positive correlation between product price and discount.

The following code performs a linear regression analysis to determine the relationship between product price and discount in the sales dataset. Key significance of the program is as follows:

- **Regression coefficient (Slope)**:
  - The slope measures how much the discount changes for every unit change in product price.
  - A positive slope indicates that as the product price increases, the discount tends to increase.
  - A negative slope suggests that higher-priced products receive lower discounts.
  - A slope of zero means no relationship between the product price and discount.

- **Intercept**:
  - The intercept is the value of the discount when the product price is zero.
  - While it may not always have a practical interpretation, it helps in forming the linear equation.

- **Decision-making**:
  - Businesses can analyze pricing strategies by understanding how discounts are applied based on product prices.

- o If the slope is significantly negative or positive, businesses may adjust their discounting policies accordingly.

- o It can also help in predicting discounts for future product pricing.

Overall, this program provides insights into how discounts are influenced by product prices and supports strategic pricing decisions. Let us dive into the code as follows:

```python
import pandas as pd
import numpy as np
from sklearn.linear_model import LinearRegression

# Read data from the sales dataset CSV file
data = pd.read_csv('sales_data.csv')

# Perform Linear Regression Analysis
X = data[['Product_Price']]
y = data['Discount']

model = LinearRegression()
model.fit(X, y)

# Compute Regression Coefficient and Intercept
regression_coefficient = model.coef_[0]
intercept = model.intercept_

print(f"Regression Coefficient (Slope): {regression_coefficient}")
print(f"Intercept: {intercept}")
```

Output:

Regression Coefficient (Slope): 0.027176200528309855
Intercept: 36.68617637540407

The results show a positive value of the regression coefficient, which means that if the product price increases, the discount also increases.

Use of comparative statistics

Comparative statistics is used when you want to compare two or more datasets to identify differences, relationships, or patterns. It is often applied to test hypotheses, make inferences, and draw conclusions based on data analysis. Here are common scenarios where comparative statistics are used:

- **Evaluating differences between groups**:
  - o When you need to compare means, variances, or distributions of two or more groups.
  - o Often used in A/B testing, experiments, or observational studies.

- **Example**: A clothing brand compares the average sales of a new collection in two different stores to see which location performed better.

- **Assessing the effectiveness of interventions**: Used to measure the impact of a change or intervention by comparing data before and after the implementation.

  - **Example**: A company introduces a new marketing campaign and compares sales data before and after the campaign to evaluate its effectiveness.

- **Identifying relationships between variables**: Comparative statistics can help determine correlations or causations between variables.

  - **Example**: A retailer compares the effect of pricing on product sales to identify the relationship between price and demand.

- **Benchmarking and competitor analysis**: Businesses use comparative statistics to measure their performance against competitors.

  - **Example**: A fashion website analyzes its conversion rate compared to industry benchmarks to assess its market position.

- **Conducting market research**: Used to compare customer preferences or purchasing behavior across different demographics or regions.

  - **Example**: A fashion brand surveys customers in urban and rural areas to compare clothing style preferences.

- **Decision making in product development**: Product developers may compare different prototypes or versions to select the best one.

  - **Example**: A company tests two different designs of a jacket and compares customer satisfaction scores using statistical tests.

- **Medical and social research**: Researchers use comparative statistics to study the effect of treatments or social interventions.

  - **Example**: A study compares the health outcomes of two groups, one receiving a new medication and the other receiving a placebo.

- **Measuring changes over time**: Comparative statistics help in analyzing trends by comparing data across multiple time periods.

  - **Example**: A fashion brand compares annual sales from 2023 and 2024 to identify growth or decline.

Descriptive statistics vs. comparative statistics

The key differences between descriptive statistics and comparative statistics are summarized as follows in *Table 6.2*:

Feature	Descriptive statistics	Comparative statistics
Purpose	Summarizes data	Compares data
Methods used	Mean, median, mode, standard deviation	t-test, ANOVA, correlation, regression
Example	The average customer spends $50	Do male and female customers spend differently?

Table 6.2: Difference between descriptive statistics and comparative statistics

Clustering

Clustering and association are two key techniques in data science, primarily used for analyzing and extracting valuable insights from data. They fall under **unsupervised learning**, where the algorithm explores the data without labeled outputs. In formal words, clustering is the process of **grouping similar data points** together based on their characteristics or patterns. The objective is to create clusters where data points within a cluster are more similar to each other than to those in other clusters.

The purpose is as follows:

- To identify patterns or natural groupings in data.
- Useful for market segmentation, image recognition, anomaly detection, and more.

Some examples are:

- A clothing retailer clusters customers based on their purchase behavior to create targeted marketing campaigns.
- In image recognition, clustering can group similar-looking images together.

Popular clustering algorithms are listed as follows:

- **K-means clustering**: Divides data into *k* predefined clusters.
- **Hierarchical clustering**: Builds a tree of clusters based on data similarity.
- **Density-based spatial clustering of applications with noise (DBSCAN)**: Groups dense regions of data points.

Now we will explain each of these clustering algorithms in detail.

K-means clustering

K-means clustering is a popular unsupervised machine learning algorithm used to group data points into clusters based on similarity. The algorithm aims to partition data into K clusters, where each data point belongs to the cluster with the nearest mean (center). The following is an explanation of K-means clustering with an example with code, thereafter.

Example

Suppose we have a dataset of 2D points (x, y), and we want to cluster them into three groups. The algorithm will find the centers of these groups based on the data points' similarities and form three clusters as follows:

1. **Initialization**: Choose K initial cluster centers (centroids). These can be randomly selected from the data or using other methods.

2. **Assignment step**: For each data point, find the nearest centroid and assign it to that cluster.

3. **Update step**: Recalculate the centroids of each cluster by taking the mean of all data points assigned to that cluster.

4. **Repeat**: Repeat steps 2 and 3 until convergence (when centroids no longer change significantly or a specified number of iterations is reached).

Let us understand through code as follows:

```
import matplotlib.pyplot as plt
from sklearn.cluster import KMeans
import numpy as np

# Generate example data
data = np.array([[2, 3], [5, 7], [8, 8], [3, 4], [4, 5], [10, 11], [8, 9],
[2, 2], [9, 8], [8, 10]])

# Specify the number of clusters (K)
k = 3

# Create a K-Means model
kmeans = KMeans(n_clusters=k)

# Fit the model to the data
kmeans.fit(data)

# Get cluster assignments for each data point
labels = kmeans.labels_

# Get cluster centers
centers = kmeans.cluster_centers_

# Plot the data points and cluster centers
plt.scatter(data[:, 0], data[:, 1], c=labels, cmap='viridis', marker='o',
s=100)
plt.scatter(centers[:, 0], centers[:, 1], c='red', marker='X', s=200)
```

```
plt.title(f'K-Means Clustering with K={k}')
plt.show()

# Display cluster assignments
for i in range(k):
    print(f'Cluster {i + 1} contains the following data points:')
    cluster_points = data[labels == i]
    print(cluster_points)
    print()
```

The output is as follows:

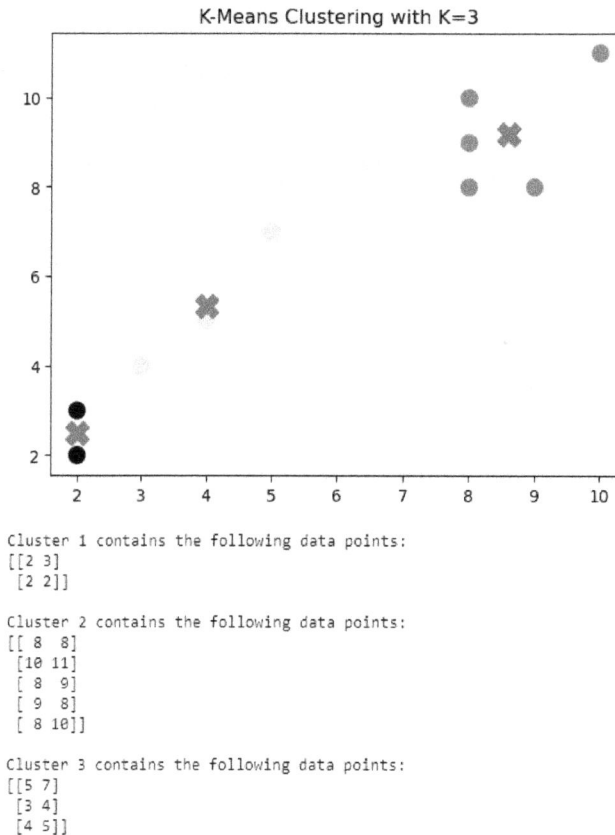

```
Cluster 1 contains the following data points:
[[2 3]
 [2 2]]

Cluster 2 contains the following data points:
[[ 8  8]
 [10 11]
 [ 8  9]
 [ 9  8]
 [ 8 10]]

Cluster 3 contains the following data points:
[[5 7]
 [3 4]
 [4 5]]
```

Figure 6.4: Output of the above code

In this code, we create a synthetic dataset with 2D points, specify the number of clusters (K), create a K-means model, fit it to the data, and visualize the clusters using a scatter plot. The code also prints the data points assigned to each cluster. The output shows how K-means clustering groups the data points into K clusters based on their proximity to cluster centers. This example demonstrates a simple case with two features, but K-means can be applied to datasets with more dimensions.

Hierarchical clustering

Hierarchical clustering is a class of unsupervised machine learning algorithms used to create a hierarchy of clusters in a dataset. Unlike partition-based methods, which produce a single set of clusters, hierarchical clustering methods create a tree-like structure of clusters known as a **dendrogram**. There are two main approaches to hierarchical clustering: agglomerative and divisive:

- **Agglomerative clustering (bottom-up approach)**: Agglomerative clustering starts with each data point as its own cluster and then iteratively merges the closest clusters until all data points are in a single cluster. The result is a hierarchical structure where data points are grouped at different levels of granularity. Commonly used linkage methods for merging clusters include single linkage (minimum pairwise distance), complete linkage (maximum pairwise distance), average linkage (average pairwise distance), and Ward's linkage (minimizes the variance within clusters).

- **Divisive clustering (top-down approach)**: Divisive clustering begins with all data points in a single cluster and then recursively divides clusters into smaller ones. The process continues until individual data points are in separate clusters. Unlike agglomerative clustering, divisive clustering is less common in practice due to its complexity and computational demands.

The dendrogram visually represents the hierarchy of clusters. You can choose a threshold on the dendrogram to determine the number of clusters you want to create.

The key characteristics of hierarchical clustering methods are as follows:

- **Hierarchical structure**: The result is a dendrogram that shows the hierarchy of clusters at various levels of granularity. The user can choose the desired number of clusters by setting a threshold on the dendrogram.

- **Proximity-based**: Clusters are merged or divided based on a proximity measure, such as Euclidean distance, correlation, or other distance metrics.

- **Non-parametric**: Hierarchical clustering does not require specifying the number of clusters in advance, making it useful for exploratory data analysis.

The applications of hierarchical clustering methods are listed as follows:

- **Taxonomy and classification**: Hierarchical clustering is used to create hierarchical taxonomies in biological classification, document categorization, and species classification.

- **Image segmentation**: In computer vision, hierarchical clustering is employed for image segmentation, where regions of an image are grouped into hierarchical structures.

- **Gene expression analysis**: Hierarchical clustering is used to analyze gene expression data, grouping genes with similar expression profiles and revealing underlying patterns in biological data.

- **Document clustering**: In natural language processing, hierarchical clustering can group similar documents and categorize them into thematic clusters.

- **Customer segmentation**: Hierarchical clustering can be applied to segment customers based on various attributes, such as purchasing behavior or demographics.

- **Anomaly detection**: By identifying and isolating anomalies, hierarchical clustering can be used for fraud detection, quality control, and outlier detection.

Hierarchical clustering methods offer insights into data structure at multiple levels of granularity, making them valuable for data exploration and visualization. The choice between agglomerative and divisive clustering depends on the problem and the desired analysis goals.

The following Python code presents hierarchical clustering:

```python
import matplotlib.pyplot as plt
from sklearn.cluster import AgglomerativeClustering
import numpy as np

# Generate example data
data = np.array([[2, 3], [5, 7], [8, 8], [3, 4], [4, 5], [10, 11], [8, 9],
[2, 2], [9, 8], [8, 10]])

# Create an AgglomerativeClustering model with the desired number of
clusters (n_clusters)
n_clusters = 3
model = AgglomerativeClustering(n_clusters)

# Fit the model to the data and obtain cluster assignments
labels = model.fit_predict(data)

# Visualize the data and dendrogram
plt.figure(figsize=(8, 5))
plt.scatter(data[:, 0], data[:, 1], c=labels, cmap='viridis', marker='o',
s=100)
plt.title(f'Hierarchical Clustering with {n_clusters} Clusters')
plt.show()
```

The output is as follows:

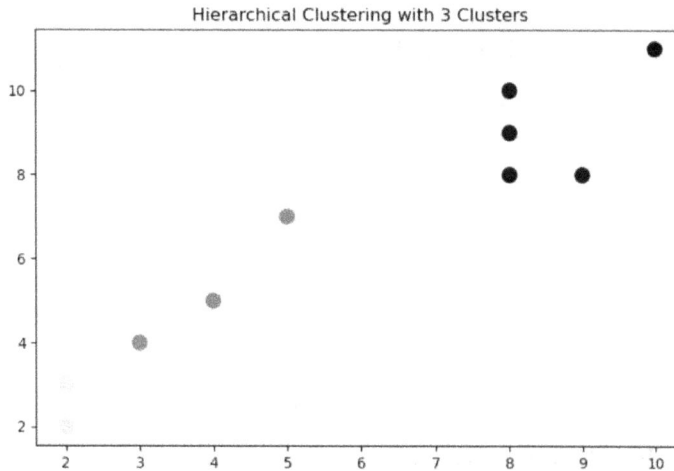

Figure 6.5: *Output of the code*

In this code, we create a synthetic dataset with 2D points, create an agglomerative clustering model with the desired number of clusters, fit the model to the data, and visualize the clusters using a scatter plot. The dendrogram is not explicitly shown in this example, but you can explore hierarchical clustering with dendrogram visualizations using libraries like **scipy** and **matplotlib**. Hierarchical clustering is a valuable tool for exploring data structure and relationships, especially when the number of clusters is not known in advance. It provides insights into how data points are related at various levels of granularity.

Density-based clustering

Density-based clustering methods are a category of unsupervised machine learning algorithms used to identify clusters in data based on the local density of data points. Unlike partition-based methods (e.g., K-means) that assume clusters as areas of high point density separated by areas of low density, density-based methods can find clusters of arbitrary shapes and handle noise effectively. Two prominent density-based clustering algorithms are DBSCAN and **ordering points to identify the clustering structure** (**OPTICS**). They are described in brief as follows:

- **DBSCAN**: DBSCAN groups data points that are close to each other in high-density regions. It defines three types of points:

  o **Core points**: Data points with a sufficient number of neighbors within a specified distance (a user-defined parameter, **eps**).

  o **Border points**: Data points within the **eps** distance of a core point but without enough neighbors to be core points.

o **Noise points**: Data points that are neither core nor border points.

The algorithm starts with an arbitrary data point, finds all points within **eps** distance, and recursively expands the cluster if it contains a core point.

- **OPTICS**: OPTICS extends the idea of DBSCAN by creating a hierarchical representation of the clustering structure.

  o It generates a reachability plot that orders data points based on their reachability distances.

  o Reachability distance measures the distance to the nearest core point. The plot provides an overview of the data points' densities and the natural clusters.

The key characteristics and benefits of density-based clustering methods are as follows:

- **Ability to find clusters of varying density**: These methods can identify clusters of different shapes and sizes and adapt to varying densities within the data.

- **Noise handling**: Density-based methods are robust to noise because noise points are typically isolated and do not belong to any cluster.

- **Automated cluster count**: Unlike some other methods that require specifying the number of clusters in advance, density-based methods can find the number of clusters based on the data structure.

- **Handling outliers**: Noise points, representing outliers or rare events, are explicitly identified.

The applications of density-based clustering methods are as follows:

- **Anomaly detection**: Identifying outliers or anomalies in various domains, such as fraud detection, network security, and quality control.

- **Geospatial clustering**: Clustering geographical data based on location and density, useful in areas like urban planning and location-based services.

- **Image segmentation**: Segmenting images into regions based on pixel intensity or color density.

- **Customer segmentation**: Grouping customers based on their purchasing behavior or geographical proximity.

- **Environmental data analysis**: Analyzing environmental sensor data to detect regions of high and low pollutant concentrations.

- **Natural language processing**: Document clustering to group similar articles, documents, or social media posts.

Density-based clustering methods are versatile and powerful for data exploration, particularly when data does not conform to the assumptions of traditional partition-based methods. The choice between DBSCAN and OPTICS depends on the specific problem, the desired level of granularity, and the need for a hierarchical clustering view. The following code represents the use of DBSCAN:

```
import matplotlib.pyplot as plt
from sklearn.cluster import DBSCAN
from sklearn.datasets import make_moons

# Generate a synthetic dataset
X, _ = make_moons(n_samples=200, noise=0.05, random_state=0)

# Create a DBSCAN model with the desired parameters (eps and min_samples)
dbscan = DBSCAN(eps=0.3, min_samples=5)

# Fit the model to the data and obtain cluster assignments
labels = dbscan.fit_predict(X)

# Visualize the clusters
plt.scatter(X[:, 0], X[:, 1], c=labels, cmap='viridis', marker='o')
plt.title('DBSCAN Clustering')
plt.show()
```

The output is as follows:

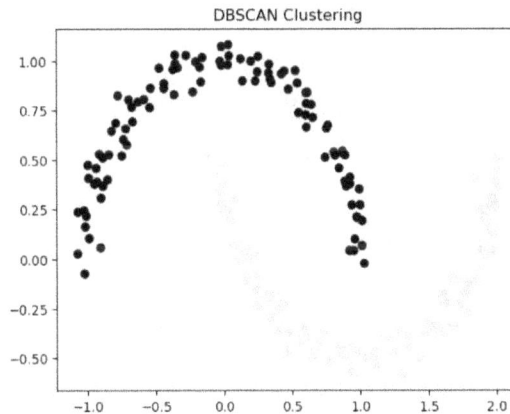

Figure 6.6: Output of above code

In this code, we generate a synthetic dataset with two moon-shaped clusters using **make_moons**. We create a DBSCAN model with the specified **eps** (maximum distance between two samples for one to be considered as in the neighborhood of the other) and **min_samples** (the number of samples in a neighborhood for a point to be considered a core point). We fit the DBSCAN model to the data and obtain cluster assignments. Finally, we visualize the clusters using a scatter plot.

DBSCAN is particularly effective at discovering clusters of arbitrary shapes and handling noise, making it a valuable tool in various applications. The `eps` and `min_samples` parameters should be adjusted according to your specific dataset and problem.

Uses of clustering

Clustering is used in data science for several practical applications where identifying natural groupings or patterns in data is beneficial. It is especially useful when working with **unlabeled data** (data without predefined categories). The primary goal is to organize data into meaningful structures to gain insights, detect patterns, or simplify complex datasets. Here are the key reasons why clustering is used:

- **Customer segmentation**:
  - **Purpose**: Group customers based on purchasing behavior, demographics, or preferences.
  - **Benefit**: Helps in targeted marketing, personalized recommendations, and customer retention.
  - **Example**: A fashion website clusters users into groups like Budget Shoppers, Luxury Buyers, or Frequent Shoppers for personalized promotions.

- **Anomaly detection**:
  - **Purpose**: Identify unusual data points that do not fit any cluster.
  - **Benefit**: Helps detect fraud, network intrusions, or manufacturing defects.
  - **Example**: Banks use clustering to identify fraudulent transactions by detecting anomalies in spending patterns.

- **Data simplification and visualization**:
  - **Purpose**: Reduce large datasets into smaller, manageable groups.
  - **Benefit**: Enables easier data visualization and interpretation.
  - **Example**: Clustering millions of social media users into groups based on similar interests for visual representation.

- **Recommendation systems**:
  - **Purpose**: Provide personalized product or content recommendations.
  - **Benefit**: Enhances user experience and boosts sales.
  - **Example**: Streaming platforms cluster users with similar viewing habits to suggest movies or shows.

- **Image and video segmentation**:
  - **Purpose**: Separate objects or regions within images or videos.
  - **Benefit**: Useful in image recognition, medical imaging, and video analysis.

o **Example**: Medical imaging systems use clustering to differentiate tumors from healthy tissue in MRI scans.

- **Market research and trend analysis**:

  o **Purpose**: Identify emerging trends and market segments.

  o **Benefit**: Supports strategic decision-making for product launches or market expansion.

  o **Example**: A clothing brand clusters fashion trends based on online search patterns and social media activity.

- **Document and text analysis**:

  o **Purpose**: Group similar text documents for easy retrieval and analysis.

  o **Benefit**: Streamlines document management and enhances information retrieval.

  o **Example**: News articles can be clustered by topics like politics, sports, or technology for recommendation systems.

- **Biological and medical research**:

  o **Purpose**: Identify patterns in biological data.

  o **Benefit**: Helps in disease classification, genetic analysis, and medical diagnosis.

  o **Example**: Researchers cluster DNA sequences to detect genetic disorders.

Association

Association is a rule-based method used to discover relationships or patterns between variables in large datasets. It identifies frequent patterns, correlations, or associations within the data.

The purpose is as follows:

- Mainly used for market basket analysis and recommendation systems.

- Helps businesses understand purchasing behavior.

Some examples are as follows:

- A grocery store discovers that customers who buy bread and butter are also likely to buy jam. This association can help in cross-selling or product placement.

- E-commerce platforms use association rules to suggest **Frequently Bought Together** products.

Common association rule mining algorithms are as follows:

- **Apriori algorithm**: Finds frequent item sets and generates rules from them.

- **Eclat algorithm**: A more memory-efficient alternative to Apriori.

- **FP Growth algorithm**: Builds a tree-like structure to discover frequent patterns efficiently.

Key metrics in association rules are as follows:

- **Support**: Frequency of a rule appearing in transactions.

- **Confidence**: Likelihood that one item is purchased when another is.

- **Lift**: Strength of a rule compared to random chance.

Apriori algorithm

Among all the above-mentioned algorithms Apriori is the most significant one. Therefore, in this chapter, we will explain this algorithm in detail. The Apriori algorithm is a classic data mining and association rule learning algorithm used to discover frequent itemsets in transactional databases. It is particularly useful for market basket analysis, where you aim to find associations or patterns among items that are frequently purchased together. The Apriori algorithm uses a breadth-first search strategy to explore the space of itemsets and efficiently identify those that meet a user-defined minimum support threshold. We explain the key concepts of the Apriori algorithm and provide a Python code example. The basic concepts and key components of association rule mining are given as follows, which are common in all association mining algorithms:

- **Frequent itemsets**: A frequent itemset is a set of items or attributes that occur together in the dataset with a frequency greater than or equal to a predefined threshold (support). For example, in a retail dataset, a frequent itemset might represent a group of products often purchased together.

- **Association rules**: Association rules are logical implications or patterns that describe how items or attributes are related. Each rule consists of two parts:

    o **Antecedent (IF part)**: It specifies the condition or itemset that, when present in a transaction, implies the occurrence of the consequent.

    o **Consequent (THEN part)**: It represents the item or attribute that is likely to co-occur with the antecedent.

- **Support**: Support is a measure that indicates how frequently an itemset or rule appears in the dataset. It is calculated as the proportion of transactions that contain the itemset or satisfy the rule. High support values indicate that the itemset or rule is common in the data.

- **Confidence**: Confidence is a measure that quantifies the strength of an association rule. It represents the conditional probability that the consequent occurs given the presence of the antecedent. High confidence values indicate a strong relationship between the items.

- **Lift**: Lift measures the extent to which the presence of the antecedent affects the likelihood of the consequent occurring. A lift value greater than 1 indicates a positive association, while a value less than 1 suggests a negative association.

- **Minimum support and minimum confidence**: These are user-defined thresholds used to filter and select association rules. Rules that do not meet these minimum support and confidence criteria are typically discarded.

- **Apriori property**: The Apriori algorithm uses a key property called the Apriori property: if an itemset is frequent, then all of its subsets must also be frequent. This property allows the algorithm to efficiently prune the search space.

The Apriori algorithm steps are as follows:

- **Initialize**: Start with frequent itemsets of size 1 (i.e., individual items) and scan the dataset to find their support.

- **Generate candidates**: Generate candidate itemsets of size (k+1) from frequent itemsets of size k. Candidate generation involves self-joining and pruning, taking advantage of the Apriori property.

- **Prune**: Remove candidate itemsets that contain subsets with low support (i.e., prune infrequent itemsets).

- **Calculate support**: Scan the dataset to find the support of each candidate itemset.

- **Repeat**: Repeat steps 2-4 until no new frequent itemsets can be found.

The following code represents the implementation of the Apriori algorithm with a sample dataset and the **mlxtend** library. You need to install the **mlxtend** library using the following command on Jupyter:

'pip install mlxtend'

```
from mlxtend.frequent_patterns import apriori
from mlxtend.preprocessing import TransactionEncoder
import pandas as pd

# Sample transaction dataset
transactions = [
    ['bread', 'milk', 'eggs'],
    ['bread', 'butter', 'eggs'],
    ['milk', 'butter', 'eggs'],
    ['bread', 'milk', 'butter', 'eggs'],
    ['bread', 'milk', 'butter']
]

# Convert transactions to one-hot encoding format
te = TransactionEncoder()
te_ary = te.fit(transactions).transform(transactions)
```

```
df = pd.DataFrame(te_ary, columns=te.columns_)
# Applying Apriori algorithm to find frequent itemsets
min_support = 0.2
frequent_itemsets = apriori(df, min_support=min_support, use_colnames=True)

# Displaying the frequent itemsets
print("Frequent Itemsets:")
print(frequent_itemsets)

# Generating association rules
from mlxtend.frequent_patterns import association_rules

# Specify the metric and threshold for generating rules
rules = association_rules(frequent_itemsets, metric="confidence", min_
threshold=0.7)

# Displaying the association rules
print("\nAssociation Rules:")
print(rules)
```

The output is as follows:

```
Frequent Itemsets:
    support                 itemsets
0      0.8                  (bread)
1      0.8                 (butter)
2      0.8                   (eggs)
3      0.8                   (milk)
4      0.6          (butter, bread)
5      0.6            (eggs, bread)
6      0.6            (milk, bread)
7      0.6           (eggs, butter)
8      0.6           (milk, butter)
9      0.6             (milk, eggs)
10     0.4     (eggs, butter, bread)
11     0.4     (milk, butter, bread)
12     0.4       (milk, eggs, bread)
13     0.4      (milk, eggs, butter)
14     0.2  (milk, eggs, butter, bread)

Association Rules:
    antecedents consequents  antecedent support  consequent support  support  \
0      (butter)     (bread)                 0.8                 0.8      0.6
1       (bread)    (butter)                 0.8                 0.8      0.6
2        (eggs)     (bread)                 0.8                 0.8      0.6
3       (bread)      (eggs)                 0.8                 0.8      0.6
4        (milk)     (bread)                 0.8                 0.8      0.6
5       (bread)      (milk)                 0.8                 0.8      0.6
6        (eggs)    (butter)                 0.8                 0.8      0.6
7      (butter)      (eggs)                 0.8                 0.8      0.6
8        (milk)    (butter)                 0.8                 0.8      0.6
9      (butter)      (milk)                 0.8                 0.8      0.6
10       (milk)      (eggs)                 0.8                 0.8      0.6
11       (eggs)      (milk)                 0.8                 0.8      0.6

    confidence    lift  leverage  conviction  zhangs_metric
0         0.75  0.9375     -0.04         0.8          -0.25
1         0.75  0.9375     -0.04         0.8          -0.25
2         0.75  0.9375     -0.04         0.8          -0.25
3         0.75  0.9375     -0.04         0.8          -0.25
4         0.75  0.9375     -0.04         0.8          -0.25
5         0.75  0.9375     -0.04         0.8          -0.25
6         0.75  0.9375     -0.04         0.8          -0.25
7         0.75  0.9375     -0.04         0.8          -0.25
8         0.75  0.9375     -0.04         0.8          -0.25
9         0.75  0.9375     -0.04         0.8          -0.25
10        0.75  0.9375     -0.04         0.8          -0.25
11        0.75  0.9375     -0.04         0.8          -0.25
```

Figure 6.7: Output of the above code

In this code, necessary libraries are imported, including **apriori** for the Apriori algorithm, **TransactionEncoder** for one-hot encoding, and Pandas for handling data. A sample transaction dataset is defined, where each list represents a transaction. A one-hot encoded **DataFrame** is created using the **TransactionEncoder**. This format is necessary for the Apriori algorithm. Then, the Apriori algorithm is applied to find frequent itemsets with a minimum support of 0.2. The discovered frequent itemsets are printed. Thereafter, association rules using the frequent itemsets are generated, specifying the metric as **confidence** and setting a minimum confidence threshold of 0.7. The generated association rules, including antecedent, consequent, support, confidence, and lift, are printed as output at the end of the code.

This code illustrates a basic implementation of the Apriori algorithm for mining association rules in a transaction dataset. It finds frequent itemsets and generates rules based on specified metrics and thresholds.

Frequent Pattern Growth

Frequent Pattern Growth (**FP Growth**) is an efficient and scalable algorithm used in frequent pattern mining, particularly in market basket analysis, to discover frequent itemsets in a transaction dataset without candidate generation (unlike Apriori). The goal of FP Growth is to find all frequent itemsets (item combinations that occur together frequently in transactions) that meet a minimum support threshold.

FP Growth algorithm steps

The following three steps are performed for FP Growth:

1. **Build the frequency table**:
   a. Scan the transaction database once.
   b. Count the frequency (support count) of each item.
   c. Discard items that do not meet the minimum support threshold.
   d. Sort the remaining items in descending order of frequency.

2. **Construct the Frequent Pattern Tree (FP-Tree)**: An FP-Tree is a **compressed representation** of the transaction database.
   a. Create a root node labeled null.
   b. For each transaction:
      i. Remove infrequent items.
      ii. Sort remaining items by descending frequency.
      iii. Insert the sorted transaction into the FP-Tree:
         • Share common prefixes with existing paths.

- Increment counts along the paths.

iv. Maintain node-links to connect all nodes with the same item name.

This step compresses the dataset and reveals itemset patterns through the tree structure.

3. **Mine the FP-Tree recursively**: Use a divide-and-conquer approach to extract frequent itemsets:

   a. For each item (starting from the least frequent):

      i. Construct its conditional pattern base (subsets of paths in the FP-Tree ending with that item).

      ii. Build a conditional FP-Tree from this pattern base.

      iii. Recursively mine the conditional FP-Tree for frequent patterns.

   b. Concatenate the suffix pattern (current item) with frequent patterns generated from the conditional tree.

This allows for efficient recursive pattern discovery without generating large candidate sets like Apriori does.

Certain advantages and limitations of FP Growth are given as follows:

- **Advantages of FP Growth**:
  - **No candidate generation**: Faster than Apriori for large datasets.
  - Compresses data efficiently using the FP-tree.
  - Can handle large volumes of data and long itemsets.

- **Limitations**:
  - Building and storing FP-trees can be memory-intensive.
  - Not as intuitive as Apriori for small datasets.
  - Complex when data is highly diverse or lacks common prefixes.

The following code represents the implementation of FP Growth:

```
!pip install mlextend
import pandas as pd
from mlxtend.preprocessing import TransactionEncoder
from mlxtend.frequent_patterns import fpgrowth, association_rules

# Step 1: Define the transactions
transactions = [
    ['milk', 'bread', 'nuts'],
    ['milk', 'bread', 'butter'],
    ['milk', 'bread'],
```

```
    ['bread', 'butter'],
    ['milk', 'bread', 'butter', 'nuts']
]

# Step 2: Convert the transaction list into a format suitable for the
algorithm
te = TransactionEncoder()
te_ary = te.fit(transactions).transform(transactions)
df = pd.DataFrame(te_ary, columns=te.columns_)

# Step 3: Apply FP-Growth algorithm
frequent_itemsets = fpgrowth(df, min_support=0.6, use_colnames=True)

# Step 4: Generate association rules (optional)
rules = association_rules(frequent_itemsets, metric="confidence", min_
threshold=0.7)

# Display results
print("Frequent Itemsets:")
print(frequent_itemsets)

print("\nAssociation Rules:")
print(rules[['antecedents', 'consequents', 'support', 'confidence',
'lift']])
```

The output is as follows:

```
Frequent Itemsets:
    support          itemsets
0     0.8             {bread}
1     0.8              {milk}
2     0.6            {butter}
3     0.6       {milk, bread}
4     0.6     {bread, butter}
5     0.6      {milk, butter}


Association Rules:
     antecedents    consequents  support  confidence    lift
0        {milk}        {bread}      0.8        0.75  0.9375
1       {bread}         {milk}      0.8        1.0   0.9375
2        {milk}       {butter}      0.6        0.75    1.25
3      {butter}         {milk}      0.6        1.0     1.25
4       {bread}       {butter}      0.6        0.75    1.25
5      {butter}        {bread}      0.6        1.0     1.25
```

Figure 6.8: Output of above code

In the above code, following observation are taken:

- **min_support=0.6**: Itemsets must appear in at least 60% of transactions.

- **confidence=0.7**: Only rules with at least 70% confidence are shown.

- The lift value tells us how much more often items are bought together than expected by chance.

Uses of association rule mining

Association in data science is used to discover relationships, patterns, and correlations between items in large datasets. It is particularly effective in analyzing transactional data to identify how items are related to each other. The primary goal of the association is to generate actionable insights that can enhance decision-making processes. Here are the key reasons why association is used in data science:

- **Market basket analysis**:
  - **Purpose**: Identify which products are frequently purchased together.
  - **Benefit**: Helps in cross-selling, product bundling, and targeted promotions.
  - **Example**: A supermarket finds that customers who buy bread and butter often buy jam, leading to bundle offers or shelf placement optimization.

- **Recommendation systems**:
  - **Purpose**: Provide personalized recommendations based on user behavior.
  - **Benefit**: Enhances customer experience and increases sales.
  - **Example**: E-commerce platforms suggest Frequently Bought Together products based on association rules.

- **Fraud detection**:
  - **Purpose**: Detect suspicious or unusual behavior patterns.
  - **Benefit**: Helps in identifying fraudulent transactions in financial data.
  - **Example**: If an unusual combination of purchases occurs, it may trigger a fraud alert.

- **Healthcare and medical diagnosis**:
  - **Purpose**: Discover correlations between symptoms, diseases, and treatments.
  - **Benefit**: Supports early diagnosis and personalized treatment plans.
  - **Example**: A hospital may find that patients with high blood pressure often have a higher risk of diabetes, leading to preventive care strategies.

- **Web and social media analysis**:
  - o **Purpose**: Analyze user behavior and preferences.
  - o **Benefit**: Enhances user engagement and content recommendations.
  - o **Example**: Social media platforms suggest connections or content based on users' interactions and similar activity patterns.

- **Inventory management**:
  - o **Purpose**: Optimize stock levels based on frequently bought items.
  - o **Benefit**: Reduces waste and ensures product availability.
  - o **Example**: Retailers track product demand patterns using association rules to adjust inventory levels efficiently.

- **Drug discovery and genomics**:
  - o **Purpose**: Identify relationships between genetic sequences and diseases.
  - o **Benefit**: Accelerates medical research and drug development.
  - o **Example**: Association analysis can detect gene mutations associated with rare diseases.

- **Customer behavior analysis**:
  - o **Purpose**: Understand purchasing patterns and preferences.
  - o **Benefit**: Allows businesses to customize their marketing strategies.
  - o **Example**: A clothing website uses association rules to recommend similar styles based on past purchases.

Clustering vs. association

The key differences between clustering and association are given as follows:

Feature	Clustering	Association
Goal	Group similar data points	Find relationships between data
Data type	Unlabeled data	Transactional or categorical data
Example use case	Customer segmentation	Market basket analysis
Output	Clusters of similar data	Association rules (e.g., A → B)
Key algorithms	K-means, Hierarchical, DBSCAN	Apriori, FP Growth, Eclat

Table 6.3: Comparison of clustering and association

Hypothesis generation

Hypothesis generation is the process of formulating testable statements or assumptions based on observations, existing knowledge, or preliminary data analysis. These hypotheses serve as the foundation for further analysis and experiments in a data-driven project.

In data science, hypothesis generation helps you make informed decisions by testing whether a particular relationship or effect exists between variables. It is a key step in EDA and problem-solving.

Steps in hypothesis generation

In order to generate a hypothesis, the following seven key steps are to be followed:

1. **Understand the problem**:
   a. Clearly define the problem you are trying to solve.
   b. Identify key business objectives or research questions.
   c. **Example**: Why are customer churn rates increasing?

2. **Perform EDA**:
   a. Analyze patterns, trends, and correlations within the data using visualization tools.
   b. Detect anomalies or unusual behaviors.
   c. **Example**: A sudden drop in sales might coincide with a website issue.

3. **Gather domain knowledge**:
   a. Collaborate with domain experts or conduct market research.
   b. Understand factors influencing the data.
   c. **Example**: Festivals or promotions may impact sales patterns.

4. **Identify variables**:
   a. Determine the dependent variable (target) and independent variables (features).
   b. **Example**: Sales (dependent) may depend on factors like ad spend, seasonality, or customer reviews.

5. **Formulate hypotheses**:
   a. Develop statements that predict relationships between variables.
   b. Create both **null hypothesis** (H_0) and **alternative hypothesis** (H_1).
   c. **Example**:

      i.   H₀: Social media engagement has no effect on product sales.

      ii.   H₁: Higher social media engagement leads to increased product sales.

6. **Prioritize and refine hypotheses**:

   a. Select hypotheses that are most relevant and feasible for testing.

   b. Ensure hypotheses are measurable and specific.

7. **Test the hypotheses**:

   a. Perform statistical analysis using methods like t-tests, chi-square tests, regression analysis, or machine learning models.

   b. Evaluate whether the data supports or rejects the hypotheses.

Examples of hypotheses

Hypothesis generation provides a structured approach to analyzing data, helping to identify key variables that influence outcomes. It enables informed decision-making through rigorous statistical testing, ensuring that conclusions are backed by evidence rather than assumptions. By offering objective validation, it helps prevent biased interpretations of data. Overall, statistical analysis supports data-driven problem-solving across a wide range of industries, enhancing the accuracy and reliability of business and research decisions. In the following section, we elaborate on certain examples of hypotheses to better understand them:

- **E-commerce**:

  o **Null hypothesis (H_0)**: Discounts have no effect on customer purchase behavior.

  o **Alternative hypothesis (H_1)**: Offering discounts increases the number of purchases.

  o H_0: There is no relationship between product rating and sales.

  o H_1: Higher-rated products have significantly more sales.

  o H_0: The website's page loading speed does not affect the conversion rate.

  o H_1: Faster website loading speed increases the conversion rate.

- **Healthcare**:

  o H_0: There is no difference in blood sugar levels between patients following a low-carb diet and those on a regular diet.

  o H_1: Patients on a low-carb diet have lower blood sugar levels than those on a regular diet.

- o **H₀**: Telemedicine has no effect on patient satisfaction compared to in-person visits.

- o **H₁**: Patients using telemedicine report higher satisfaction than those with in-person visits.

- **Finance**:

  - o **H₀**: There is no correlation between interest rates and loan default rates.

  - o **H₁**: Higher interest rates lead to higher loan default rates.

  - o **H₀**: Stock prices are not influenced by social media sentiment.

  - o **H₁**: Positive social media sentiment results in increased stock prices.

- **Marketing**:

  - o **H₀**: Email marketing campaigns have no impact on customer retention.

  - o **H₁**: Personalized email marketing campaigns improve customer retention.

  - o **H₀**: Advertisement spending has no effect on brand awareness.

  - o **H₁**: Higher advertisement spending leads to increased brand awareness.

- **Education**:

  - o **H₀**: The implementation of e-learning platforms does not improve student performance.

  - o **H₁**: E-learning platforms lead to better academic performance compared to traditional learning.

  - o **H₀**: Class size has no effect on student academic achievement.

  - o **H₁**: Smaller class sizes lead to higher student academic achievement.

- **Social media**:

  - o **H₀**: There is no relationship between posting frequency and follower growth.

  - o **H₁**: Increased posting frequency leads to higher follower growth.

  - o **H₀**: The time of day a post is published does not affect its engagement.

  - o **H₁**: Posts published during peak hours have higher engagement rates.

Conclusion

This chapter presented a detailed exploration of EDA, demonstrating how to extract meaningful insights from raw data using both statistical techniques and visual methods. Beginning with descriptive statistics, readers learned to summarize data distributions using mean, median, standard deviation, and visual tools like histograms and box plots.

Comparative statistical methods, including t-tests, F-tests, and ANOVA, were applied to evaluate group differences, with code examples illustrating how to interpret significance levels and assumptions. The chapter then progressed to correlation and regression analysis, showing how to quantify and model relationships between variables. Clustering techniques such as K-means were introduced to uncover natural groupings in data, while association rule mining helped identify frequent co-occurrences within datasets. Throughout the chapter, Python code and outputs were provided for each method to ensure practical understanding. Finally, the chapter emphasized hypothesis generation based on observed patterns, setting the stage for confirmatory analysis. Overall, the chapter offered a hands-on, analytical foundation for making informed, data-driven decisions.

In the subsequent chapter, we will study designing visualizations including time series data, geolocated data, hierarchies, and networks.

Multiple choice questions

1. **Which of the following measures is not affected by outliers?**

    a. Mean

    b. Standard deviation

    c. Median

    d. Range

2. **Which statistic best describes the spread of a dataset?**

    a. Mode

    b. Mean

    c. Standard deviation

    d. Frequency

3. **A t-test is used to:**

    a. Compare more than two groups

    b. Measure the strength of correlation

    c. Compare the means of two groups

    d. Test for association between items

4. **An F-test is primarily used to:**

    a. Test correlation

    b. Compare group variances

    c. Predict outcomes

    d. Visualize data

5. **One-way ANOVA is appropriate when**:
    a. Comparing two groups
    b. Testing one categorical variable against one numerical variable across 3+ groups
    c. Performing regression analysis
    d. Finding a correlation between variables

6. **A Pearson correlation coefficient of -0.95 indicates**:
    a. Strong negative linear relationship
    b. Strong positive linear relationship
    c. No relationship
    d. Non-linear relationship

7. **Correlation measures**:
    a. Causation
    b. Frequency
    c. Strength and direction of linear relationship
    d. Differences between groups

8. **In simple linear regression, the dependent variable is**:
    a. The variable used to predict
    b. Always categorical
    c. The variable being predicted
    d. Unrelated to the independent variable

9. **The R^2 value in a regression model tells us**:
    a. If the model is overfitting
    b. The number of variables used
    c. The proportion of variance explained by the model
    d. The average error of prediction

10. **K-means clustering is a**:
    a. Supervised learning algorithm
    b. Classification method
    c. Unsupervised learning algorithm
    d. Statistical test

11. **The elbow method is used to:**

    a. Test statistical significance

    b. Normalize features

    c. Determine optimal number of clusters

    d. Visualize regression models

12. **In association rules, lift is a measure of:**

    a. Statistical variance

    b. Strength of association compared to random chance

    c. Distribution spread

    d. Linear relationship strength

13. **The rule {Milk} ⇒ {Bread} with high confidence means:**

    a. Bread causes people to buy milk

    b. If bread is bought, milk is always bought

    c. If milk is bought, bread is likely to be bought

    d. There is a strong negative relationship

14. **Hypothesis generation is typically done during:**

    a. The final model evaluation

    b. Data collection

    c. Exploratory data analysis

    d. Statistical inference

15. **A good hypothesis should be:**

    a. Based on intuition only

    b. Vague and flexible

    c. Testable and specific

    d. Proven before testing

Answers

1. c

2. c

3. c

4. b

5. b

6. a

7. c

8. c

9. c

10. c

11. c

12. b

13. c

14. c

15. c

Questions

1. What is the difference between mean, median, and mode? When might each be more appropriate to use?

2. How do standard deviation and variance help in understanding data dispersion?

3. Given a dataset, how would you identify the presence of outliers using box plots or z-scores?

4. When should you use a t-test versus an ANOVA?

5. How does an F-test differ from a t-test, and what is it commonly used for?

6. Given two independent samples, how would you test if their means are significantly different?

7. How would you interpret the p-value in an ANOVA output?

8. What is the difference between correlation and causation?

9. How do you interpret Pearson's correlation coefficient? What are its limitations?

10. If two variables have a correlation coefficient of -0.85, what does this imply?

11. What is the purpose of linear regression? How do you interpret its coefficients?

12. How would you check if a regression model fits the data well?

13. What assumptions must be met for a linear regression model to be valid?

14. What is the K-means clustering algorithm, and how does it work?

15. How would you decide the optimal number of clusters in a dataset?

16. What is the difference between hierarchical and non-hierarchical clustering?

17. What is association rule mining? Give an example of a practical application.

18. Explain support, confidence, and lift in the context of association rules.

19. How can association rules be used in market basket analysis?

20. What is the role of hypothesis generation in exploratory data analysis?

21. How would you formulate a hypothesis from a visual trend observed in data?

22. Why is it important to differentiate between hypothesis generation and hypothesis testing?

Programming exercises

1. Load a CSV dataset (e.g., Iris or Titanic):

   a. Calculate mean, median, mode, variance, and standard deviation for numeric columns.

   b. Plot histograms and box plots for selected variables.

   c. Identify outliers using the IQR method.

2. Use a housing price dataset or similar:

   a. Fit a simple linear regression model (e.g., Price ~ Area).

   b. Fit a multiple linear regression model with at least three predictors.

   c. Evaluate the model using R^2, residual plots, and RMSE.

3. Use the Iris dataset or any multi-feature dataset:

   a. Apply K-means clustering.

4. Using a dataset with at least two groups (e.g., test scores of two schools):

   a. Perform an independent t-test to compare the means.

   b. Check if the variances of the two groups are equal using an **F-test**.

5. Use a dataset with multiple groups (e.g., test scores from three teaching methods).

   a. Perform one-way ANOVA to test for significant differences among the groups.

   b. Visualize group means with error bars.

6. Using a dataset like Iris or a housing dataset:

   a. Compute the Pearson correlation matrix for numeric variables.

   b. Identify and interpret the strongest positive and negative correlations.

7. Use a synthetic or real transaction dataset (e.g., groceries):

   a. Convert transactions into a one-hot encoded DataFrame.

    b.   Apply the Apriori algorithm to find frequent itemsets.

    c.   Generate association rules and interpret support, confidence, and lift.

8.   Choose any dataset (e.g., Titanic, sales data, or healthcare):

    a.   Use EDA visualizations (e.g., bar plots, scatter plots, pair plots) to explore the data.

    b.   Based on visual patterns, formulate 2–3 testable hypotheses (e.g., Survival is related to passenger class).

    c.   Briefly explain why these hypotheses are worth testing.

Join our Discord space

Join our Discord workspace for latest updates, offers, tech happenings around the world, new releases, and sessions with the authors:

https://discord.bpbonline.com

CHAPTER 7
Data Visualization

Introduction

Data visualization is the process of converting raw data into meaningful and interpretable graphical formats such as charts, graphs, maps, and dashboards. This transformation plays a vital role in making data-driven insights more accessible and easier to understand, especially for stakeholders who may not be well-versed in statistical or technical analysis. By presenting data visually, it becomes much easier to spot trends, detect correlations, and highlight anomalies or outliers that may otherwise go unnoticed in raw numerical form.

The importance of data visualization lies in its ability to simplify complex datasets. Large volumes of data can be overwhelming, but visual tools allow users to quickly interpret and analyze the key information without having to dig through spreadsheets or databases. This simplification supports enhanced decision-making by enabling faster and more accurate insights, thus helping organizations respond promptly to changing conditions or emerging opportunities. Furthermore, visualizations are powerful tools for identifying hidden patterns and trends over time, which can be essential for predictive analysis or strategic planning.

Another major benefit is improved communication. Visual representations of data are easier to present in meetings, reports, or dashboards, helping communicate findings more clearly and effectively to both technical and non-technical audiences. Overall, well-crafted data visualizations not only enrich the understanding of data but also facilitate collaboration, clarity, and impactful storytelling in both business and research environments.

Structure

The chapter covers the following topics:

- Principles of data visualization
- Feature selection
- Time series analysis
- Geolocated data analysis
- Correlations and connections
- Networks and hierarchies
- Interactivity

Objectives

The objective of this chapter is to provide a comprehensive understanding of advanced data visualization techniques and their practical applications in data science. It aims to equip learners with the ability to design clear, accurate, and meaningful visual representations of data. The chapter focuses on enabling students to analyze **time series data** to identify temporal trends, apply **geolocated visualizations** for spatial insights, and explore **correlations and connections** using statistical graphics. It also introduces the concepts of **network and hierarchical visualizations** to model complex relationships and structures. Additionally, the chapter emphasizes the significance of **interactivity** in modern visualization tools to promote dynamic exploration, user engagement, and data-driven decision-making. By the end of the chapter, learners should be able to select appropriate visualization methods for various data types, build interactive dashboards, and communicate analytical results effectively through visual storytelling.

Principles of data visualization

Creating effective data visualizations requires following certain foundational principles that ensure the data is not only presented attractively but also interpreted correctly and efficiently by the audience. These principles act as guidelines to enhance the quality, usability, and impact of visual data communication, described as follows:

- **Clarity**: It is the foremost principle and involves designing visuals that are simple, intuitive, and free of unnecessary complexity. A clear visualization allows viewers to quickly grasp the main message without confusion. Overuse of colors, labels, or decorative elements can obscure insights, so the goal should always be to present information as transparently and straightforwardly as possible.

- **Accuracy**: It is critical because misleading visuals can distort the truth and lead to incorrect conclusions. This means using appropriate scales, chart types, and data representations that faithfully reflect the data's true meaning. For example, manipulating axis ranges or using inconsistent intervals may exaggerate or understate trends, which compromises the integrity of the visualization.

- **Relevance**: It emphasizes the importance of focusing only on the essential data required to convey the intended message. Including too much information or irrelevant metrics can lead to visual clutter, which distracts the viewer and dilutes the key insights. Good visualizations prioritize the most valuable data and remove anything that does not directly contribute to understanding the issue at hand.

- **Consistency**: It helps create a professional and cohesive look across multiple visual elements. This includes maintaining uniform colors, font styles, legends, symbols, and labeling across all charts and graphics. Consistency not only improves readability but also ensures that viewers can easily compare and interpret different pieces of data without reorienting themselves each time.

- **Interactivity**: It is a modern and increasingly important principle, especially in digital formats. Providing interactive features such as filters, tooltips, drill-downs, and responsive dashboards allows users to explore the data more deeply according to their needs or interests. Interactivity enhances user engagement and supports dynamic exploration, which can lead to more personalized and insightful analysis.

Together, these principles ensure that data visualizations are not only aesthetically appealing but also functional, trustworthy, and insightful, ultimately leading to better understanding and smarter decision-making.

Types of data visualization

Data visualizations can be categorized based on their complexity and functionality, ranging from simple charts to advanced interactive dashboards. Each type serves a different analytical purpose, helping users explore and communicate data in the most meaningful way for the context.

Basic charts and graphs

These are foundational visual tools commonly used for data analysis and presentation due to their simplicity and effectiveness:

- **Bar chart**: Bar charts are ideal for comparing data across different categories. Each bar's height or length corresponds to the value it represents, making it easy to see which categories perform better or worse. They are especially useful for summarizing survey results, comparing revenues, or displaying population figures by region.

- **Line chart**: Line charts are widely used to illustrate trends over time, such as stock market changes, temperature variations, or sales growth. They help identify upward or downward movements, cycles, and patterns by connecting data points with a continuous line.

- **Pie chart**: Pie charts display proportions of a whole as slices of a circle. While visually appealing, they should be used cautiously, especially when there are many segments or similar-sized categories, as this can make comparisons difficult. They work best when showing a limited number of categories with distinct differences in proportions.

- **Scatter plot**: Scatter plots show the relationship between two continuous variables, making them effective for identifying correlations, trends, or clusters. Each point represents a data pair, which helps in understanding associations such as height vs. weight or advertising spend vs. sales revenue.

Advanced visualizations

Advanced visualizations are used for more complex datasets and can reveal deeper insights that basic charts may not capture:

- **Choropleth maps**: These maps use color gradients to represent data values across geographic regions, such as countries, states, or districts. Commonly used in demographics and public health, choropleths can visually compare variables like population density, literacy rates, or COVID-19 infection rates across locations.

- **Box plot**: A box plot (or box-and-whisker plot) provides a compact summary of the distribution of a dataset, showing the median, quartiles, and any outliers. It is particularly useful for comparing distributions between groups or spotting variability in data.

- **Heatmap**: Heatmaps use color intensity to show the concentration or strength of values within a matrix. They are often used to display correlation matrices, website activity, or resource usage, where darker or lighter shades indicate higher or lower values.

- **Network graph**: Network graphs visualize relationships or connections among entities. Nodes represent entities, and edges (lines) represent relationships. They are commonly used in social network analysis, citation networks, or supply chain mapping to uncover structural patterns.

Interactive dashboards

Interactive dashboards offer dynamic and real-time data visualization, allowing users to explore and manipulate data without needing programming knowledge, as explained here:

- **Tableau, Power BI**: These are popular business intelligence tools that allow users to create drag-and-drop dashboards. They support real-time data integration and offer a wide range of customizable visuals. These tools are widely used in business environments for performance tracking, forecasting, and decision-making.

- **Plotly, Dash**: These are Python-based libraries that allow for the creation of web-based interactive visualizations and dashboards. Dashboards built with Plotly or Dash can include features like filters, sliders, and live updates, making them suitable for data science and analytics applications.

- **D3.js**: D3.js is a powerful JavaScript library for building highly customized, interactive visualizations on the web. It allows for precise control over every visual element, enabling complex animations and real-time user interaction. While it requires coding expertise, D3 is ideal for projects that demand flexibility and a unique visual experience.

Note: **Choosing the right type of data visualization depends on the nature of your data, your audience, and the insight you want to communicate. From simple comparisons to complex data interactions, each visualization type plays a unique role in transforming raw data into actionable understanding.**

Tools for data visualization

Data visualization is a vital part of data analysis and communication, and numerous tools are available to support this task depending on the complexity of the data, the type of visualization needed, and the user's skill level. These tools can be broadly categorized based on their functionality and usage into programming libraries, business intelligence platforms, geospatial tools, and web-based visualization frameworks.

Python libraries for visualizations

Python is one of the most popular languages for data science, and it offers a rich ecosystem of libraries for data visualization:

- **Matplotlib** is the foundational plotting library in Python. It enables the creation of static, animated, and interactive visualizations. It is highly customizable and is often used for generating basic plots such as line graphs, bar charts, and histograms. While it requires more coding effort, it offers full control over plot appearance.

- **Seaborn** is built on top of Matplotlib and simplifies the creation of aesthetically pleasing and statistically informative graphics. It provides high-level functions for drawing attractive visualizations like heatmaps, violin plots, and pair plots. Seaborn also integrates well with Pandas DataFrames, making it suitable for quick exploratory data analysis.

- **Plotly** is a powerful library for creating interactive web-based visualizations. It supports a wide variety of chart types, including 3D plots, maps, and dashboards. Plotly allows users to hover, zoom, and explore data interactively, which makes it ideal for presentations and web applications.

- **Bokeh** is another Python library focused on interactive visualizations that can be embedded into web applications. It excels at handling large streaming datasets and supports interactive tools such as sliders, selectors, and hover functionality, making it suitable for building dynamic dashboards.

Business intelligence tools

These tools are designed for users who may not have programming experience but need to analyze and visualize data efficiently:

- **Tableau** is a widely used BI tool that allows users to create drag-and-drop dashboards and detailed reports. It connects easily to a variety of data sources and offers advanced analytics features like forecasting and trend analysis. Tableau's interface makes it possible to build complex visuals without writing code, which is ideal for business users and analysts.

- **Power BI** is Microsoft's BI tool that integrates seamlessly with Excel, SQL Server, and other Microsoft products. It enables users to create interactive reports and dashboards with real-time data updates. Power BI is especially favored in enterprise environments due to its integration capabilities and cost-effectiveness.

Geospatial tools

Geospatial data visualizations are crucial when working with location-based datasets, such as population maps or delivery routes:

- **Geopandas** extends the capabilities of Pandas to allow spatial operations on geometric types. It enables users to visualize and analyze geographic data using shapefiles, coordinate systems, and map overlays. It is well-suited for working with regions, boundaries, and spatial joins.

- **Folium** is a Python library built on the Leaflet.js framework and is used to create interactive maps. It supports features like marker clustering, choropleth maps, and popups. Folium makes it easy to overlay data on real-world maps, which is useful for transportation, public health, or demographic analysis.

- **Google Maps API** allows developers to embed and customize maps in web applications. It provides features such as directions, distance calculation, heatmaps, and street views. It is commonly used in logistics, travel apps, and location-based services.

Web-based visualization frameworks

These tools are best for creating highly customized, interactive data visualizations on web platforms:

- **D3.js (Data-Driven Documents)** is a powerful JavaScript library that provides developers with the ability to create complex, interactive, and animated visualizations using HTML, SVG, and CSS. D3 gives precise control over every visual element, which makes it ideal for custom visual storytelling. However, it requires a solid understanding of JavaScript and DOM manipulation.

- **Highcharts** is another JavaScript-based charting library that is user-friendly and supports a wide range of chart types, from line graphs to stock charts and maps. It is widely used in commercial applications due to its polished visual output and ease of integration. Highcharts also offers support for accessibility and responsive design.

Feature selection

Feature selection in data science is the technique of identifying and selecting the most relevant variables from a dataset that contribute significantly to a predictive model's performance. It helps reduce the dimensionality of data, which in turn lowers computational cost and improves model efficiency. By removing irrelevant, noisy, or redundant features, feature selection also minimizes the risk of overfitting and enhances generalization to unseen data. Common methods include filter-based techniques (e.g., correlation), wrapper methods (e.g., recursive feature elimination), and embedded methods (e.g., using model coefficients or feature importances). It is a crucial step in building accurate and interpretable machine learning models. The following code example shows using **SelectFromModel** from scikit-learn along with visualization of selected features using a bar plot. We use a **SelectFromModel**, **RandomForestClassifier** on the Iris dataset, and visualize the feature importances before and after feature selection:

```
import numpy as np
import pandas as pd
import matplotlib.pyplot as plt
from sklearn.datasets import load_iris
from sklearn.ensemble import RandomForestClassifier
from sklearn.feature_selection import SelectFromModel

# Load dataset
iris = load_iris()
X = pd.DataFrame(iris.data, columns=iris.feature_names)
y = iris.target

# Fit RandomForest model
model = RandomForestClassifier(n_estimators=100, random_state=42)
model.fit(X, y)

# Visualize all feature importances
importances = model.feature_importances_
```

```
plt.figure(figsize=(8, 5))
plt.barh(X.columns, importances, color='skyblue')
plt.title('Feature Importances Before Selection')
plt.xlabel('Importance')
plt.show()

# SelectFromModel to keep only important features
selector = SelectFromModel(model, threshold='median', prefit=True)
X_selected = selector.transform(X)
selected_features = X.columns[selector.get_support()]

# Show selected features
print("Selected Features:", list(selected_features))

# Visualize selected features
selected_importances = importances[selector.get_support()]
plt.figure(figsize=(6, 4))
plt.barh(selected_features, selected_importances, color='lightgreen')
plt.title('Selected Feature Importances')
plt.xlabel('Importance')
plt.show()
```

The output is shown in the following figures:

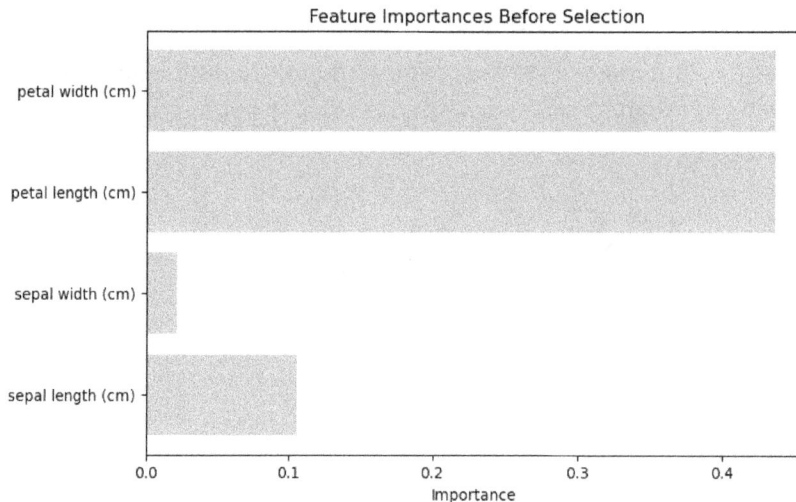

Figure 7.1: *Bar chart representation of all features of the dataset*

```
Selected Features: ['petal length (cm)', 'petal width (cm)']
```

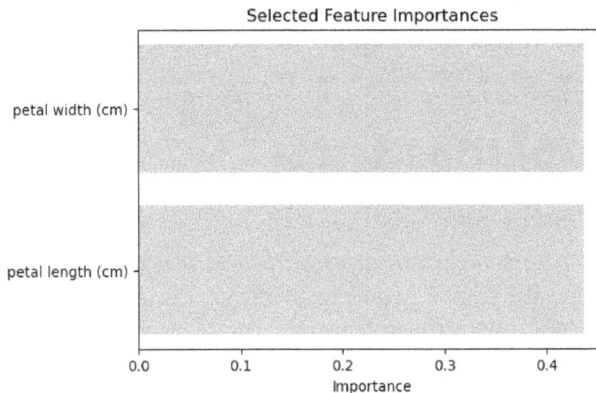

Figure 7.2: Bar chart representation of selected features of the dataset

The output in *Figures 7.1* and *7.2* shows complete features and selected features through bar graphs. A **RandomForestClassifier** is trained on the Iris dataset to evaluate feature importance. The model identifies how much each feature contributes to the prediction by calculating feature importances. Using **SelectFromModel**, only the features with importance above the median threshold are retained for further analysis. Finally, a bar plot is generated to visualize the selected important features, highlighting the most influential variables in the dataset.

Time series analysis

Time series data analysis is a statistical technique used to analyze datasets that are collected at successive, evenly spaced points in time. This type of data captures how a particular variable changes over a period, whether it is hourly, daily, monthly, or yearly, and is used to identify trends, patterns, seasonal effects, and forecast future values. Time series analysis is widely applied in fields such as finance (stock prices), economics (GDP), weather forecasting, healthcare monitoring, traffic flow, energy consumption, and more.

Key characteristics of time series data

The time series data exhibits certain important characteristics, which are given as follows:

- **Temporal order**: Time series data are ordered chronologically. The position of data points in time is crucial, unlike in typical datasets where the order of rows may not matter.

- **Dependence on time**: Values in a time series are often dependent on previous time points, meaning past values can influence future outcomes. This temporal dependence differentiates time series analysis from other types of statistical analysis.

- **Stationarity**: A key concept in time series analysis is **stationarity**, where the statistical properties of the series (mean, variance, autocorrelation) are constant over time. Many modeling techniques assume stationarity, and non-stationary data often need transformation (e.g., differencing or detrending) to meet this condition.

Components of time series

Time series data is generally decomposed into several components:

- **Trend**: The long-term progression of the data, showing upward or downward movement over time. For example, the overall increase in global temperatures over decades indicates a rising trend.

- **Seasonality**: Regular, repeating patterns or cycles over specific intervals (e.g., sales peaking every December). These are predictable and often tied to calendar seasons or business cycles.

- **Cyclic patterns**: Long-term fluctuations that are not fixed in frequency (unlike seasonality), such as economic booms and recessions.

- **Irregular or random noise**: Unpredictable variations caused by unknown or random factors. These are the residual components that remain after removing trend and seasonality.

Steps in time series analysis

The steps involved in time series analysis are given as follows:

- **Data visualization**: Plotting the time series helps understand the underlying trend, seasonality, and anomalies.

- **Smoothing**: Techniques like moving average or exponential smoothing are used to reduce noise and better highlight trends.

- **Stationarity testing**: Methods such as the **Augmented Dickey-Fuller** (**ADF**) test check whether a time series is stationary.

- **Decomposition**: Time series can be decomposed into trend, seasonal, and residual components using additive or multiplicative models.

- **Modeling**: Several models can be applied:

  o **Autoregressive Integrated Moving Average (ARIMA)**: A popular model for univariate forecasting, useful for non-seasonal stationary series.

  o **Seasonal ARIMA (SARIMA)**: An extension of ARIMA that handles seasonality.

  o **Exponential smoothing (Holt-Winters)**: For series with trends and seasonality.

- o **Machine learning models**: Random Forest, XGBoost, and LSTM neural networks are also increasingly used for time series forecasting.

- **Forecasting**: Once a model is built and validated, it can be used to predict future values of the time series.

The following code makes you understand all the steps involved in time series analysis:

1. **Import required libraries**:

```
import pandas as pd
import numpy as np
import matplotlib.pyplot as plt
import seaborn as sns
from statsmodels.tsa.seasonal import seasonal_decompose
from statsmodels.tsa.stattools import adfuller
from statsmodels.tsa.arima.model import ARIMA
```

2. **Load time series data (you can replace with your own CSV file)**:

```
# Example: Monthly airline passengers data
url = 'https://raw.githubusercontent.com/jbrownlee/Datasets/master/
airline-passengers.csv'
df = pd.read_csv(url, parse_dates=['Month'], index_col='Month')
```

3. **Plot the original time series**:

```
plt.figure(figsize=(10, 4))
plt.plot(df, label='Monthly Passengers')
plt.title('Monthly Airline Passengers')
plt.xlabel('Date')
plt.ylabel('Number of Passengers')
plt.legend()
plt.show()
```

4. **Decompose the time series**:

```
decomposition = seasonal_decompose(df, model='multiplicative')
decomposition.plot()
plt.tight_layout()
plt.show()
```

5. **Perform stationarity test (ADF test)**:

```
result = adfuller(df['Passengers'])
print("ADF Statistic:", result[0])
print("p-value:", result[1])
if result[1] < 0.05:
    print("The series is stationary.")
```

```
else:
    print("The series is non-stationary.")
```

6. **Differencing to make series stationary (if needed)**:

```
df_diff = df.diff().dropna()

plt.figure(figsize=(10, 4))
plt.plot(df_diff, label='Differenced Series')
plt.title('Differenced Time Series')
plt.legend()
plt.show()
```

7. **Fit ARIMA model**:

```
model = ARIMA(df, order=(1, 1, 1))  # (p, d, q)
model_fit = model.fit()
```

8. **Summary and diagnostics**:

```
print(model_fit.summary())
model_fit.plot_diagnostics(figsize=(10, 6))
plt.show()
```

9. **Forecasting the next 12 months**:

```
forecast = model_fit.forecast(steps=12)
forecast_index = pd.date_range(start=df.index[-1], periods=13,
freq='MS')[1:]

plt.figure(figsize=(10, 4))
plt.plot(df, label='Original Series')
plt.plot(forecast_index, forecast, label='Forecast', color='red')
plt.title('Forecast for Next 12 Months')
plt.legend()
plt.show()
```

The output is as follows:

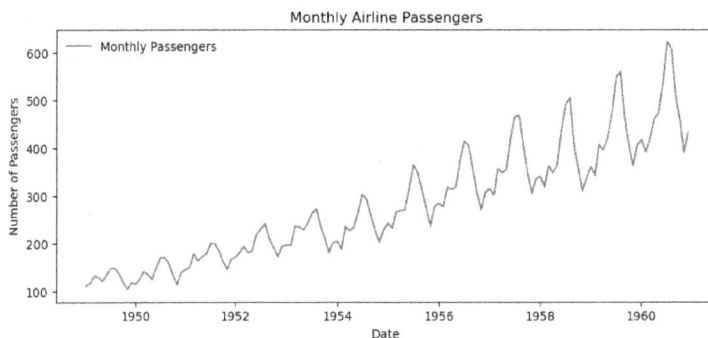

Figure 7.3: *Representation of monthly airline passengers*

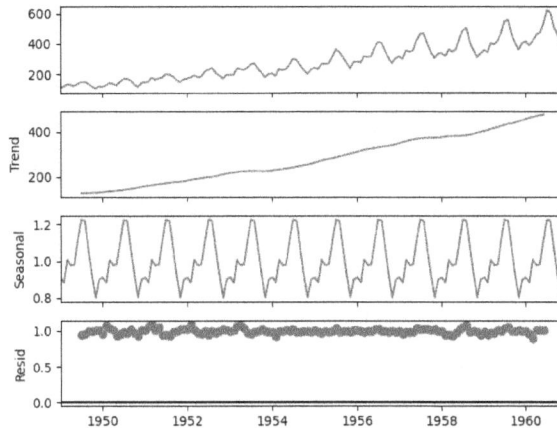

Figure 7.4: Representation of residual. Seasonal, trend analysis

```
ADF Statistic: 0.8153688792060547
p-value: 0.9918802434376411
The series is non-stationary.
```

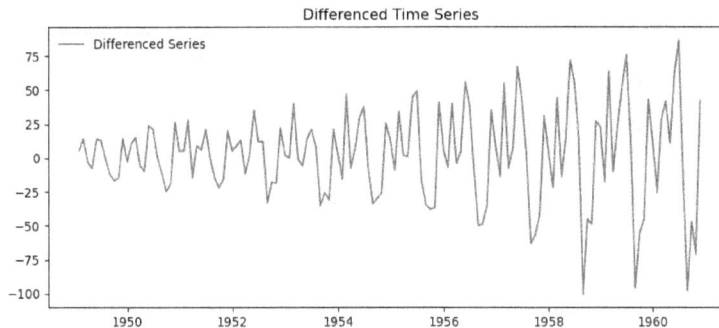

Figure 7.5: Representation of different series

SARIMAX Results

```
==============================================================================
Dep. Variable:                Passengers   No. Observations:            144
Model:                  ARIMA(1, 1, 1)   Log Likelihood          -694.341
Date:                Thu, 05 Jun 2025   AIC                      1394.683
Time:                        12:23:36   BIC                      1403.571
Sample:                    01-01-1949   HQIC                     1398.294
                         - 12-01-1960
Covariance Type:                  opg
==============================================================================
                 coef    std err          z      P>|z|      [0.025      0.975]
------------------------------------------------------------------------------
ar.L1         -0.4742      0.123     -3.847      0.000      -0.716      -0.233
ma.L1          0.8635      0.078     11.051      0.000       0.710       1.017
sigma2       961.9270    107.433      8.954      0.000     751.362    1172.492
==============================================================================
Ljung-Box (L1) (Q):                   0.21   Jarque-Bera (JB):             2.14
Prob(Q):                              0.65   Prob(JB):                     0.34
Heteroskedasticity (H):               7.00   Skew:                        -0.21
Prob(H) (two-sided):                  0.00   Kurtosis:                     3.43
------------------------------------------------------------------------------
```

Figure 7.6: Results of the SARIMAX model

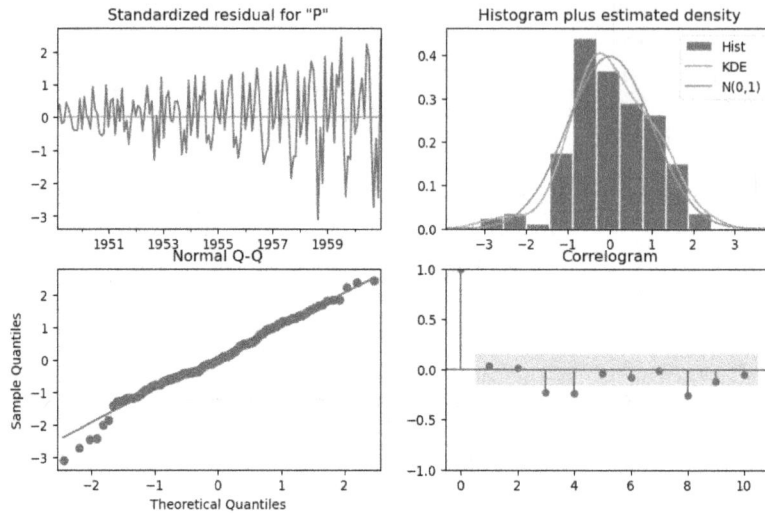

Figure 7.7: Representation of sample quartiles and histograms

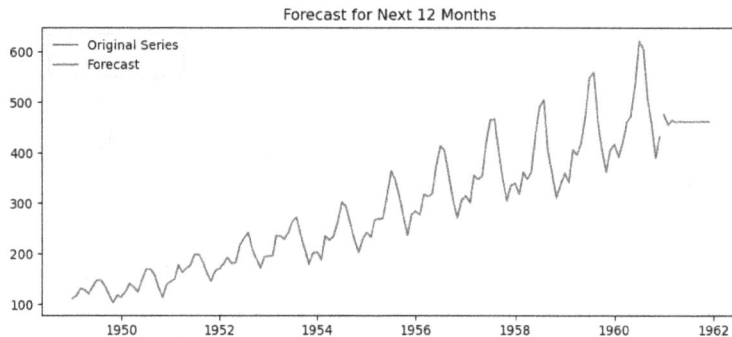

Figure 7.8: Representation of forecast for the next 12 months

The code and output (given from *Figures 7.3* through *7.8*) are explained as follows:

1. Required libraries are imported:

   a. **pandas, numpy**: For data manipulation and calculations.

   b. **matplotlib, seaborn**: For plotting graphs and visualizations.

   c. **seasonal_decompose**: To break the time series into trend, seasonal, and residual components.

   d. **adfuller**: For stationarity testing using the ADF test.

   e. **ARIMA**: To model and forecast the time series data.

2. Monthly airline passenger data is loaded from GitHub. **parse_dates** converts the **Month** column into a datetime format. **index_col** sets the datetime as the index, which is essential for time series analysis.

3. The original data is plotted to visualize the general pattern, which helps detect trends, seasonality, and anomalies visually.

4. Time series is decomposed into:

    - **Trend**: Long-term progression.
    - **Seasonality**: Regular repeating patterns.
    - **Residual**: Random noise.

    This is useful for understanding the internal structure of the data.

5. It is checked if the time series is **stationary**, which is a key assumption for many models like ARIMA. `ADF Statistic`: A large negative value indicates stationarity. `p-value`: If < 0.05, the series is stationary.

6. Differencing is done if required. If the series is **non-stationary**, differencing helps by subtracting the current value from the previous one. It makes the data stable over time (i.e., stationary), ready for modeling.

7. ARIMA model is fit as ARIMA(p, d, q):

    - p = number of autoregressive terms (lags of the series)
    - d = number of times the series needs to be differenced
    - q = number of lagged forecast errors in the model

8. The model is summarized, and a diagnostic is performed, which provides a summary of model coefficients and statistics. Diagnostic plots show:

    - Residual normality
    - Autocorrelation
    - Model fit quality

9. Future values are forecasted, which generates forecasts for the next 12 months. The forecasted values are plotted alongside the original data to visualize future trends.

Applications of time series analysis

The important applications of time series analysis are given as follows:

- **Finance**: Predicting stock prices, market trends, or interest rates.
- **Healthcare**: Monitoring vital signs over time (e.g., heart rate, glucose levels).
- **Weather and climate**: Forecasting temperature, rainfall, and natural events.
- **Sales and marketing**: Demand forecasting, customer behavior prediction, and campaign impact analysis.
- **Operations management**: Inventory forecasting, capacity planning, and quality control.

Geolocated data analysis

Geolocated analysis, also known as **geospatial analysis** or **location-based analysis**, refers to the process of collecting, analyzing, and interpreting data that has a geographical or spatial component. It involves mapping data points to specific locations on the Earth's surface and analyzing patterns, relationships, or trends based on their geographic distribution. This type of analysis combines traditional data analytics with **geographic information system** (**GIS**) technology to add the dimension of *where* to decision-making.

Key concepts in geolocated analysis

The key points are described as follows:

- Geolocation is the process of identifying the physical location of an object or person using data like GPS coordinates (latitude and longitude), IP address, Wi-Fi, RFID, or mobile network data.

- **Spatial data**: This refers to data that is connected to a location, such as coordinates, addresses, zip codes, or administrative boundaries (e.g., cities, states, countries). Spatial data is usually categorized into:
    - **Point data** (e.g., ATM locations, accident spots)
    - **Line data** (e.g., roads, rivers)
    - **Polygon data** (e.g., country borders, districts)

- **GIS**: A system that captures, stores, manipulates, analyzes, and presents spatial or geographic data. It forms the foundation for geolocated analysis.

Tools for geolocated analysis

Various tools are used for geolocated data analysis, as follows:

- **Python libraries**:
    - **Geopandas**: Extends Pandas to handle geospatial data.
    - **Folium**: Creates interactive maps using Leaflet.js.
    - **Shapely, PyProj**: Handle geometry and projections.
    - **Plotly, Matplotlib**: Support map visualizations.

- **Web APIs**:
    - **Google Maps API**: For geocoding, route optimization, and mapping.
    - **OpenStreetMap**: Free geographic data.

- **GIS software**:
    - QGIS (open-source)
    - ArcGIS (commercial)

Steps in performing geolocated analysis

Various steps for geolocated data analysis are given as follows:

1. **Data collection**: Collect location-based data (e.g., GPS, mobile app data, satellite images).

2. **Data cleaning and geocoding**: Convert addresses into coordinates (geocoding) or filter out incomplete entries.

3. **Mapping and visualization**: Plot data on maps to observe spatial distributions (e.g., choropleth maps, heatmaps).

4. **Spatial analysis**: Perform proximity analysis, clustering (e.g., DBSCAN), buffer zones, or route optimization.

5. **Insights and decision making**: Derive actionable insights, such as choosing the best site for a new store or identifying underserved regions.

Now, let us understand through the following code how geolocated data analysis is performed:

```
!pip install folium
```

1. **Import libraries**:

```
import pandas as pd
import folium
```

2. **Load dataset (Earthquake data with location info)**:

```
url = "https://earthquake.usgs.gov/earthquakes/feed/v1.0/
summary/2.5_month.csv"
df = pd.read_csv(url)

# Show basic info
print(df[['place', 'mag', 'time', 'latitude', 'longitude']].head())
```

3. **Create a base map centered globally**:

```
m = folium.Map(location=[0, 0], zoom_start=2)
```

4. **Add markers for each earthquake**:

```
for index, row in df.iterrows():
    folium.CircleMarker(
        location=[row['latitude'], row['longitude']],
        radius=row['mag'] * 2,   # magnitude as size
        popup=f"{row['place']} (Mag: {row['mag']})",
        color='red',
        fill=True,
        fill_opacity=0.7
    ).add_to(m)
```

5. **Save and display the map**:

```
m.save("earthquake_map.html")
print("Map saved as 'earthquake_map.html'")
```

The output is as follows:

```
                           place   mag                      time   latitude  \
0       54 km NW of Toyah, Texas  2.60  2025-06-05T06:43:47.629Z  31.668000
1     35 km NW of Mýrina, Greece  4.70  2025-06-05T05:18:38.412Z  40.132500
2   52 km S of Gazipaşa, Turkey  4.30  2025-06-05T04:32:32.358Z  35.802100
3     63 km NW of Ocampo, Mexico  4.90  2025-06-05T03:26:21.976Z  27.648400
4      3 km SE of Tres Pinos, CA  2.55  2025-06-05T01:01:27.690Z  36.774666

     longitude
0  -104.191000
1    24.812400
2    32.229800
3  -102.914600
4  -121.289169
Map saved as 'earthquake_map.html'
```

Figure 7.9: *Longitude and latitude analysis and results*

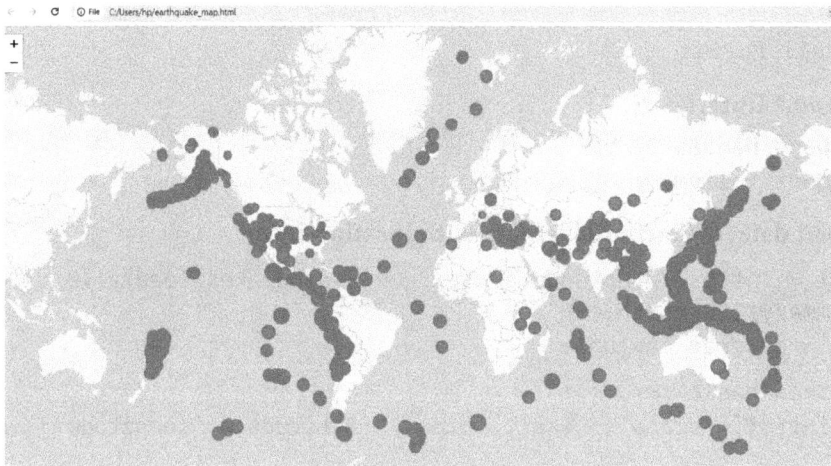

Figure 7.10: *Contents of earquake_map.html file*

The code loads recent earthquake data from USGS (includes latitude/longitude). Then initializes an interactive map using folium. It plots each earthquake with a circle marker sized by magnitude. Thereafter, it saves the output as an HTML file, which you can open in your browser as shown in *Figure 7.9* and *Figure 7.10*.

Applications of geolocated analysis

There are various applications of geolocated analysis given as follows:

- **Urban planning**: Analyze traffic patterns, population density, and land use to support city planning and infrastructure development.

- **Healthcare**: Map disease outbreaks (e.g., COVID-19 hotspots), access to healthcare services, or patient distribution.

- **Retail and marketing**: Identify store performance by location, optimize delivery routes, and target location-based advertisements.

- **Logistics and transportation**: Optimize delivery paths, track vehicle movement, and manage supply chains more effectively.

- **Environmental monitoring**: Analyze deforestation, pollution hotspots, or wildlife movement patterns using satellite imagery and sensor data.

- **Security and emergency response**: Map crime zones, plan resource deployment, and identify high-risk disaster areas.

Correlations and connections

Correlation refers to a statistical relationship between two variables. It measures how changes in one variable are associated with changes in another. Correlation is typically quantified using a correlation coefficient, which ranges between:

- +1 → Perfect positive correlation (as one increases, so does the other)
- 0 → No correlation (no linear relationship)
- –1 → Perfect negative correlation (as one increases, the other decreases)

The most common correlation metric is Pearson's correlation coefficient, but others include Spearman's rank and Kendall's tau.

Note: **There is a positive correlation between height and weight—taller people generally weigh more.**

The types of correlations are summarized in *Table 7.1*:

Type	Description	Example
Positive	Both variables move in the same direction	Income ↑ and spending ↑
Negative	One variable increases as the other decreases	Exercise ↑ and weight ↓ (in some cases)
Zero/No correlation	No linear relationship between variables	Shoe size and intelligence
Nonlinear (Curvilinear)	Relationship exists but not in a straight line (e.g., quadratic)	Age and memory (improves then declines)

Table 7.1: Types of correlations

Importance of correlation in data analysis

Correlation is performed due to the following reasons:

- **Identifies meaningful relationships**: Helps find how variables relate to each other.
- **Feature selection**: In machine learning, correlated features may be dropped or engineered to improve model accuracy.
- **Predictive modeling**: Understanding relationships aids in regression and forecasting.
- **Anomaly detection**: Unexpected correlations can indicate errors or new insights.

Visualization of correlations

Correlation can be visualized by the following plots:

- **Scatter plots**: They show relationships between two numerical variables, where the pattern direction shows the nature of the correlation.
- **Correlation matrix (Heatmap)**: A grid showing correlation coefficients between multiple variables. Visualized using color gradients (e.g., with **seaborn. heatmap()**).
- **Line graphs/pairplots**: They help visualize how multiple variables move together over time or across observations.

The following code represents the correlation between age, income, and spending of employees in terms of scatter plot, heatmap, and line plot:

```python
import pandas as pd
import seaborn as sns
import matplotlib.pyplot as plt

# Sample DataFrame
data = {
    'Age': [25, 30, 45, 50, 22],
    'Income': [35000, 45000, 70000, 80000, 32000],
    'Spending': [2000, 2500, 4000, 4200, 1800]
}
df = pd.DataFrame(data)

# ----- 1. Scatter Plot Matrix -----
sns.pairplot(df)
plt.suptitle("Scatter Plot Matrix", y=1.02)
plt.show()

# ----- 2. Correlation Heatmap -----
```

```
corr = df.corr()
sns.heatmap(corr, annot=True, cmap='coolwarm')
plt.title("Correlation Heatmap")
plt.show()

# ----- 3. Line Plot for Trends -----
plt.figure(figsize=(8, 5))
plt.plot(df['Age'], label='Age', marker='o')
plt.plot(df['Income'], label='Income', marker='s')
plt.plot(df['Spending'], label='Spending', marker='^')
plt.title("Line Plot of Variables")
plt.xlabel("Index")
plt.ylabel("Values")
plt.legend()
plt.grid(True)
plt.tight_layout()
plt.show()
```

The output is as follows:

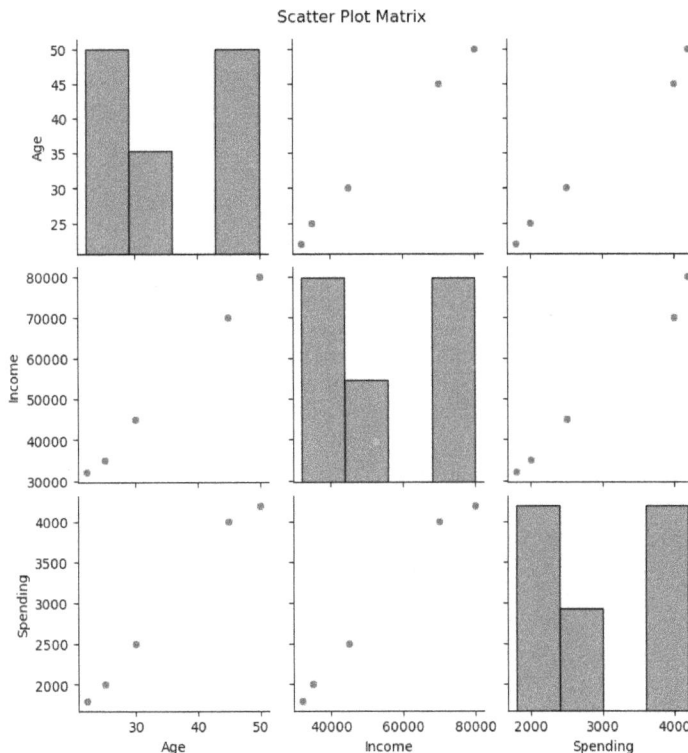

Figure 7.11: *Matrix of scatter plots showing relationships between all pairs of variables (age, income, and spending)*

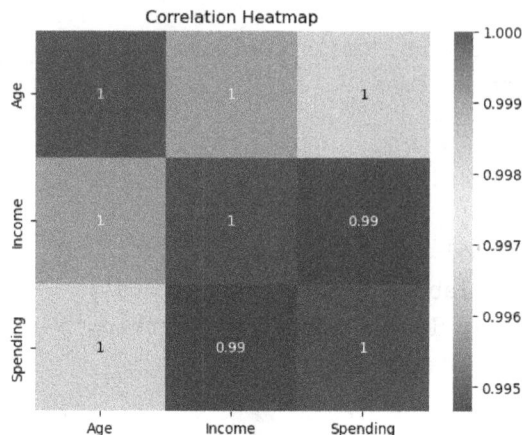

Figure 7.12: Heatmap representing which variables are positively or negatively correlated

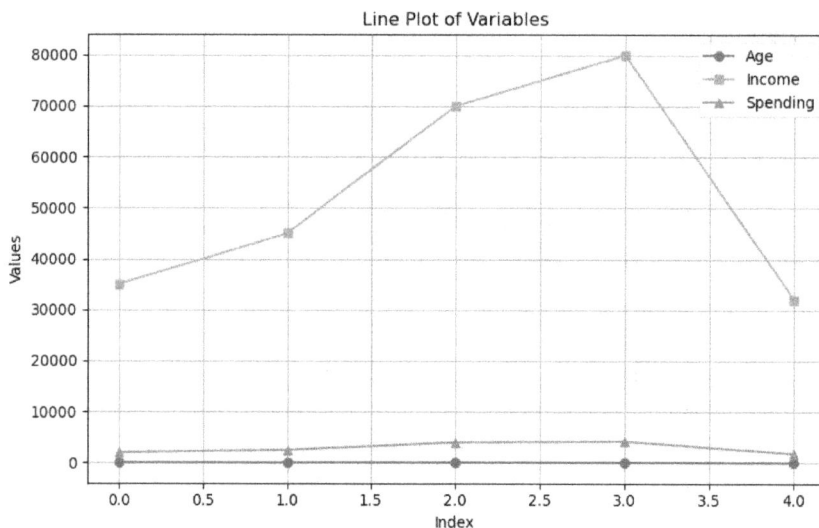

Figure 7.13: Line plot showing the trend of each variable across the data index

In the code, a simple dataset is created with three variables: Age, Income, and Spending, given in *Figures 7.11 to 7.13*. This data is converted into a **pandas DataFrame** for easy analysis. **pairplot()** from seaborn creates a matrix of scatter plots showing relationships between all pairs of variables. It also includes histograms or KDE plots on the diagonal. It helps visually identify linear and non-linear correlations. **df.corr()** calculates the correlation matrix (Pearson by default) between all numeric variables. **sns.heatmap()** visualizes this matrix:

- **annot=True** displays the actual correlation values inside the cells.
- **cmap='coolwarm'** gives a blue-to-red gradient indicating strength and direction of the correlation.

It helps quickly see which variables are positively or negatively correlated. This part creates a line plot showing the trend of each variable across the data index (like user or time). Each variable is plotted with a different marker for clarity. It is useful for comparing how the values move together (e.g., does spending rise as income increases?)

Connections

While correlation indicates linear relationships, connections refer to broader, more complex relationships among data points or entities:

- **Causal connections** (e.g., smoking → lung cancer)
- **Network connections** (e.g., social media friends, communication patterns)
- **Association rules** (e.g., people who buy bread also buy butter)
- **Hierarchical or spatial connections** (e.g., regions within countries, parts within wholes)

These connections often require:

- **Graph theory** (e.g., network graphs)
- **Clustering** and **association rule mining**
- **Causal inference techniques** like Granger causality or **structural equation modeling (SEM)**

Important notes:

Correlation ≠ Causation: Just because two variables move together does not mean one causes the other. Always investigate underlying mechanisms.

Outliers can distort correlation.

Non-linear relationships may require other statistical methods to capture.

Correlation is a fundamental statistical tool to measure the strength and direction of relationships between numerical variables. Connections, on the other hand, encompass a wider array of relationships, including causal, associative, structural, or spatial, which go beyond what simple correlation coefficients can capture.

Both concepts are essential for discovering insights, building predictive models, and making informed decisions in data science, social sciences, marketing, healthcare, and beyond.

Networks and hierarchies

A network is a system of interconnected entities, often represented as nodes (points) and edges (connections or relationships). Examples include the following:

- **Social networks**: People (nodes) connected by friendships (edges)

- **Internet**: Devices (nodes) connected by cables or wireless links (edges)
- **Biological networks**: Genes or proteins (nodes) connected through interactions (edges)
- **Citation networks**: Academic papers (nodes) linked via references (edges)

Key features of networks

The main network features are:

- **Directed vs. undirected**: Is the connection one-way or two-way? (e.g., Twitter vs. Facebook)
- **Weighted edges**: Some links may be stronger or more significant than others.
- **Degree centrality**: How many connections a node has.
- **Clustering**: Subgroups of nodes are tightly connected to each other.
- **Path length**: How many steps it takes to go from one node to another.

Tools for network analysis

Various tools are available for network analysis as described below:

- **NetworkX (Python)**: For graph-based computations and visualization.
- **Gephi**: A GUI-based tool for interactive network visualization.
- **Neo4j**: A graph database system.

Networks are important because they provide a powerful way to visualize and analyze relationships and interactions among entities, whether individuals, systems, or data points. By mapping these connections, networks help uncover key patterns such as central influencers, bottlenecks, and tightly-knit communities within larger systems. This makes them invaluable in diverse fields like epidemiology, where they track disease spread; logistics, for optimizing supply chains; sociology, to study social influence and group dynamics; cybersecurity, to identify vulnerable links in digital systems; and artificial intelligence, where they model neural and relational structures. Overall, networks offer deep insight into how systems behave, evolve, and respond to change.

Hierarchies

A hierarchy is a structured arrangement where entities are ranked or organized into levels, with each level subordinate to the one above. Examples include the following:

- **Organizational chart**: CEO at the top, followed by VPs, managers, and staff
- **Taxonomy of living things**: Kingdom → Phylum → Class → Order → Family → Genus → Species

- **File system**: Root → Folder → Sub-folder → File
- **Decision trees**: Root node → Branches → Leaves

Key features of hierarchies

The main network features are:

- **Tree-like structure**: One root, branching downward.
- **Parent-child relationships**: Every node (except the root) has exactly one parent.
- **Levels/Depth**: Number of layers in the structure.
- **Flow of control or authority**: Often top-down in nature.

The tools for hierarchy representation are as follows:

- Dendrograms (from clustering)
- Decision trees (e.g., using scikit-learn)
- Org charts (e.g., with Graphviz or diagrams.net)
- **Treemaps**: Space-filling visualizations for hierarchical data

Hierarchies are important because they help represent the order, importance, and dependencies among different elements within a system. By organizing information or entities into structured levels, hierarchies make it easier to understand relationships and control flows. They are widely used in areas such as management, to define authority and reporting structures; biology, for classifying organisms; file storage, to arrange data systematically; and classification systems, for organizing knowledge. Hierarchies also play a critical role in designing web navigation and user interfaces, providing clear pathways for users to access information, and are fundamental in AI models like decision trees, where decisions flow from general to specific in a logical structure. The differences between networks and hierarchies are summarized as follows in *Table 7.2*:

Feature	Hierarchies	Networks
Structure	Tree-like (top-down)	Web-like (complex connections)
Relationships	Parent-child	Many-to-many
Directionality	Strict, downward	Flexible, bidirectional
Example	Organizational chart	Social media connections

Table 7.2: Comparison of hierarchies and networks

Interactivity

Interactivity in data science refers to the ability of users to actively engage with data visualizations, models, and dashboards, rather than just viewing static charts or reports. It transforms data analysis from a one-way presentation into a two-way exploration, where users can manipulate inputs, drill into details, and gain deeper insights tailored to their specific questions.

Key aspects of interactivity

The main roles of interactivity are explained as follows:

- **User engagement**: Interactive elements like dropdowns, sliders, checkboxes, zooming, filtering, and tooltips allow users to explore data from multiple angles. For example, users can dynamically adjust time ranges, select specific categories, or view detailed values by hovering over points in a graph.

- **Real-time feedback**: With interactive dashboards and tools, changes made by the user (e.g., selecting a different region or metric) can trigger instant updates to charts, summaries, or models. This enables faster decision-making and what-if scenario testing without needing to write new code or regenerate reports.

- **Exploratory data analysis (EDA)**: Interactivity is especially powerful during EDA. Tools like Plotly, Dash, Tableau, or Power BI allow analysts to visually slice and dice data to find trends, correlations, and outliers that might be missed in static plots.

Tools for interactive data science

There are various tools used to make a system interactive in data science, as follows:

- **Python libraries**:
  - Plotly, Bokeh, and Dash for interactive web-based visualizations.
  - ipywidgets in Jupyter for creating interactive notebooks.

- **Web frameworks**: D3.js and React for custom interactive visualizations.

- **BI platforms**: Tableau and Power BI offer drag-and-drop dashboards with built-in interactivity.

Benefits of interactivity

The benefits of interactivity are given as follows:

- **Enhanced understanding**: Users can explore data on their own and uncover hidden insights.

- **Data-driven decisions**: Real-time interaction supports rapid and informed decision-making.

- **Accessibility**: Non-technical stakeholders can easily interpret and engage with complex data.

- **Customization**: Enables tailoring the analysis to specific business or research questions.

Interactivity is no longer just a nice-to-have in data science; it is a vital component that bridges the gap between data and decision-making. By empowering users to ask questions, test ideas, and view data dynamically, interactive data science tools foster better exploration, clearer communication, and smarter outcomes.

Conclusion

This chapter explored the multifaceted world of data visualization, emphasizing its role in uncovering insights and enhancing decision-making. It begins with principles of designing effective visualizations, highlighting clarity, accuracy, and relevance to ensure that visual outputs communicate data meaningfully. Time series analysis is discussed as a method to track trends and patterns over chronological sequences, making it invaluable in forecasting and monitoring. Geolocated analysis leverages spatial data to reveal regional trends and geographic disparities, often through maps and spatial plots. The chapter also looks into correlations and connections, using scatter plots, heatmaps, and statistical techniques to understand relationships between variables. Networks and hierarchies are examined to visualize complex systems, networks reveal relationships and influences among entities, while hierarchies represent structured, ordered systems such as organizational charts or decision trees. Lastly, the importance of interactivity is emphasized, showing how dynamic tools and dashboards allow users to manipulate data in real time, encouraging deeper engagement and exploration. Together, these visualization strategies provide a comprehensive toolkit for analyzing, interpreting, and communicating data effectively across diverse domains.

In the next chapter, we will work on real-world projects in order to understand data preparation and analysis (data science) in more depth.

Multiple choice questions

1. **What is the primary goal of designing effective data visualizations?**

    a. To decorate reports

    b. To increase the data size

    c. To communicate insights clearly and accurately

    d. To create complex charts

2. **Which of the following is not a principle of good data visualization?**

    a. Clarity

    b. Relevance

    c. Complexity

    d. Accuracy

3. **Consistency in visual design refers to**:

    a. Using many types of charts

    b. Applying uniform styles, fonts, and colors

    c. Including unrelated data

    d. Avoiding color use entirely

4. **Which visualization is best suited for comparing categories?**

    a. Line chart

    b. Scatter plot

    c. Pie chart

    d. Bar chart

5. **What does avoid clutter mean in visualization design?**

    a. Use lots of colors

    b. Include all data in one chart

    c. Show only essential elements

    d. Maximize the use of 3D effects

6. **What type of data is used in time series analysis?**

    a. Spatial data

    b. Categorical data

    c. Data collected over time

    d. Textual data

7. **Which plot is best for showing trends over time?**

    a. Pie chart

    b. Heatmap

    c. Line plot

    d. Box plot

8. **What is the main purpose of time series analysis?**

    a. Sorting categorical values

    b. Predicting future values based on historical trends

    c. Analyzing image data

    d. Counting categories

9. **Seasonality in time series refers to**:

    a. Random noise in the data

    b. Long-term shifts in data

    c. Regular patterns that repeat over intervals

    d. Incorrect data points

10. **Which Python library is most commonly used for plotting time series?**

    a. seaborn

    b. matplotlib

    c. geopandas

    d. nltk

11. **What does geolocated data contain?**

    a. File paths

    b. Time zones

    c. Geographic coordinates

    d. Character strings

12. **Which visualization is commonly used for mapping geographic data?**

    a. Scatter plot

    b. Choropleth map

    c. Box plot

    d. Line chart

13. **Which tool is widely used for geospatial analysis in Python?**

    a. pandas

    b. plotly

    c. geopandas

    d. sklearn

14. **What is the key benefit of geolocated analysis?**

    a. Shows relationships over time

    b. Tracks user interface clicks

    c. Reveals spatial patterns and regional trends

    d. Stores large datasets

15. **Heatmaps in geolocation data typically represent**:
    a. Cold and hot weather zones
    b. Intensity or frequency of a variable across locations
    c. Line paths on maps
    d. Pie chart equivalents

16. **Which plot is best to visualize the relationship between two continuous variables?**
    a. Pie chart
    b. Line plot
    c. Scatter plot
    d. Histogram

17. **A correlation coefficient near -1 indicates**:
    a. No relationship
    b. Strong negative relationship
    c. Strong positive relationship
    d. Non-linear relationship

18. **What does a heatmap of a correlation matrix show?**
    a. Bar heights
    b. Category frequency
    c. Strength of relationships between variables
    d. Spatial data

19. **Which Python library is commonly used for correlation heatmaps?**
    a. NumPy
    b. seaborn
    c. TensorFlow
    d. OpenCV

20. **Which of the following implies no correlation?**
    a. 0
    b. 1
    c. -1
    d. 0.8

21. **A network graph consists of**:

    a. Levels and branches

    b. Nodes and edges

    c. Maps and charts

    d. Tables and queries

22. **Which tool is commonly used for network visualization in Python?**

    a. scikit-learn

    b. pandas

    c. networkx

    d. folium

23. **Hierarchical structures are best visualized using**:

    a. Scatter plots

    b. Bar charts

    c. Tree diagrams or dendrograms

    d. Line graphs

24. **In a hierarchy, each child node typically**:

    a. Has multiple parents

    b. Has one parent

    c. Is disconnected

    d. Links to all nodes

25. **Organizational charts are examples of**:

    a. Network graphs

    b. Flat structures

    c. Hierarchies

    d. Heatmaps

26. **Interactivity in data visualizations allows**:

    a. Static views only

    b. User-driven exploration and filtering

    c. Faster image processing

    d. Manual annotation of datasets

27. **Which is a web-based Python library for interactive dashboards?**

    a. Dash

    b. NumPy

    c. seaborn

    d. sklearn

28. **Interactivity improves**:

    a. Data loss

    b. Processing time only

    c. Engagement and understanding

    d. File size

29. **Which of the following is an example of interactivity?**

    a. Exporting CSV

    b. Using a pie chart

    c. Applying filters in a dashboard

    d. Counting values

30. **Which platform provides drag-and-drop tools for interactive dashboards?**

    a. Jupyter

    b. PyTorch

    c. Tableau

    d. VS Code

Answers

1. c
2. c
3. b
4. d
5. c
6. c
7. c
8. b
9. c
10. b

11. c

12. b

13. c

14. c

15. b

16. c

17. b

18. c

19. b

20. a

21. b

22. c

23. c

24. b

25. c

26. b

27. a

28. c

29. c

30. c

Questions

1. What is the main purpose of data visualization in data science?
2. Define clarity in the context of data visualization.
3. Name any two types of charts commonly used for comparing categorical data.
4. What is time series analysis?
5. Mention one Python library used to visualize time series data.
6. What does seasonality mean in time series data?
7. What is geolocated data?
8. Name one tool used for geospatial visualization in Python.
9. Define a correlation matrix.
10. What type of plot is used to display the correlation between two numeric variables?
11. What are nodes and edges in a network graph?

12. Give one example where hierarchical visualization is used.

13. How does interactivity benefit a data dashboard?

14. Mention any two interactive visualization tools used in Python.

15. What does a heatmap represent in data visualization?

Programming exercises

1. Create a bar chart and a pie chart using a dataset that includes sales by product categories. Compare which one communicates the information more clearly.

2. Load a dataset (e.g., Iris or Titanic) and apply at least three principles of good visualization: clarity, relevance, and consistency. Explain each design choice.

3. Load a time series dataset (e.g., stock prices or weather data). Plot the trend over time using a line chart and identify any seasonal patterns.

4. Perform a rolling average smoothing on a time series and visualize the smoothed trend along with the original line plot.

5. Using a dataset that includes latitude and longitude (e.g., world cities), plot these locations on a map using Folium.

6. Visualize population density by region using a choropleth map. Use a geoJSON file for boundaries and join it with population data.

7. Create a correlation matrix heatmap for a multivariable dataset (e.g., cars dataset: speed, weight, fuel efficiency, etc.).

8. Generate scatter plots to analyze pairwise relationships between variables. Use color or size to add a third dimension.

9. Create a simple social network graph with nodes and edges using networkx. Label nodes and visualize the network.

10. Build a tree hierarchy.

Join our Discord space

Join our Discord workspace for latest updates, offers, tech happenings around the world, new releases, and sessions with the authors:

https://discord.bpbonline.com

CHAPTER 8
Projects

Introduction

In today's digital era, businesses and service providers are increasingly relying on intelligent systems to understand and engage with their customers more effectively. This chapter delves into the development and analysis of three practical, real-world projects that are centered around enhancing customer experience and decision-making through data-driven technologies. These projects are designed to demonstrate the application of machine learning, natural language processing, and data analytics in solving common business problems.

The first project focuses on building a **movie recommender system**, which uses user preferences, genres, and ratings to suggest relevant content. This system showcases how collaborative and content-based filtering techniques can personalize experiences and boost user engagement.

The second project introduces a **customer FAQ chatbot**, developed using a user-friendly interface that allows customers to interact through buttons and receive immediate responses. This project illustrates the use of conversational interfaces and rule-based logic to automate customer service and support.

The third project involves a **customer segmentation system**, where we perform K-means clustering on a retail or e-commerce dataset to identify distinct customer groups. This helps businesses tailor their marketing strategies and product offerings by understanding various customer behaviors and patterns.

Through these projects, readers will gain hands-on experience with data preprocessing, visualization, machine learning, and user interface design, equipping them with the skills needed to build intelligent customer-centric applications.

Structure

The chapter covers the following topics:

- Movie recommender system
- Customer support chatbot
- Customer segmentation system

Objectives

This chapter aims to provide readers with practical insights and skills in building intelligent systems that enhance customer interaction and support business decision-making. Through three hands-on projects, developing a recommendation system, designing a customer FAQ chatbot, and implementing a customer segmentation system, readers will learn to analyze and preprocess customer data, build personalized recommendation engines, create interactive chat interfaces for automated customer support, and apply clustering techniques to identify distinct customer groups. The chapter emphasizes real-world applications of data analysis, machine learning, and natural language processing, enabling readers to visualize patterns, extract insights, and develop solutions that are both data-driven and user-centric. By the end, readers will be equipped with a foundational understanding of how to use AI-driven tools to improve customer experience and business outcomes.

Movie recommender system

In the digital age, where users are inundated with vast choices of content, recommender systems have emerged as essential tools for enhancing user experience and engagement. Among the most widely used applications of recommendation engines is in the entertainment domain, particularly in movie recommendation platforms such as *Netflix*, *IMDb*, and *Amazon Prime Video*.

In this chapter, we explore the design and functioning of a movie recommender system that intelligently suggests films by leveraging three core criteria: genre relevance, top-rated selections, and user-based ratings. The system is a hybrid approach, combining elements of content-based filtering and popularity-based ranking to create a balanced and dynamic recommendation mechanism.

The **genre-based filtering** component ensures that users receive suggestions aligned with their thematic preferences, be it action, drama, comedy, or science fiction. By identifying and matching movie genres with user interests, the system ensures relevance in content delivery.

Next, the **top-rated filtering** mechanism considers aggregated ratings from a broader user base, highlighting critically acclaimed or popularly endorsed films. This not only improves the quality of recommendations but also builds trust in the system's suggestions.

Lastly, where user history or ratings are available, the system integrates **individual preferences** by analyzing a user's past interactions and feedback. This personalized layer refines recommendations further, making them uniquely tailored to each viewer's tastes.

Together, these components work in synergy to offer a movie recommendation system that is both reliable and customized, helping users discover films they are likely to enjoy without the overwhelm of choice.

MovieLens dataset

In this recommender system, we utilize the **MovieLens dataset**, a widely used benchmark dataset for evaluating recommendation algorithms. Curated by the *GroupLens Research Project* at the *University of Minnesota*, the MovieLens dataset contains real-world data collected from users who have rated movies over a period of time.

The dataset includes several files that provide comprehensive information about users, movies, and their interactions. The key files and their respective fields are:

- **movies.dat**: Contains metadata about movies, with each entry typically including:
  - **MovieID**: A unique identifier for each movie.
  - **Title**: The title of the movie, often including the year of release.
  - **Genres**: A pipe-separated list of genres associated with the movie (e.g., Action | Adventure | Sci-Fi).
- **ratings.dat**: Captures user preferences in the form of ratings, with fields:
  - **UserID**: An anonymized unique identifier for each user.
  - **MovieID**: References the movie that was rated.
  - **Rating**: The user's rating of the movie, typically on a scale of 1 to 5.
  - **Timestamp**: The time when the rating was made (in Unix time format).
- **users.dat (in some versions)**: Includes demographic information about users, such as age, gender, occupation, and ZIP code.

The most commonly used version, MovieLens 100K, contains 100,000 ratings from 943 users on 1,682 movies. Larger versions such as MovieLens 1M, 10M, and 20M also exist, offering progressively more data for building and evaluating scalable recommender systems. In our project, we use the Movielens 1M dataset. Before implementing the recommender system, we convert the `movies.dat` file into `movies.csv` (*Table 8.1*) and the `ratings.dat` file into `ratings.csv` (*Table 8.2*), and their sample contents are shown as follows:

movieId	title	genres
1	Toy Story (1995)	Animation	Children's	Comedy
2	Jumanji (1995)	Adventure	Children's	Fantasy
3	Grumpier Old Men (1995)	Comedy	Romance
4	Waiting to Exhale (1995)	Comedy	Drama
5	Father of the Bride Part II (1995)	Comedy
6	Heat (1995)	Action	Crime	Thriller
7	Sabrina (1995)	Comedy	Romance
8	Tom and Huck (1995)	Adventure	Children's
9	Sudden Death (1995)	Action
10	GoldenEye (1995)	Action	Adventure	Thriller
11	American President, The (1995)	Comedy	Drama	Romance
12	Dracula: Dead and Loving It (1995)	Comedy	Horror
13	Balto (1995)	Animation	Children's
14	Nixon (1995)	Drama
15	Cutthroat Island (1995)	Action	Adventure	Romance
16	Casino (1995)	Drama	Thriller
17	Sense and Sensibility (1995)	Drama	Romance
18	Four Rooms (1995)	Thriller
19	Ace Ventura: When Nature Calls (1995)	Comedy
20	Money Train (1995)	Action
21	Get Shorty (1995)	Action	Comedy	Drama
22	Copycat (1995)	Crime	Drama	Thriller
23	Assassins (1995)	Thriller

Table 8.1: *Sample contents of movies.csv file*

userId	movieId	rating	timestamp
1	1193	5	978300760
1	661	3	978302109
1	914	3	978301968
1	3408	4	978300275
1	2355	5	978824291
1	1197	3	978302268
1	1287	5	978302039

userId	movieId	rating	timestamp
1	2804	5	978300719
1	594	4	978302268
1	919	4	978301368
1	595	5	978824268
1	938	4	978301752
1	2398	4	978302281
1	2918	4	978302124
1	1035	5	978301753
1	2791	4	978302188
1	2687	3	978824268
1	2018	4	978301777
1	3105	5	978301713
1	2797	4	978302039
1	2321	3	978302205
1	720	3	978300760

Table 8.2: Sample contents of ratings.csv file

The following code implements a movie recommender system:

```
#load dataset
import pandas as pd

# Load CSVs
movies = pd.read_csv("movielens/movies.csv")     # columns: movieId, title,
genres
ratings = pd.read_csv("movielens/ratings.csv")  # columns: userId, movieId,
rating, timestamp

# Merge ratings and movies
df = pd.merge(ratings, movies, on='movieId')

#preprocess data

import re

def extract_year(title):
    match = re.search(r"\((\d{4})\)", title)
    return int(match.group(1)) if match else None

movies['year'] = movies['title'].apply(extract_year)

#top rated movies with minimum threshold
```

```
def recommend_top_rated(df, min_ratings=100, top_n=10):
    movie_stats = df.groupby('title').agg({'rating': ['mean', 'count']})
    movie_stats.columns = ['avg_rating', 'num_ratings']
    filtered = movie_stats[movie_stats['num_ratings'] >= min_ratings]
    top_movies = filtered.sort_values(by='avg_rating', ascending=False).
head(top_n)
    return top_movies
```

```
#Genre based recommender
```

```
from sklearn.metrics.pairwise import cosine_similarity
from sklearn.feature_extraction.text import CountVectorizer
```

```
# Use CountVectorizer to transform genres
cv = CountVectorizer(tokenizer=lambda x: x.split('|'))
genre_matrix = cv.fit_transform(movies['genres'])
genre_sim = cosine_similarity(genre_matrix)
```

```
def recommend_similar_by_genre(movie_title, top_n=10):
    if movie_title not in movies['title'].values:
        return f"'{movie_title}' not found in the dataset."

    idx = movies[movies['title'] == movie_title].index[0]
    sim_scores = list(enumerate(genre_sim[idx]))
    sim_scores = sorted(sim_scores, key=lambda x: x[1], reverse=True)
[1:top_n+1]

    recommended = movies.iloc[[i[0] for i in sim_scores]]
    return recommended[['title', 'genres', 'year']]
```

```
#latest movies
```

```
def recommend_latest_movies(movies_df, top_n=10):
    return movies_df.sort_values(by='year', ascending=False).
dropna(subset=['year']).head(top_n)[['title', 'genres', 'year']]
```

```
#function calls for execution
```

```
# Top rated
print("Top Rated Movies:")
print(recommend_top_rated(df))
```

```
# Genre-based
print("\nMovies similar to 'Sudden Death (1995)':")
print(recommend_similar_by_genre('Sudden Death (1995)'))
```

```
# Latest
print("\nLatest Movies:")
print(recommend_latest_movies(movies))
```

The output is as follows:

Top Rated Movies:

title	avg_rating	num_ratings
Seven Samurai (The Magnificent Seven) (Shichini...	4.560510	628
Shawshank Redemption, The (1994)	4.554558	2227
Godfather, The (1972)	4.524966	2223
Close Shave, A (1995)	4.520548	657
Usual Suspects, The (1995)	4.517106	1783
Schindler's List (1993)	4.510417	2304
Wrong Trousers, The (1993)	4.507937	882
Sunset Blvd. (a.k.a. Sunset Boulevard) (1950)	4.491489	470
Raiders of the Lost Ark (1981)	4.477725	2514
Rear Window (1954)	4.476190	1050

Movies similar to 'Sudden Death (1995)':

	title	genres	year
19	Money Train (1995)	Action	1995
70	Fair Game (1995)	Action	1995
143	Bad Boys (1995)	Action	1995
202	Under Siege 2: Dark Territory (1995)	Action	1995
224	Drop Zone (1994)	Action	1994
248	Hunted, The (1995)	Action	1995
312	Specialist, The (1994)	Action	1994
380	Bad Company (1995)	Action	1995
389	Street Fighter (1994)	Action	1994
390	Coldblooded (1995)	Action	1995

Latest Movies:

	title	genres	year
3882	Contender, The (2000)	Drama|Thriller	2000
3528	Whipped (2000)	Comedy	2000
3577	Big Momma's House (2000)	Comedy	2000
3170	Isn't She Great? (2000)	Comedy	2000
3555	Shanghai Noon (2000)	Action	2000
3554	Mission: Impossible 2 (2000)	Action|Thriller	2000
3549	Small Time Crooks (2000)	Comedy	2000
3548	Road Trip (2000)	Comedy	2000
3547	Loser (2000)	Comedy|Romance	2000
3546	Dinosaur (2000)	Animation|Children's	2000

The code is explained as follows:

1. This system combines three types of recommendations:

   - Top-rated movies (based on average rating + number of ratings)

- Genre-based recommendations (content-based filtering using cosine similarity). Cosine similarity is scale-invariant—it focuses on orientation rather than magnitude, making it ideal for comparing documents or embeddings where length may vary.

- Latest releases (newest movies sorted by release year)

2. We used the MovieLens `.dat` files, specifically as described in *Table 8.3*:

File	Description
`movies.dat`	Movie metadata: movieId, title, genres
`ratings.dat`	User ratings: userId, movieId, rating, timestamp

Table 8.3: Fields of movies.dat and ratings.dat files

3. We converted `.dat` to `.csv` using proper encoding (ISO-8859-1) and custom separator (::).

4. Recommend movies that are highly rated by many users. Its working is as follows:

   a. Merge ratings with movies on movieId.

      i. Group by title, calculate:
         - avg_rating (mean rating)
         - num_ratings (count of ratings)

      ii. Filter out movies with fewer than N ratings (to ensure popularity).

      iii. Sort by average rating, return top N.

5. Recommend movies similar in genre to a given movie. Its working is given as follows:

   a. Convert the genres text into numerical vectors using **CountVectorizer**. E.g., Action | Comedy becomes a binary vector.

   b. Compute the cosine similarity between these vectors.

   c. Given a target movie, retrieve the top N most similar genre vectors

6. Show recently released movies. Its working is as follows:

   a. Extract the year from the movie title using regex.

   b. Sort movies in descending order of year.

7. For more understanding, a summary of the used techniques is given as follows in *Table 8.4*:

Recommender	Method	Library used
Top-rated	GroupBy + Filter + Sort	**pandas**
Genre-based	CountVectorizer + Cosine	**sklearn**
Latest releases	Regex + Sort	**re, pandas**

***Table 8.4**: Summary of methods used in recommender systems*

An extension of a movie recommender system enhances its basic functionality by adding features like hybrid models (combining content and collaborative filtering), context-awareness (using time, location, and mood), group recommendations, and explainability. Advanced extensions include using deep learning, real-time suggestions, sentiment analysis from reviews, and supporting multiple domains like TV shows or games. These improvements aim to make recommendations more personalized, dynamic, and user-friendly.

Customer support chatbot

In this section, we create a simple **graphical user interface** (**GUI**) application using Python's Tkinter library, designed to simulate a basic customer support assistant. It allows users to interact with the chatbot not by typing, but by clicking on buttons representing **frequently asked questions** (**FAQs**). Each button corresponds to a typical customer query, and when clicked, the chatbot displays an appropriate pre-defined response. It includes the following key features:

- **GUI interface**:
    - The chatbot runs in a windowed interface (Tkinter GUI).
    - It displays a chat window (text box) that shows both the user's query (as a button label) and the bot's response.

- **Button-based input**: The user does not have to type; instead, a series of buttons is displayed with common questions such as:
    - What is the return policy?
    - How long does a refund take?
    - How do I track my order?
    - Can I change my shipping address?
    - **Newly added**: Refund and Return

- **Predefined responses**: Each button has a corresponding predefined response, for example:
    - **Return**: Returns can be made within 15 days of receiving the product.

- o **Refund**: Refunds are processed after a quality check and will be completed within standard business hours.

- **Chat history**: The chat window maintains a running conversation by showing both user queries (triggered by button clicks) and chatbot answers.

  - o **Scalability**: More buttons (FAQs) can be added easily to the interface, and responses can be customized or expanded to include rich content like links or contact info.

The code of the chatbot is given as follows:

```python
import tkinter as tk

class FAQChatbot(tk.Tk):
    def __init__(self):
        super().__init__()
        self.title("FAQ-Based Customer Support Chatbot")
        self.geometry("600x600")
        self.configure(bg="white")

        tk.Label(self, text="Customer Support - FAQ", font=("Helvetica",
18, "bold"), bg="white").pack(pady=10)

        self.faq_data = {
            "What are your business hours?": "Our support is available from
9 AM to 6 PM, Monday to Friday.",
            "What is your return policy?": "You can return the product
within 15 days of purchase. Please ensure it is unused and in original
packaging.",
            "What is your refund policy?": "Refunds are processed after
quality check of the returned product, and will be credited during business
hours.",
            "How can I contact customer support?": "You can reach us at
support@example.com or call +1-800-123-456.",
            "How can I check my order status?": "Please provide your order
ID to track the status of your order."
        }

        self.create_faq_section()

    def create_faq_section(self):
        container = tk.Frame(self, bg="white")
        container.pack(fill="both", expand=True, padx=20)

        for question, answer in self.faq_data.items():
            self.add_faq_item(container, question, answer)
```

```python
    def add_faq_item(self, parent, question, answer):
        frame = tk.Frame(parent, bg="white", bd=1, relief="solid")
        frame.pack(fill="x", pady=5)

        # Question Button
        is_expanded = tk.BooleanVar(value=False)

        def toggle():
            if is_expanded.get():
                answer_label.pack_forget()
                is_expanded.set(False)
            else:
                answer_label.pack(fill="x", padx=10, pady=5)
                is_expanded.set(True)

        question_btn = tk.Button(frame, text=question, font=("Helvetica",
12, "bold"), anchor="w", command=toggle, bg="#f0f0f0", relief="flat")
        question_btn.pack(fill="x", padx=10, pady=5)

        # Hidden Answer Label
        answer_label = tk.Label(frame, text=answer, font=("Helvetica", 11),
wraplength=550, justify="left", bg="white")
# Run the chatbot GUI
if __name__ == "__main__":
    app = FAQChatbot()
    app.mainloop()
```

The output is as follows:

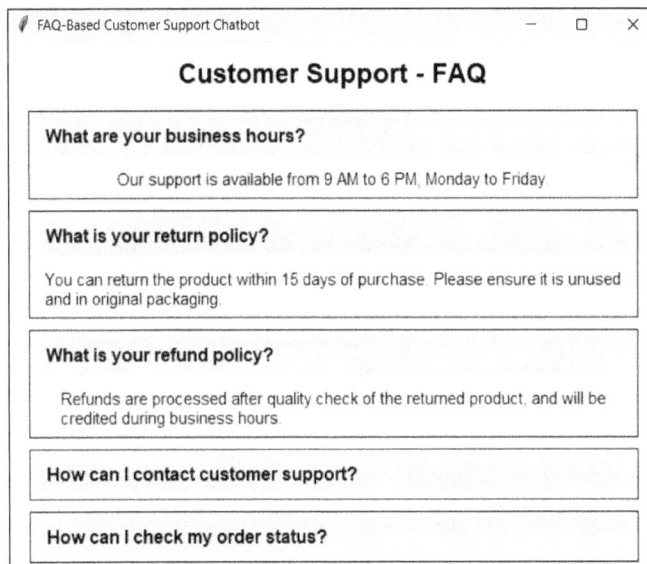

Figure 8.1: It shows the output of the above code (collapsible chatbot)

This Python code creates a graphical chatbot interface using Tkinter that allows users to interact with FAQs. Each question can be clicked to show or hide the answer, providing a collapsible interface similar to modern FAQ sections on websites. The explanation of the code is given as follows:

- **Importing Tkinter**: The **tkinter** library is imported as follows:

    - **tkinter** is Python's standard GUI library.

    - **tk** is the alias used here for simplicity.

- **Class definition**: Class is defined as follows:

    - **class FAQChatbot(tk.Tk)**: This creates a new class FAQChatbot that inherits from **tk.Tk**, which means it behaves like a main Tkinter window.

- **Constructor method**: Constructor methods are used as follows:

```
def __init__(self):
    super().__init__()
```

    - **__init__** initializes the GUI.

    - **super().__init__()** calls the **tk.Tk** initializer.

```
self.title("FAQ-Based Customer Support Chatbot")
self.geometry("600x600")
self.configure(bg="white")
```

    - Sets the window title, size, and background color.

```
tk.Label(self, text="Customer Support - FAQ",
font=("Helvetica", 18, "bold"), bg="white").pack(pady=10)
```

    - Adds a title label at the top of the window.

- **FAQ data**: FAQ data is generated as follows:

```
self.faq_data = {
    "What are your business hours?": "Our support is available from 9
AM to 6 PM...",
    ...}
```

    - A dictionary storing question-answer pairs.

- **Creating the FAQ section**:

```
self.create_faq_section()
```

    - Calls a method to display all FAQ items.

- **Creating container for FAQs**:

```
def create_faq_section(self):
    container = tk.Frame(self, bg="white")
```

o This creates a **Frame** to hold all FAQ items.

o Iterates through each FAQ and adds it using **self.add_faq_item()**.

- **Adding each FAQ item**:

    o Defines how each individual FAQ looks and behaves:

    ```
    def add_faq_item(self, parent, question, answer):
    ```

    o Outer frame with a border for separation:

    ```
    frame = tk.Frame(parent, bg="white", bd=1, relief="solid")
    ```

    o Boolean variable to track whether the answer is visible:

    ```
    is_expanded = tk.BooleanVar(value=False)
    ```

    o Function to show/hide the answer when the question is clicked:

    ```
    def toggle():
        if is_expanded.get():
            answer_label.pack_forget()
            is_expanded.set(False)
        else:
            answer_label.pack(...)
            is_expanded.set(True)
    ```

    o Button for the question. Clicking this will run the **toggle()** function:

    ```
    question_btn = tk.Button(..., command=toggle)
    ```

    o This label contains the answer, but it is not packed initially, so it is hidden.

    ```
    answer_label = tk.Label(...)
    ```

- **Running the application**: Runs the chatbot window when the script is executed:

```
if __name__ == "__main__":
    app = FAQChatbot()
    app.mainloop()
```

The above code explanation is self-explanatory. The button-based chatbots are widely used in e-commerce and customer care support websites/apps for most of the online platforms, which serve the purpose of an FAQ as well.

Extensions of a chatbot system enhance its capabilities through features like context awareness, multi-turn conversations, API integration, voice/multimodal support, sentiment detection, personalization, multilingual support, and human handoff, making chatbots more intelligent, interactive, and useful in real-world applications.

Customer segmentation system

A customer segmentation system is a powerful analytical tool used by businesses to divide their customer base into distinct groups or segments based on shared characteristics. These characteristics can include demographics (age, gender, income), behavioral traits (purchase history, product preferences), geographic location, or psychographics (lifestyle, interests). The ultimate goal of segmentation is to understand customers better, tailor marketing strategies, and offer more personalized products or services to improve customer satisfaction and business performance.

In today's data-driven economy, customer segmentation is at the heart of successful marketing and **customer relationship management** (**CRM**). Instead of treating all customers the same, businesses use segmentation to identify patterns and group similar customers together. For example, a retailer might segment its customers into budget-conscious shoppers, frequent buyers, and premium customers, each requiring a different communication strategy.

One of the most common techniques used in customer segmentation systems is K-means clustering, a type of unsupervised machine learning algorithm. K-means works by grouping customers into *K* clusters based on the similarity of selected features such as age, income, and spending behavior. Before clustering, data is often preprocessed, cleaned, normalized, and sometimes reduced in dimensionality using methods like **principal component analysis** (**PCA**) for easier visualization.

The system first evaluates different values of K (the number of clusters) using techniques such as the **elbow method**, which helps determine the optimal number of clusters by examining how clustering performance improves as K increases. Once the optimal K is found, the algorithm assigns each customer to a cluster. These clusters are then analyzed to understand the distinguishing traits of each segment.

For example, a segment with high income and high spending scores might be ideal for luxury product marketing, while a low-income, high-spending group might indicate price-sensitive but brand-loyal customers. The following project code represents the concept of customer segmentation:

```
import pandas as pd
import numpy as np
import matplotlib.pyplot as plt
import seaborn as sns
from sklearn.preprocessing import StandardScaler
from sklearn.cluster import KMeans
from sklearn.decomposition import PCA

# Step 1: Load sample e-commerce data (simulated)
data = {
    'CustomerID': range(1, 201),
```

```
        'Age': np.random.randint(18, 70, 200),
        'Annual Income (k$)': np.random.randint(15, 150, 200),
        'Spending Score (1-100)': np.random.randint(1, 100, 200)
}
df = pd.DataFrame(data)

# Step 2: Data Preprocessing
features = ['Age', 'Annual Income (k$)', 'Spending Score (1-100)']
X = df[features]

# Normalize features
scaler = StandardScaler()
X_scaled = scaler.fit_transform(X)

# Step 3: Elbow Method to choose optimal K
wcss = []
for k in range(1, 11):
    kmeans = KMeans(n_clusters=k, random_state=42, n_init=10)
    kmeans.fit(X_scaled)
    wcss.append(kmeans.inertia_)

# Plot Elbow Curve
plt.figure(figsize=(8, 4))
plt.plot(range(1, 11), wcss, marker='o')
plt.title('Elbow Method For Optimal K')
plt.xlabel('Number of clusters (K)')
plt.ylabel('WCSS')
plt.grid(True)
plt.show()

# Step 4: Apply KMeans with optimal K (let's assume 5)
kmeans = KMeans(n_clusters=5, random_state=42, n_init=10)
clusters = kmeans.fit_predict(X_scaled)
df['Cluster'] = clusters

# Step 5: Visualize Clusters using PCA
pca = PCA(n_components=2)
principal_components = pca.fit_transform(X_scaled)
df['PCA1'] = principal_components[:, 0]
df['PCA2'] = principal_components[:, 1]

plt.figure(figsize=(8, 6))
sns.scatterplot(data=df, x='PCA1', y='PCA2', hue='Cluster', palette='Set2',
s=100)
plt.title('Customer Segments (via PCA)')
```

```
plt.xlabel('PCA Component 1')
plt.ylabel('PCA Component 2')
plt.legend(title='Cluster')
plt.grid(True)
plt.show()

# Step 6: Summary
print(df.groupby('Cluster')[features].mean())
```

The output is as follows:

Figure 8.2 represents the elbow method, and *Figure 8.3* represents principal component analysis:

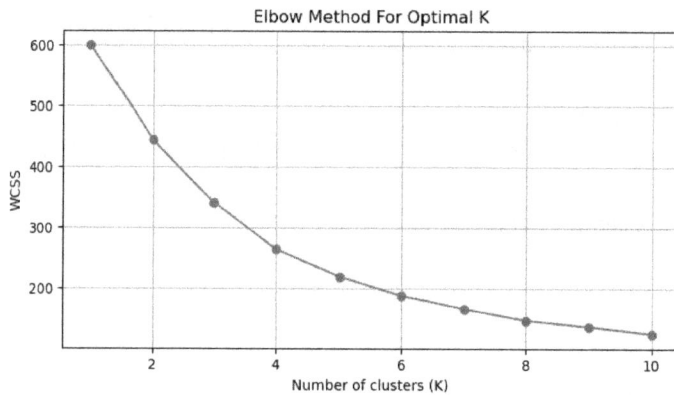

Figure 8.2: *Number of optimal clusters using the elbow method*

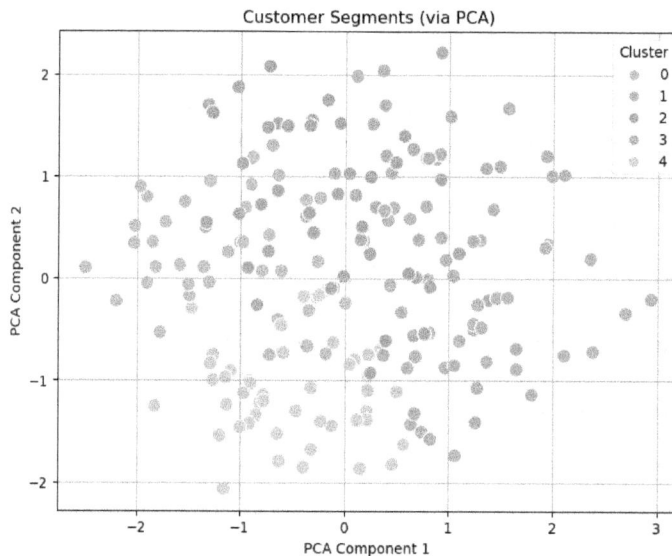

Figure 8.3: *Dimensionality reduction and visualization using PCA*

	Age	Annual Income (k$)	Spending Score (1-100)
Cluster			
0	45.692308	121.076923	23.820513
1	29.189189	42.000000	56.756757
2	57.893617	88.297872	75.085106
3	27.064516	107.225806	70.548387
4	53.652174	52.173913	27.695652

In the above code, data is generated in the code itself; however, one can replace it with a real-world dataset (CSV file).

The provided code implements a customer segmentation system using K-means clustering on a simulated e-commerce dataset. It begins by generating synthetic data for 200 customers, including their age, annual income, and spending score. These three features are selected for clustering and normalized using **StandardScaler** to ensure consistent scale. The elbow method is then used to determine the optimal number of clusters by calculating the **within-cluster sum of squares** (**WCSS**) for cluster values ranging from 1 to 10, and the results are visualized in a line plot. Based on the elbow plot, the number of clusters is assumed to be 5, and K-means clustering is applied to group the customers accordingly. To visualize the resulting clusters in two dimensions, PCA is used to reduce the feature space, and a scatter plot is generated where each point represents a customer and is colored by cluster. Finally, the code prints the mean values of the features for each identified cluster, providing insight into the characteristics of each customer group. This process allows businesses to segment their customers for targeted marketing and personalized strategies.

Note: In the above code, PCA is used after K-means here purely for visualization. The clustering was done in the full feature space, and PCA helps project that result into two dimensions to make the clusters easy to understand in a 2D plot.

Extensions of a customer segmentation system include predictive modeling, real-time updates, hyper-personalization, geo-segmentation, CRM integration, and behavioral insights, making segmentation more dynamic, actionable, and tailored to business needs.

Conclusion

In conclusion, this chapter has explored three foundational projects, recommendation systems, customer FAQ chatbots, and customer segmentation systems, that illustrate the practical application of data science and artificial intelligence in solving real-world business challenges. Through these projects, readers have gained hands-on experience in data preprocessing, machine learning, and clustering. The recommendation system demonstrated how to personalize user experiences based on behavior and preferences. The FAQ chatbot showcased the power of conversational AI in automating customer support. The customer segmentation project highlighted the value of unsupervised learning in understanding diverse customer groups for targeted marketing strategies. Together, these projects not only strengthen technical competencies but also provide a holistic perspective on how intelligent systems can enhance customer engagement and drive business value.

Join our Discord space

Join our Discord workspace for latest updates, offers, tech happenings around the world, new releases, and sessions with the authors:

https://discord.bpbonline.com

Appendix

References

The references are as follows:

- *Peter Bruce (Author), Andrew Bruce (Author), Peter Gedeck, Practical Statistics for Data Scientists: 50+ Essential Concepts Using R and Python, Second Edition, 2020*

- *Jonathan Schwabish, Data Visualization in Excel: A Guide for Beginners, Intermediates, and Wonks, Paperback, 2023*

- *Alberto Boschetti (Author), Luca Massaron (Author), Python Data Science Essentials - Second Edition: Learn the fundamentals of Data Science with Python, 2016*

- *Joel Grus, Data Science From Scratch: First Principles with Python, Second Edition (Greyscale Indian Edition), 2019*

- **www.github.com**

- **www.kaggle.com**

Join our Discord space

Join our Discord workspace for latest updates, offers, tech happenings around the world, new releases, and sessions with the authors:

https://discord.bpbonline.com

Index

www.ingramcontent.com/pod-product-compliance
Lightning Source LLC
Chambersburg PA
CBHW061806210326
41599CB00034B/6900